Educator's
Self-Teaching Guide
to
Individualizing Instructional Programs

Educator's
Self-Teaching Guide
to
Individualizing Instructional Programs

Stafford

Rita Dunn and Kenneth Dunn

Parker Publishing Company, Inc.
West Nyack, New York

Also by the authors:

Practical Approaches to Individualizing Instruction: Contracts and Other Effective Teaching Strategies, Parker Publishing Company, Inc., 1972

By Kenneth J. Dunn and Jack Tanzman:

Using Instructional Media Effectively, Parker Publishing Company, Inc., 1971

© 1975, *by*

PARKER PUBLISHING COMPANY, INC.
West Nyack, N.Y.

Library of Congress Cataloging in Publication Data

Dunn, Rita Stafford
    Educator's self-teaching guide to individualizing
    instructional programs.

    Bibliography: p.
    1. Individualized instruction.   I. Dunn, Kenneth J.,
joint author. II. Title.
LB1031.D79 1975   371.39'4   74-17165
ISBN 0-13-240663-2

Printed in the United States of America

"Individualized instruction is the one-to-one relationship between a student and what he learns."

Educators also walk to the tune of different drummers. Some teachers and administrators hear the varied beats and orchestrate learning to provide for the differences among students. It is to them and to total individualization that we dedicate this book.

Illustration 1-1. Open space that flexibly provides cozy nooks for individuals, quiet alcoves for small groups, and larger areas where ten or more students may study together maximizes the instructional potential of the newer architectural designs. (Photograph of P.S. 219, Paul Klapper Satellite Schools, New York. Courtesy of Caudil Rowlett Scott, Architects, New York. John Bintliff, photographer.)

A Word from the Authors

This book serves as a self-instructional and self-evaluating guide to managing, observing, and evaluating quality individualized instructional programs. It is written for experienced educators who have, to varying degrees, joined the movement away from "whole-class" instruction. This practical handbook enables administrators *and* teachers to assess the strengths and weaknesses of individualized programs and details clear action guidelines for improving their effectiveness.

Each chapter begins with functional behavioral objectives to describe what can be learned from the book and how the reader will be able to measure his own progress. The information, suggestions, and techniques which follow are directly related to the objectives, as are the self-teaching strategies that measure individual or group achievement of the stated objectives.

This guide may be used in many ways.

1. Educators who wish to increase their knowledge and skill relative to the individualization process may study alone, in pairs, or in small groups either for part or all of the book. This technique provides self-selection of learning style and pacing.

2. Districts that wish to expand their teachers' and supervisors' abilities to organize, manage, and evaluate programs effectively may use this approach as an in-service plan, because the behavioral objectives and evaluation devices with answers are included and may be used as the basis for demonstrating increased skill and proficiency.

3. Teacher centers may use this guide as a learning alternative, a means whereby teachers may learn independently or in small groups and demonstrate their abilities through performance tasks which can then be evaluated. In essence, this book is a competency-based program that provides clearly stated behavioral objectives, resources, and a criterion-referenced instrument to measure the reader's individual progress for each chapter.

4. Districts that are concerned about expanding their community's knowledge of instructional programs may use the exercises to provide

innovative activities for "Open School Week" or parent training sessions. The extensive footnotes in Appendix A provide practitioners with a substantial research base for the individualization methods they propose in their own schools.

    5. Teachers and supervisors who visit "innovative" programs may use the suggested guidelines and instruments in Chapters 6, 7 and 8 to determine the effectiveness of what is observed and the potential of visited programs for adoption in local schools.

    6. The exercises which supplement each chapter are equally suited to the development of appropriate skills among paraprofessionals and student teachers.

    The book provides clear descriptions of the five major methods of individualizing teaching and learning, as well as the solid reasoning for stressing this important approach. Seven steps to individualization are described for immediate use in any classroom or school. This practical step-by-step process begins with the introduction of small-group techniques and moves through cooperative teacher-student planning toward instructional independence for students.

    The book provides a large variety of practical tips, suggestions, photographs and drawings designed to meet the specific needs of super-

Illustration 1-2. The educational potential of well-designed open space can be diminished by the inappropriate use of furniture in conventional ways. (Photograph of Westlake High School, Ohio. Courtesy of Lesko Associates, Cleveland, Ohio.)

visors and teachers who are responsible for newly developing programs.
For example:

1. The redesign of instructional space to facilitate individualized learning
    is blueprinted for instant adoption or adaptation.
2. Reliable methods of recognizing a student's learning style and using it
    to his advantage are described for application by teachers and students.
3. Newly developed behavior observation instruments are included to aid
    teachers and evaluators in improving the teaching-learning process.
4. Finally, the book uses a variety of self-instructional techniques which
    make learning individualized and enjoyable for the reader.

This book, then, is more than an instructional guide; it is an exciting,
effective way for educators with experience to expand their knowledge of
individualization and apply strategies for evaluating and strengthening
their efforts. The teacher and supervisor are actually put through some of
the most successful processes of individualization. Thus, educators are
provided with the practical means of aiding themselves and their students in
moving forward with the most important new approach to teaching and
learning in the past fifty years.

Rita Dunn
Kenneth Dunn

ACKNOWLEDGMENTS

With special thanks to
Ruth Allen and John Macellari.

Except where otherwise indicated, all photographs
by Kenneth J. Dunn.

Table of Contents

5. Developing Student Independence (*cont.*)

6. Observing Individualized Teaching and Learning: What to Look For 218

7. Supervising an Individualized Instruction Program: How to Record and Interpret Teacher and Student Behaviors...........................241

8. Analyzing Individualized Programs Through Case Studies.............273

8. Analyzing Individualized Programs (*cont.*)

Participating in Four Case Studies at Different Levels ● 275

Analyzing the Innovative Primary School ● Visiting the Beach Elementary School ● Diagnosing a New Social Studies Program at the Urban Junior High School Level ● Adding Structure to a Community High School Program

In Conclusion ● 310

Educator's
Self-Teaching Guide
to
Individualizing Instructional Programs

TOTAL INDIVIDUALIZATION

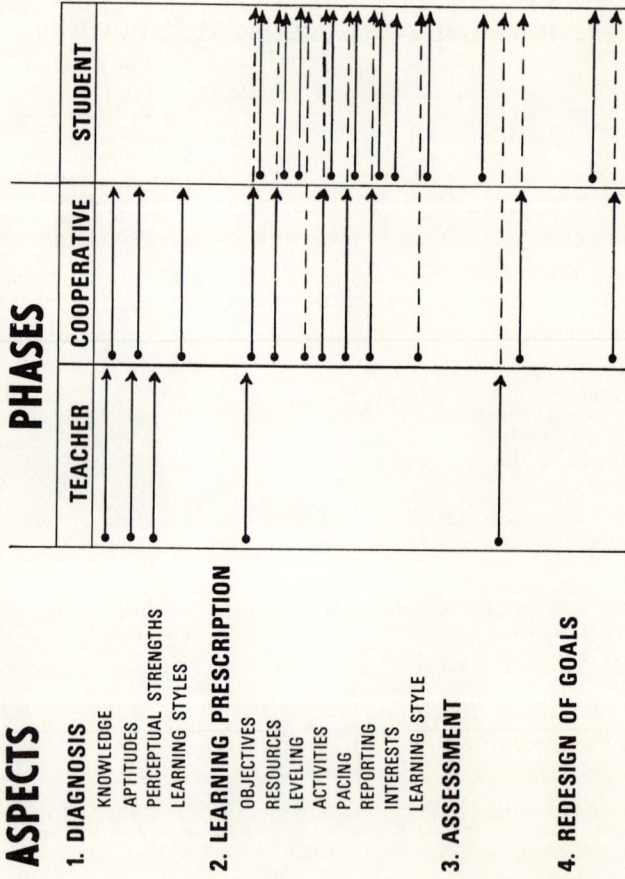

PHASES

ASPECTS

	TEACHER	COOPERATIVE	STUDENT

1. DIAGNOSIS
- KNOWLEDGE
- APTITUDES
- PERCEPTUAL STRENGTHS
- LEARNING STYLES

2. LEARNING PRESCRIPTION
- OBJECTIVES
- RESOURCES
- LEVELING
- ACTIVITIES
- PACING
- REPORTING
- INTERESTS
- LEARNING STYLE

3. ASSESSMENT

4. REDESIGN OF GOALS

Designed by Rita Dunn and Kenneth Dunn

Figure 1-1

ONE

Defining Individualized Instruction: Five Alternative Methods

Behavioral Objectives for Chapter 1

1. You will be able to identify at least ten procedures that many traditional schools follow which actually *prevent* a student from learning easily.
2. You will be able to list the five methods through which programs may be individualized.
3. You will be able to describe ten aspects of an individualized instructional program.
4. You will be able to cite at least ten advantages of individualization.

. . . .

EXPLAINING THE RATIONALE

The process of educating children is evolving from teacher-determined instruction toward student-selected procedures for achieving objectives-based learning. It is only recently that we have begun to apply our knowledge that each youngster learns in a manner that is uniquely his own, through perceptual strengths that either fortify or discourage his acquisition of knowledge and skills, and with a learning style that tends to dominate his every effort to achieve. Individualization is more than a philosophy, more than an instructional process, and more than a means whereby both the teacher and the student become responsible, cooperative human beings who are both dependent upon and accountable to each other and themselves. Individualization is the recognition that for each student, whether child or adult, learning is a pervasive, developmental process that varies, often completely.

Because of the soundness of this philosophy and partially due to the widespread professional attention devoted to the development of alternative forms of education, teachers across the nation have been experimenting extensively with new techniques for moving toward varied forms of independent student programs. Unfortunately, energetic enthusiasm and much of the current literature provide little practical assistance in effectively organizing a functional system. Too often what emerges is an informal, relaxed environment. This is a step in the right direction but an environment is *not* a program.

Too few "how to do it" instructional resources or experienced personnel have been available to teachers striving toward the development of individualization. In addition to this lack, guidelines for administrators that describe the differences among the supervision of a traditional, transitional, or individualized setting have been virtually nonexistent. Like many colleges of education, the literature and the "experts" assume that educators will be able to translate theory and philosophy into practice and emerge with their own creative contribution to the field. Not so. This kind of translation is not possible until one has the knowledge and experience to develop insight and to adapt what is known to his own unique situation.

As a result of the enormous amount of ardor for individualization and the concomitant lack of know-how, few educators are able to compare the programs they have developed with others that range on a continuum from the traditional to the transitional, to true individualization.

One of the purposes of this book, therefore, is to provide teachers and administrators with precise guidelines for organizing, managing, supervising, and evaluating individualized programs so that they may knowledgeably begin to improve the programs they have implemented.

Before educators are able to analyze what exists they need to review (a) the fallacies[1] that are still largely a part of our psychological "set" with the realities of how students learn and (b) the alternatives that individualization permits.

Fallacy	Reality	Individualization Alternatives
1. Students learn by listening.	Some students learn by listening, others learn by seeing, others must learn by touching or acting out and many by differing combinations of these. Children and adults learn through different perceptions and although repetition through varied perceptions tends to *reinforce* learning, information, skills, and values should be introduced through major perceptual strengths.	Students are given options within a structure to elect how they will learn selected material. Reinforcement through additional perceptual means is provided, but the youngsters determine how they will initially begin the learning process related to their instructional objectives. This process leads to student decision-making, responsibility, and ultimate accountability, given other important factors such as realistic teacher expectations.

Fallacy	*Reality*	*Individualization Alternatives*
2. A class of 25 students can learn identical content in the same specified amount of time.	Children (and adults) absorb varying amounts of content at different rates and at different times; they also vary in the amount and type of content they *retain*.	Students are given approximate time intervals during which they may complete their instructional objectives, but are permitted to pace themselves and to determine the amount of study and number of objectives with which they can cope. This process is guided by the teacher to encourage continuous achievement.
3. All students can learn in depth if they will only concentrate.	All students can learn *something* about a given topic, but each has a greater or lesser capacity to absorb details, concepts, and nuances. Here, too, much depends on the interest, the frame of reference, the maturity level, and the elements of training and experience for each youngster.	In conservative individualized programs, students are given instructional requirements and are then permitted some instructional options. In an open-ended individualized program, youngsters are permitted to study what most stimulates and absorbs them. A happy medium would lie somewhere between, based on the recognition that most schools follow a definite (though flexible) curriculum, but that people learn most easily when they are interested in the subject.
4. A quiet school is a good school.	A consistently quiet school is often a subdued school where students have been trained or coerced into patterns of behavior that are often unnatural to healthy youth.	Some students require a quiet environment in which to learn, while others need verbal and sometimes social interaction; most youngsters require one or the other and combinations of each at different times. An effective individualized program permits the learners to determine whether they will work alone, in pairs, or in small groups. Unnecessary noise is as inconsistent with a well-functioning program as is continuing silence. The busy, self-controlled sound of student and teacher interaction and activity is part of an effective learning environment.
5. Children should be admitted to school when they are five years of age. or	Children should be admitted to school when they are "ready" to learn. or	Students should be repeatedly diagnosed, prescribed for, and guided through the learning process. Some children should enter a formal or semiformal educational program earlier or later than other children, remain in school for varying amounts of time, be provided different kinds of experiences, and be encouraged to formulate
6. Students should be in school for the same amount of time each day. or	Students should be in school for the amount of time during which they are capable of being attentive, studious, positively involved and relaxed. or	

Fallacy	*Reality*	*Individualization Alternatives*
7. Youngsters should be maintained in school until they are 16 years of age.	Youngsters should be maintained in school until they can no longer obtain positive learning experiences. Alternative programs, both in and out of school, should be provided for students who would benefit from them.	programs that vary extensively in terms of environment, objectives, resources, activities, focus, and self-direction.
8. It is better for children to remain on "grade level" with youngsters of the same chronological age than to study with either much younger or much older learners.	It is better for children to be working at their maximum individual capacities with different age groups than to be either bored by the lack of intellectual challenge or frustrated by being unable to compare themselves favorably with their peers.	Interage groupings that change with subject and interest areas are common. The rhetoric about academic superiority frequently being inconsistent with emotional maturity holds little weight; there is no evidence to substantiate that keeping the bright, immature child with his age peers contributes to either his maturity or his adjustment.
9. There are special teaching methods that are panaceas for instructing children, e.g., "discovery" in social studies, "phonics" in reading, "experimentation" in science, etc.	Since children learn most easily through their strongest perceptual strength, the instructional method should relate directly to that mode. A cognitive, conceptual learner who enjoys reading may learn easily through discovery, the child who learns by talking and listening may not. A child who learns visually may experience difficulty with an essentially phonics approach. The youngster who learns tactually will delight in the experimentation, whereas the phonetically oriented learner may become bored or frustrated when required to go through an entire touching-doing process.	Children are made aware of their instructional objectives, provided with alternative resources through which to learn, and are then permitted to select the way(s) in which they will complete the learning process. Students are eventually trained to select goals and methods with appropriate support and guidance from teachers.
10. The teacher should be accountable for a student's learning.	The student should be *equally* as accountable for his learning.	Teachers are required to diagnose accurately, prescribe appropriately, and guide students through varied effective instructional techniques. Youngsters are apprised of both their options *and* their responsibilities. Learners who do not meet their responsibilities are cautioned, aided or reassigned into a more structured program.

Fallacy	*Reality*	*Individualization Alternatives*
11. A "great" teacher must be an excellent actor or actress.	A great teacher establishes rapport, respect, and a climate that creates an eased, personalized joy of learning and achieving for each of his students. Because many students do not learn unless they are actively involved in the process, the dramatic teacher may be amusing but is not necessarily an effective instructor for most learners.	Students are permitted extensive and frequent opportunities to be involved directly with their teachers. The quiet, undramatic teacher may be as effective, or more so than her counterpart, depending on the personality ranges of her students and the degree of rapport, caring, aiding, self-achievement and desire to learn that are evident.
12. Young children need a "mother substitute" and therefore the self-contained classroom, where one teacher is responsible for most of the instruction, is the best organizational pattern for primary grades.	Young *and* older children need a variety of challenging activities, many warm and responsive adults, other positive children, loving parents, and opportunities to become independent and responsible.	Children are exposed to a variety of adults and relate beautifully when the adults are responsive, caring, and effective in their assigned roles.
13. Each teacher knows what is "best" for the children in her class.	Every teacher is not like every other teacher; some are excellent diagnosticians, some are effective prescribers, some are outstanding guides in the learning process, and some are excellent at all or none of these functions.	Children are being granted an increasingly larger role in determining some, many, or all of their objectives in conjunction with their teachers. The more involvement the student gains, the more likely he is to be a motivated learner.
14. Students learn best through repeated, sequential periods that are spaced throughout the school day (week) (year) and are "articulated" with the same (or other) subject(s) in succeeding days and years.	Students learn in a variety of both structured and unstructured ways.	Students are repeatedly diagnosed to avoid unnecessary (and boring) repetition and are provided alternative schedules and patterns of learning.
15. Education occurs between 8:30 a.m. and 3:00 p.m. when students are in school.	Learning occurs whenever students are actively involved in stimulating experiences on their level of comprehension and interest.	Students are provided multiple options, multiple environments, and the freedom of scheduling themselves so that learning becomes more self-selective to varying degrees for different students.

RECOGNIZING ALTERNATIVE METHODS

Once the realities of learning are understood and accepted by the staff and administration, interest in developing or improving an individualized program is certain to emerge. Faculty should recognize that there are at least five basic ways to individualize instruction and that these include varied emphases on prepackaged, teacher- or student-determined diagnosis, prescription, learning resources, activities, assessment, and recycling.

1. Programed Learning

Programed learning is used here in a broad context. It refers to commercially designed materials in which, minimally, skills and related

Photos 1-1, 1-2. Joseph F. Herney Jr. and Rosalie Rogers designed a semiprogramed course of instruction for their secondary foreign language students. Sequenced materials are kept in bins or on tables. Students are diagnosed, given an individual prescription, and then permitted to acquire the required skills alone, with a classmate or two, or in a small group. (Photographs courtesy of Briarcliff High School and Briarcliff Middle School, Briarcliff Manor, New York.)

objectives are prearranged and sequenced in short or extensive groupings on a continuum ranging from the simple to the complex.

In essence, the student is diagnosed by preestablished instruments and then programed into the learning resources at the point at which the materials are either developmental or partially repetitive for him. All students proceed through essentially the same sequence but may pace themselves and learn through resources that are appropriate to their level of comprehension and achievement. Programed learning is far better than the group instruction traditionally employed in our schools, *but it is individualized only in terms of diagnosis, prescription, rate and level.*

The producers of various programed learning resources point out that despite the fact that most of their materials are visual (similar to mini-workbook units), supplementary tapes and/or filmstrips are occasionally available. The fact that students are required to learn skills through a visual approach, however, sharply reduces the effectiveness of this method.

Another deficiency of this type of individualization is that it virtually isolates the learner for long periods of instructional time. The student works with the materials, and as he completes various segments and tests

Photo 1-2

Photos 1-3, 1-4, 1-5. Joe and Rosalie, who have taught 13 and 11 years respectively, teach individuals, small groups, and large groups, as the need arises. They are constantly moving among the students, questioning, evaluating, challenging and reinforcing. (Photographs courtesy of Briarcliff High School and Briarcliff Middle School, Briarcliff Manor, New York.)

Photo 1-4

Photo 1-5

-himself he may seek assistance if he feels the need. If he believes that he is progressing correctly, or if he chooses to become absorbed in fantasy or other activities, he may spend a great deal of time without benefiting from either adult or peer interaction. There *are* youngsters who prefer to work alone, but the Scribner and Durell studies at Boston University and, more recently, the Poirier[2] methods instituted at the University of California verify that retention is greater after student discussion of what is being learned. However, any teacher who chooses to use programed learning as one means of individualizing instruction may overcome the alienation factor by incorporating small-group techniques[3] such as team learning, circle of knowledge, group analysis, case study, simulation, and brain-storming, into the program.

2. Instructional Packages

Many of the British Primary Schools and the American Open Class-room and Open Corridor schools rely heavily on student use of manipu-lative materials to promote learning. When a variety of materials are related to a specific concept (Elementary Science Study [ESS], Science; A Process Approach [SAPA], Science Curriculum Improvement Study [SCIS], etc.), sequenced, and/or "packaged," they are called "instructional packages." This method of individualization provides extensive opportunity for student selection and exploration of materials based on interest, the establishment of either teacher- or student-selected goals, self-pacing, and individual leveling. It is a less structured method than programed learning and permits options and alternative learning processes. Critics note that the teacher is not in control of what will be learned unless she designs the package. Also, many youngsters require structure and do not have the self-motivation and discipline to pursue learning by themselves over an extended period of time. Further, special skills of analysis, translation, and application are necessary to transfer a student's experiences with materials into knowledge.

Because of these considerations, some teachers have begun designing extended instructional packages to meet the specific requirements of their students. These become self-contained units of study designed to help a student master a particular concept that is stated as simplified behavioral objectives.

The youngster follows instructions given on a teacher-made tape that guides and encourages him through four multisensory activities —auditory, visual, tactual and kinesthetic. The youngster is thus permitted to learn through his strongest perceptual strength and reinforce through the others.

The teacher-made package builds in diagnosis, prescription, self-pacing, multisensory resources and activities, and an evaluation device at the end to determine the degree of mastery that has actually occurred. Essentially, the instructional package is a "fun," but effective, means of individualizing instruction, particularly for slow learners and nonreaders.

The lack of student interaction that has been claimed as a negative aspect of programed learning sequences is equally true of instructional packages, but with this method, the inclusion of small-group techniques is inappropriate. Students use instructional packages when the need for a particular skill or concept arises, and, very often, a package may be suitable for a few youngsters at the beginning of the semester, for others three weeks later, for others at midsemester, and so on; some students may never get to use a selected package at all. Since few learners are coping with the same material at the same time with this technique, the use of small-group interaction strategies cannot easily occur.

An instructional package may be assigned to a student for any one of a number of reasons.

a.   An advanced student, able to cope with new concepts or skills independently, may work well ahead of his peers through the use of this method. He need not wait to learn until either the teacher can work with him individually or the rest of his peers catch up. He also need not learn on "grade level."

Photos 1-6, 1-7. Students who are ready for advanced skills prior to their peers, or who require reinforcement in specific areas, may use instructional packages. Here Marie Cannava, who has taught for seven years, is introducing a package on "Coining Words —How Our Language Was Formed" to an eighth grader. (Photographs courtesy of H. Frank Carey High School, Franklin Square, New York.)

Photo 1-7

b. An interested student may learn more about a given topic, concept or skill at the moment in time when he wants to, not when the teacher is able to get to the subject.

c. A slow student who is still struggling with a given topic, concept or skill after most of his peers have mastered it may spend as much time as needed reinforcing the knowledge at his own leisure and pace until he, too, is ready to move ahead.

d. The average student who cares to learn something new in an interesting way may become sufficiently motivated to work on his own because of the nature of the varied, multisensory activities.

Instructional packages, therefore, may be used either as introductory or reinforcement resources, depending upon the nature of the teacher's diagnosis.

Photos 1-8, 1-9, 1-10. Instructional packages may be "signed out" for home study. Instructions on teacher-made tapes guide students through four multisensory activities—auditory, visual, tactual and kinesthetic. This package describes how nouns and verbs form sentence patterns. (Photographs courtesy of the Department of Curriculum and Teaching, St. John's University, New York.)

Photo 1-9

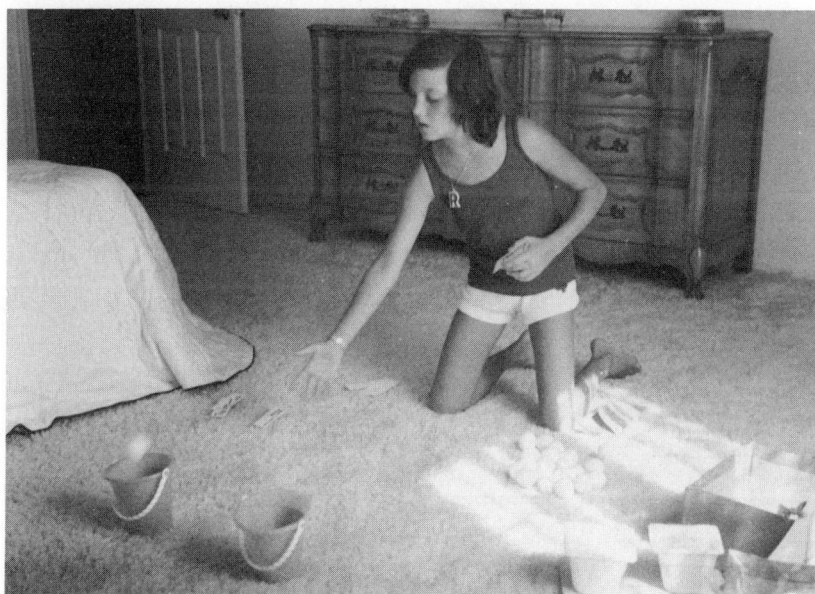

Photo 1-10

3. Contracts

A contract is a self-contained outline of study that clearly indicates to the student:

a. what he is required to learn and how he may demonstrate what he was required to learn after he has learned it. This statement (simplified for youngsters) is called a "behavioral objective." The teacher may wish to set standards for how well each youngster should learn the required material;

b. the multisensory "resource alternatives" through which he may learn what he is required to learn (books, magazines, films, filmstrips, tapes, manipulative materials, games, visits, persons, etc.);

c. the "activity alternatives" through which he *uses* what he has learned in productive ways to provide reinforcement and retention (dioramas, skits, painting, compositions, etc.); and

d. the "reporting alternatives" through which he may share and discuss with others what he has produced.

A contract, therefore, includes behavioral objectives, resource alternatives, activity alternatives, and reporting alternatives.

Photo 1-11. Valerie Scott, after six years of teaching, says that she would not return to the way she taught before using contract activity packages. "This stimulating method eliminates boredom and permits students to learn as well or better than they did before. Even more important, the kids' attitudes have become so positive!" (Photograph courtesy of Grand Avenue Junior High School, Bellmore-Merrick, New York.)

Photo 1-12. This fourth grader works independently and responsibly on a curriculum contract. (Photograph courtesy of the Floral Park-Bellerose Elementary School, Floral Park, New York.)

When a contract includes a means of diagnosing what the student *already knows* about a given topic or concept and what he *still must learn*, it becomes a ''contract activity package'' (CAP). The ''package'' usually includes diagnostic, self-assessment, and terminal teacher instruments, but one test that is directly related to the contract's stated behavioral objectives may be used instead of three separate ones. A contract activity package therefore includes:

a. A diagnostic test
b. Behavioral objectives written for the child
c. Resource alternatives
d. Activity alternatives
e. Reporting alternatives (including the use of small-group techniques)
f. A self-assessment inventory
g. A teacher assessment of the student

    if necessary

h. Enrichment or review materials

A contract is outlined by the teacher after diagnosis of the pupil's strengths, weaknesses, interests, and abilities and is developed and expanded cooperatively with the student. The student then assumes the obligation of endeavoring to fulfill it successfully. The contract may be reevaluated, redesigned, altered, or replaced entirely upon the consent of interested parties (pupil, teacher, administrator, or parent). It serves only as a guide to study for the student and a guide for evaluation to the teacher. This method provides individualized diagnosis, prescription, student-selected objectives, materials, activities, reporting, small-group interactions, self-pacing, interests, and assessment. In addition, the contract recognizes each student's learning style including perceptual strengths.

4. Work-Study Experiences

Teachers and/or students cooperatively diagnose, prescribe, and assess. The student's learning environment is advanced into the community, into industry, and/or into business. The student's prescription encompasses academically oriented requirements that may be fulfilled while being employed. This is the method utilized by the Parkway School in Philadelphia, also called "the School Without Walls." This approach provides individualized diagnosis, cooperatively designed prescriptions, environment, materials, activities, interests, leveling, and assessments. This form of individualization has been used essentially by high schools and higher education institutions.

5. Community Contributions

This method is essentially similar to the work-study experience but requires nonremunerative giving of self and time to community agencies and institutions such as orphanages, hospitals, social and welfare groups, needy citizens, etc. It, too, when implemented properly, individualizes in terms of diagnosis, cooperatively developed prescriptions, environment, materials, activities, interests, leveling and assessment, and grants academic credit in relation to the completion of established objectives. Again, this method has been initiated with older students only, two examples being the Great Neck High School North Community and Village School Programs, both of which provide community contribution as alternative means of achieving academic credit.

Any individualized program is either directly related to or an outgrowth of one of these five forms.

Photo 1-13. Paul Francis, a senior, spent five months at the State Capitol in Albany, New York, working directly under the auspices of State Assemblyman J. Edward Meyer as he fulfilled an independent study prescription that involved a full-time responsibility away from school. As the youngest legislative assistant in New York, Paul described his experience as "an opportunity to play a part in the development of the laws of New York State." He said that every student "should have an opportunity to spend part of his educational experience in a non-academic setting with adults in some form of internship in the real world." Assemblyman Meyer selected Paul for "his common sense and ability to react analytically and directly with reasoned opinion." Paul, as a result of this individualized activity, is majoring in political science at Yale. (Photograph courtesy of Horace Greeley High School, Chappaqua, New York.)

DEFINING PARTIALLY AND TOTALLY
INDIVIDUALIZED PROGRAMS

Many different types of programs have been introduced under the name of "individualization." Some permit individual pacing and/or leveling, others encourage self-selection of objectives, others provide multiple learning options, and still others permit consideration of the child's learn-

Photo 1-14. Gail Dimin, a senior in Wantagh High School, spends three and one-half hours a day assisting elementary school students to learn. Originally uncertain of whether she wanted to teach, Gail now declares, "I love it. It's what I really want to do!" (Photograph courtesy of the Forest Lake Elementary School, Wantagh, New York.)

ing style and perceptual strengths. Few programs are totally individualized through the incorporation of all of these aspects into the overall instructional scheme. The degree to which a program utilizes teacher- and/or student-determined goals, materials, activities, interests, and assessment devices determines whether it is called "individually diagnosed and prescribed," "personalized," "self-directed," "independent study," or "individualized."

The following are overviews of selected types of programs that meet *some* of the criteria for effective individualized instruction.

1. Individually Diagnosed and Prescribed Instruction[4]

Student skills and objectives are prearranged and packaged in sequences on a continuum ranging from the simple to the complex. Students are diagnosed, programed into the sequence at the level at which they are ready to learn, and then permitted to move through the prepared materials at their own pace.

Basic Characteristics of Individualization

• Diagnosis

- Self-pacing
- Leveling

2. Personalized Instruction

The student establishes his own goals within the framework of the resources available. He then follows the program and uses the resources established by the teacher. He is permitted to complete the program as quickly as he can or as slowly as is necessary.

Basic Characteristics of Individualization

- Diagnosis
- Self-selection of goals
- Self-pacing
- Leveling

3. Self-Directed Instruction

The materials and the procedures are determined by the student, but the school determines the objectives and the general structure of the environment.

Basic Characteristics of Individualization

- Diagnosis
- Self-selection of materials
- Self-selection of learning activities
- Self-pacing
- Leveling

4. Independent Study

The student determines his instructional objectives and activities, but the school usually selects a limited number of students or courses for this approach.

Basic Characteristics of Individualization

- Diagnosis
- Self-selection of goals
- Self-selection of learning materials
- Self-selection of activities
- Self-pacing
- Leveling

5. Total Individualization

An operational approach to total individualization involves the *student* in:

Diagnosis: a.   What does the student know (facts, concepts, and skills), to what degree of proficiency, and at what level in the several content areas for which the school and/or the student have established objectives?

b.   What are the student's specific interests, skills, abilities, aptitudes, and degrees of maturity and motivation?

b.   What are the student's perceptual strengths?

d.   What are the student's best learning styles[5] for various school or self-selected tasks?

Prescription: a.   What are the jointly determined objectives to be achieved by the student? Ultimately, the student may self-select his objectives.

b.   What are the alternative learning resources and activities available to reach those objectives?

c.   What are the optional methods by which the student may demonstrate that he has attained the objectives?

Self-selection: a.   How will the student plan his own progress?

b.   What alternatives will the student be permitted to use, e.g., additional media resources, learning activity alternatives, and human or environmental resources?

c.   How may the student modify or apply his objectives where and when appropriate?

d.   How will the student interact with others in the learning process?

Teacher and   a.   How will the teacher and the student assess and rede-
Cooperative   sign new objectives based on the individualized evalu-
Assessment: ation?

b.   Which objectives and procedures may the student design in the interest of his own self-fulfillment?

c.   How will the new, individualized experiences aid in additional diagnosis and prescriptions?

Basic Characteristics of Individualization

- Teacher and student diagnosis
- Teacher and student prescription
- Student selection of goals, learning materials, activities, and instructional techniques

Photo 1-15. The development of prescriptions as an outgrowth of diagnosis is an integral part of any individualized approach. Joan Lowenthal, who has taught for eight years, discusses the selection of contract objectives with this student. (Photograph courtesy of the Seaford Manor Elementary School, Seaford, New York.)

Photos 1-16, 1-17. Joan encourages students to select their own learning materials and activities and provides for the use of multimedia resources. (Photographs courtesy of the Seaford Manor Elementary School, Seaford, New York.)

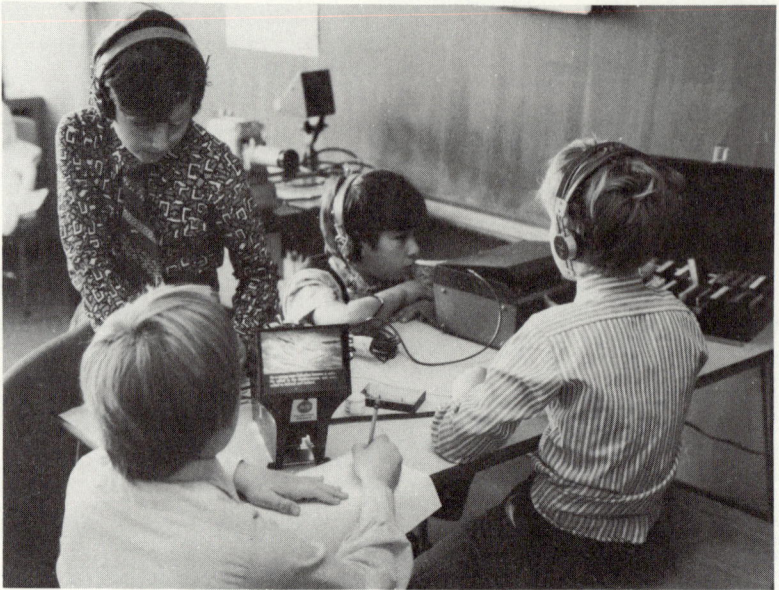

Photo 1-17

- Self-pacing
- Self-leveling
- Self-assessment followed by cooperative assessment
- Self-selection of learning process determined by learning styles(s)
- Objectives and prescription based on student interest(s)
- Student creativity incorporated into self-selection aspects

DIVIDING TOTAL INDIVIDUALIZATION INTO WORKABLE PHASES

As indicated earlier many programs include only selected characteristics of individualization, such as self-pacing or student selection of alternative objectives, and their designers do not realize that they could easily move into a well-organized, complete approach if they structured their progress on a gradual but advancing basis. A program is not totally individualized unless each of the aspects listed in Figure 1-1 (page 18) is included in its daily operational procedures.

To read the Total Individualization chart correctly, recognize that each of the unbroken line arrows indicates that the selected aspect is either (a) teacher, (b) cooperative (student and teacher) or (c) student responsibility. When the arrow for an identified aspect first appears in the "Teacher" column, the suggestion is that responsibility for that item *begins* with the teacher. When the arrow first appears in the "Cooperative" column,

Photo 1-18. Permitting students to achieve through their own learning style is another aspect of individualization. Here two junior high school students elected to work together on an instructional package on grammar. (Photograph courtesy of the Baldwin Harbor Junior High School, Baldwin, New York.)

responsibility for that aspect *begins* through joint teacher and student involvement. Where the unbroken arrow appears in the "Student" column only, it suggests that self-leveling, self-determination of learning style, and self-evaluation are preferable to either teacher-initiated or cooperatively designed leveling or learning style. Further, self-evaluation in these cases is an important part of the assessment process. There are times, however, when a student may show an inability to correctly select appropriate resources or the way in which he learns, or when he does not objectively analyze what he has mastered and what still remains to be learned, when it is necessary for the teacher to impose decisions concerning any phase of the student's progress or program.

Where an unbroken line arrow is paralleled by a broken line arrow the implication is that the choice of whether the responsibility is shared or not is left to the teacher.

Teacher Responsibilities

As the chart suggests, diagnosis of the student's knowledge, aptitude, and perceptual strengths initially should be conducted by the teacher. This could become a cooperative venture shortly after the student has had some experience with taking pretests that reveal what he knows about the topic (unit, contract, instructional package, etc.) and eliminating those objectives that directly relate to the information. Diagnosis of the first three aspects (knowledge, aptitude and perceptual strengths) remains the cooperative responsibility of the teacher and the student and should not be completely relegated to the student.

A pretest directly related to the topic's objectives could easily provide the knowledge diagnosis. Observation of his academic progress over a period of time will probably reveal as much information about a student's ability as a standardized test, for youngsters have been known to achieve either poorly or remarkably well in a given situation, depending upon their emotional, physical, sociological, or psychological reactions to any one or more of a number of given factors. Aptitude test scores have to be viewed with reservation for many students who often work far beyond or far below their test-revealed potential.

Posttests related to the student's objectives do not raise the same reservations. Although some professionals today scorn written, verbal, or performance evaluations and advocate a completely test-free educational system, individualization requires assessment. *It is necessary to determine how well each learner has achieved in terms of his own objectives.* Evaluating student academic growth is desirable for several reasons:

1.   "Nothing succeeds like success." A student who sees evidence of his own academic progress will become better able to continue learning. It is more likely that a youngster *will* succeed in an individualized program, for he is working with appropriate objectives, materials and methods and can pace himself without excessive pressure. Why should he then not see the fruits of his efforts? Why should he be denied the pleasure of praise for his achievements?

2.   Students frequently do not recognize all that they have learned in a given period, class, unit, etc. By taking a pretest and criterion-referenced posttest they can easily observe their own progress. This advancement adds to their appreciation of both school and themselves.

3.   An individualized program cannot be measured in any appropriate way other than by individual student achievement. An individualized program may be extremely effective for some students and comparatively ineffective for others. Such a program should only be discarded for those students for whom it does not work; those who succeed within it should be encouraged to continue, for in addition to academic success, these youngsters are gaining the skills of independent decision-making, task-focus, and self-determined learning. These are skills which would be desirable for all people and, for obvious reasons, are more valuable to a student than much of the information to which he is exposed on an almost daily basis.

4. Test evaluations are a direct means of communicating to the student, his parents, administrators or evaluators how well or how poorly the youngster is achieving. They eliminate teacher subjectivity and require direct student response to information.

5. By definition, the best way to determine whether or not an individualized program is effective is to measure the individual student's progress against his objectives, both cognitive and affective. Students who succeed in an individualized program as well or better than they did in a whole-group structure should be encouraged to continue learning in this way. Students who do not achieve in an individualized setting must be regrouped and assigned to another instructional environment.

Students who achieved 90 or more on a group IQ test in previous programs and who, nevertheless, scored poorly on objective achievement assessments should be tested for a determination of their perceptual strengths. The obvious discrepancy between intelligence and achievement needs to be analyzed.

The Frostig, Slingerland, and Wu screening instruments have been gaining wide professional attention as measures that indicate visual, perceptual-motor and memory-task proficiencies needed for academic success. Instruction for perceptually handicapped students must be modified based on their perceptual *strengths*, and remedial procedures to alleviate their disabilities should be prescribed by an expert in this field.

Once these diagnoses have been made, the teacher should prescribe the first set of objectives. The student should be permitted to select his objectives from the set the teacher designed. This, in effect, provides student options from among approved alternatives. This is also, in a sense, cooperative, but as the student develops increased facility in working with objectives, he will be able to suggest objectives for himself that the teacher may not have considered, and eventually he will design his own. Phase one is the first step toward helping the learner to achieve that goal. Phase two would be a more cooperative stage wherein the teacher and the student jointly develop the individual's objectives.

Some students may never be able to move into phase two, whereas others may have the insight, intelligence, and creativity to write independently a complete set of objectives for themselves after their first experience in using them. Such youngsters will move into phase three where they will design their own objectives, prescription, and/or contract without any teacher input other than approval or advice.

The assessment aspect is the final one in which the teacher should maintain continuous involvement. If teachers want to be accountable for their students' progress, they must be directly involved in the pretesting-posttesting aspects of the youngsters' programs.

Cooperative Responsibilities

Those aspects that easily could begin as a cooperative teacher-student effort include:

1. the diagnosis of student learning style[6]
2. the selection of learning resources (tapes, texts, filmstrips, etc.), activities, and small-group techniques
3. agreed-on time intervals within which self-pacing may be attempted, and
4. agreed-on means of assessment (pre- and post-).

"Leveling" is a term which means that students may learn about any topic through resources on a level of reading comprehension appropriate to them. For example, a 9-year-old youngster who is learning about rain forests may use texts that would normally be considered appropriate for 7-, 8-, 9-, 10-, and 11-year-olds; he need not read about a social studies unit only in "on-grade level" materials. A student who reads poorly need not be penalized in every subject because the information that he is expected to gather can only be obtained through grade-level books; he may read about mathematics, science, social studies, language arts, and the creative arts in books usually prescribed for younger students. "Self-leveling" is the process by which students select resources with which they feel comfortable and are permitted to learn through materials usually prescribed for younger students. When self-leveling, youngsters face fewer comprehension difficulties, but are frequently appropriately limited in the amount of information on a given topic to which they are exposed. Teachers should challenge students to reach those levels that they are capable of attaining.

As indicated above, learning style should be identified cooperatively whenever necessary. In most cases, however, students should be permitted to function in the instructional environment through their self-determined *modus operandi*, which usually closely conforms to their learning style. Where academic progress is not in harmony with the knowledge, aptitude, and perceptual-strength diagnoses, teachers should analyze the student's learning style to be able to prescribe alternative ways of achieving. For a thorough description of how to identify and use learning style see Chapter 3.

Student Responsibilities

With the exceptions of knowledge, aptitude, and perceptual-strength diagnoses, most of the aspects of individualization may eventually become the responsibility of students. Depending upon age, maturity and ability, some students are able to write their own prescriptions, assess themselves,

Photo 1-19. Encouraging students to locate, select, use, share, repair, and replace resources is one means of developing student responsibility and independence. (Photograph courtesy of the Westorchard School, Chappaqua, New York.)

and function effectively in the instructional environment when they are only 9 or 10 years old. Conversely, of course, graduate institutions have some students who are unable to assume responsibility for their own learning. Teachers must, therefore, continuously diagnose, prescribe for and guide some students through their entire educational experience. It is important that teachers recognize when to "let go" of the able learners and how to encourage the hesitant ones who have the potential to become independent and self-actualizing.

Determining who will be responsible for introducing each of the necessary aspects of individualization is the first step in designing an effective program.

TEAM LEARNING EXERCISE ON INDIVIDUALIZED INSTRUCTION

When an assessment device is directly related to previously stated objectives, it is called a "criterion-referenced" instrument. On the next few pages you will find such a test that you may use to discover whether or not you have achieved the behavioral objectives listed at the beginning of this chapter.

You may take this test alone or, if you prefer, you may work with others to determine the answers to each question. When a small group (3-8) of learners who have studied the same materials cooperatively try to develop the answers to questions directly related to the material, the technique is called "team learning." The following exercise may be used, therefore, to assess either an individual's or a group's learning.

If you prefer testing yourself alone, read the questions, write in the answers, and then compare your responses with those listed under "Comparing Answers to the Self-Instruction Guide."

If you would like to work with others, have the group seat itself together in an oval design. Select or permit one person to volunteer to serve as a "recorder." The team should tackle one question at a time by reading it, discussing possible answers, deciding on the answers that are correct, and directing the recorder to write them. When no additional answers are forthcoming for the first question, proceed to the next, and so on. When finished, check the group's answers with those given here (pages 47 through 49).

This is an interesting way to learn and an accurate means of measuring what has been learned.

TEAM LEARNING INDIVIDUALIZED INSTRUCTION: EXERCISE ON THE RATIONALE AND FIVE ALTERNATIVE METHODS

Team Members

1. _____   4. _____
2. _____   5. _____
3. _____   6. _____

Recorder: _____

Assessment

A. Identify at least ten things that many traditional schools do that actually prevent a child from learning easily.

1. _____   6. _____
2. _____   7. _____
3. _____   8. _____
4. _____   9. _____
5. _____   10. _____

B. List the five possible methods through which programs may be individualized.

1. _____
2. _____

3. _____
4. _____
5. _____

C. List at least ten aspects of an individualized instructional program.

1. _____   6. _____
2. _____   7. _____
3. _____   8. _____
4. _____   9. _____
5. _____   10. _____

D. Cite at least ten advantages of individualization.

1. _____
2. _____
3. _____
4. _____
5. _____
6. _____
7. _____
8. _____
9. _____
10. _____

Bonus: Go to the head of the class if you can name two more!

11. _____
12. _____

Comparing Answers to the Self-Instruction Guide

A. Things that many traditional schools do that may actually prevent a student from learning include:

1. using teaching methods that appeal to only one perceptual strength
2. lecturing, rather than actively involving pupils in learning
3. group pacing
4. requiring similar things and similar amounts of learning from all grouped youngsters
5. requiring an essentially noiseless environment
6. requiring extensive conformity
7. admitting all children at the same age and keeping them in school for the same time intervals
8. maintaining a grade-level system
9. using a textbook (reading) approach
10. using only one method or approach to teach a concept, subject, etc.

11. requiring the student to learn essentially from his teacher or text
12. requiring similar characteristics of all teachers
13. maintaining a conformist adult-child instructional relationship
14. expecting individual teachers (rather than a team) to diagnose, prescribe for, and guide a student through the instructional process
15. selecting the methods of instruction on the basis of teaching style rather than learning style
16. providing learning opportunities within a structured "school day" or "year" rather than on a more flexible basis
17. maintaining educational programs essentially in educational facilities

B. The five basic methods through which programs may be individualized:

1. contracts: contract activity packages (CAP), learning activity packages (LAP), teaching-learning units (TLU), etc.
2. programed learning
3. instructional packages
4. work-study experiences
5. community contribution experiences

C. Aspects of an individualized program[7]:

1. diagnosis (teacher, student, cooperative, team)
2. prescription (teacher, student, cooperative, team)
3. publicly stated objectives (teacher, student, cooperatively or team prescribed)
4. alternative resources through which to learn
5. alternative or optional activities
6. self-pacing
7. self-leveling
8. self-assessment and/or cooperative assessment, teacher and/or team assessment
9. self-selection of learning methods
10. objectives and prescription based on student abilities and interests
11. opportunities for student creativity incorporated into prescription
12. criterion-referenced evaluation
13. performance-based evaluation (student demonstration of knowledge through means other than written tests, e.g., acting, making of a project, conducting an experiment, etc.)

D. Advantages of individualization:

All of the "aspects" listed as a response to item C plus:
1. provides for student success rather than failure
2. builds self-image
3. permits peer interaction that causes retention

4. decreases student dependence on the teacher and initially transfers it to peers and eventually to self
5. provides for problem-solving experiences
6. develops internal motivation rather than peer competition
7. develops critical analysis abilities.

TWO

Organizing for Individualization: A Seven-Step Process

Behavioral Objectives for Chapter 2

1. You will be able to list each of the seven steps through which a teacher should guide children to gradually develop their ability to function effectively in an individualized program.
2. You will be able to explain why each of the steps is usually necessary.

. . . .

DEVELOPING THE BASIC ELEMENTS OF INDIVIDUALIZED INSTRUCTION

In addition to the basic aspects of individual diagnosis, prescription, options, evaluation, and redesign, there are several related characteristics that are also essential to an effective individualized instructional program. These other facets of individualized learning, and some general examples of how to achieve them, follow.

Related Characteristics	*Process Opportunities*	*Examples*
Each student should:	Students are provided with:	
1. Assume some responsibility for his own learning and relate the curriculum to his major interests.	1. Opportunities to determine some, many, or all of their instructional objectives in conjunction with their teachers. The more involvement the student gains in making instructional decisions, the more likely he is to become a responsible and motivated learner.	1. Teachers and students design projects, contracts, instructional packages, case studies, etc., with opportunities for additional student-developed personal objectives.
2. Be helped to become an independent learner, capable of progressing without being overly dependent on others.	2. Multiple options, varied environments, and the freedom of scheduling themselves so that under the teacher's guidance learning becomes increasingly self-selective and self-evaluative.	2. Varied instructional areas are provided to permit student selection of learning materials and a considerable amount of self-assessment prior to teacher-student evaluation.
3. Learn at a pace (rate, speed) that is comfortable for him.	3. Projected time intervals during which they are permitted to pace themselves and to determine the amount of study and the number of objectives they can complete. This process is guided by the teacher to encourage positive achievement.	3. Instructional objectives are partially self-selected and students determine the pace of their learning and the time requirements for most objectives.
4. Learn through materials that are related to his perceptual strengths (seeing, hearing, touching, acting out, combinations of senses, etc.).	4. Combined teacher, student and specialist diagnosis of perceptual learning strengths with subsequent joint prescription of materials and techniques that capitalize on strengths and reduce the negative effects of weaknesses.	4. Multimedia and multisensory learning resources are provided and screening procedures are used to determine which combinations of materials and packages are best suited to the student's perceptual strengths.
5. Learn in accordance with his own learning style (alone, in small groups, through media, etc.).	5. Joint diagnosis of learning style and suggestions of study procedures, e.g., a quiet area, a tutoring team, a small-group instructional procedure, different times of the day, etc.	5. A varied instructional environment is provided and diagnostic procedures are used to encourage the student to work appropriately with available facilities, adults, peers and resources.
6. Learn on a level that is appropriate to his abilities.	6. Learning objectives and multisensory resources (books, films, etc.) appropriate to varied ability levels.	6. Behavioral objectives of varied types and levels of difficulty are available for students and are accompanied by multisensory materials.

Related Characteristics	*Process Opportunities*	*Examples*
7. Be graded in terms of his own achievement and not in comparison with others.	7. Personalized instructional objectives and self-evaluation procedures as well as a teacher assessment of growth in comparison with individual diagnoses and prescriptions.	7. Tests, suggested answer cards, model solutions, and self-assessment devices are provided to allow an individual student to measure his progress in terms of his own objectives.
8. Experience a sense of achievement and thus be able to develop self-esteem and pride.	8. Packages, prescriptions, instructional groupings, goals, and self-assessment techniques that permit continuing achievement and success.	8. Teacher-student conferences, team reviews, peer and self-evaluation of progress and achievement on teacher and self-determined objectives are included as part of the prescription.

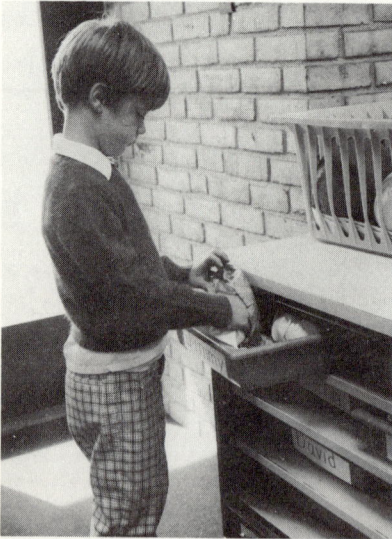

Photo 2-1. Separate, labeled tote trays in accessible cabinets aid students to organize their work and materials so that they become independent learners. (Photograph courtesy of the Westorchard School, Chappaqua, New York.)

Photo 2-2. This math learning station permits students to select the materials they will use to achieve their objectives. (Photograph courtesy of the Floral Park-Bellerose Elementary School, Floral Park, New York.)

BEGINNING THE PROCESS OF INDIVIDUALIZATION:
WHAT TO DO AND WHY

Unfortunately, most American children are unprepared for this type of independent, individualized learning approach. From the moment they are born they are, in a sense, conditioned to accept directives from others. Their hospital experiences are determined by the nursery schedule. At home they are continuously directed toward modes of acceptable behavior, dress, social interaction, verbalization, and play. In school they are immediately apprised of the rules and regulations that govern that institution and are expected to conform. For most of their young, pliable lives they awake, wash, eat, dress, leave their homes, arrive elsewhere, play, work, study, return home, and sleep essentially when and how they are told.

It is unrealistic to expect that after five to fifteen years of submissive, structured, and directed behavior children will be able to function effectively in an individualized program that requires the ability to solve problems, make decisions, and remain independently task-focused. Indeed, some children may feel disoriented when first exposed to individualized learning because of their previous experiences in structured environments. To avoid feelings of insecurity and an inability to function well, it is important that freedom to select options and to learn independently be granted to students gradually and with direction. *Good individualized programs involve effective structures and continually improving student performance toward appropriate personal and group standards.*

Students should not be expected to make intelligent self-instructional decisions without first being taught how. Guiding a youngster through the processes of selecting, decision-making, locating, cooperating, and evaluating will require varying amounts of teacher and student time, energy, and competence, but effective teacher and administrator training in these operations is essential if each student is to achieve success in an individualized environment.

There are seven sound steps to consider in teaching students to be responsible for self-instruction. Following are the steps and their description (see Figure 2-1).

Step 1: Learning in Small Groups

Students who have been parent- or teacher-directed for most of their lives first should learn to make simple decisions and to assume the responsibility for completing simple tasks free of constant adult supervision. Use of selected techniques such as circles of knowledge, team learning, case studies, brainstorming and simulations[1] provides a structure wherein learn-

Photo 2-3. Students should be provided many opportunities to make decisions. These second graders are cooperatively trying to agree on appropriate alternative responses to a "treasure hunt" problem. (Photograph courtesy of the Westorchard School, Chappaqua, New York.)

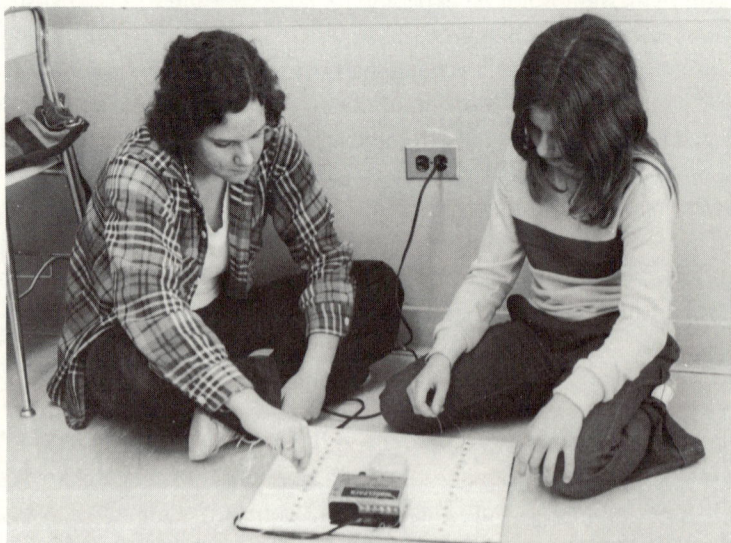

Photo 2-4. Using a game that requires problem-solving skills, these students are exploring possible answers together. (Photograph courtesy of Seaford Junior High School, Seaford, New York.)

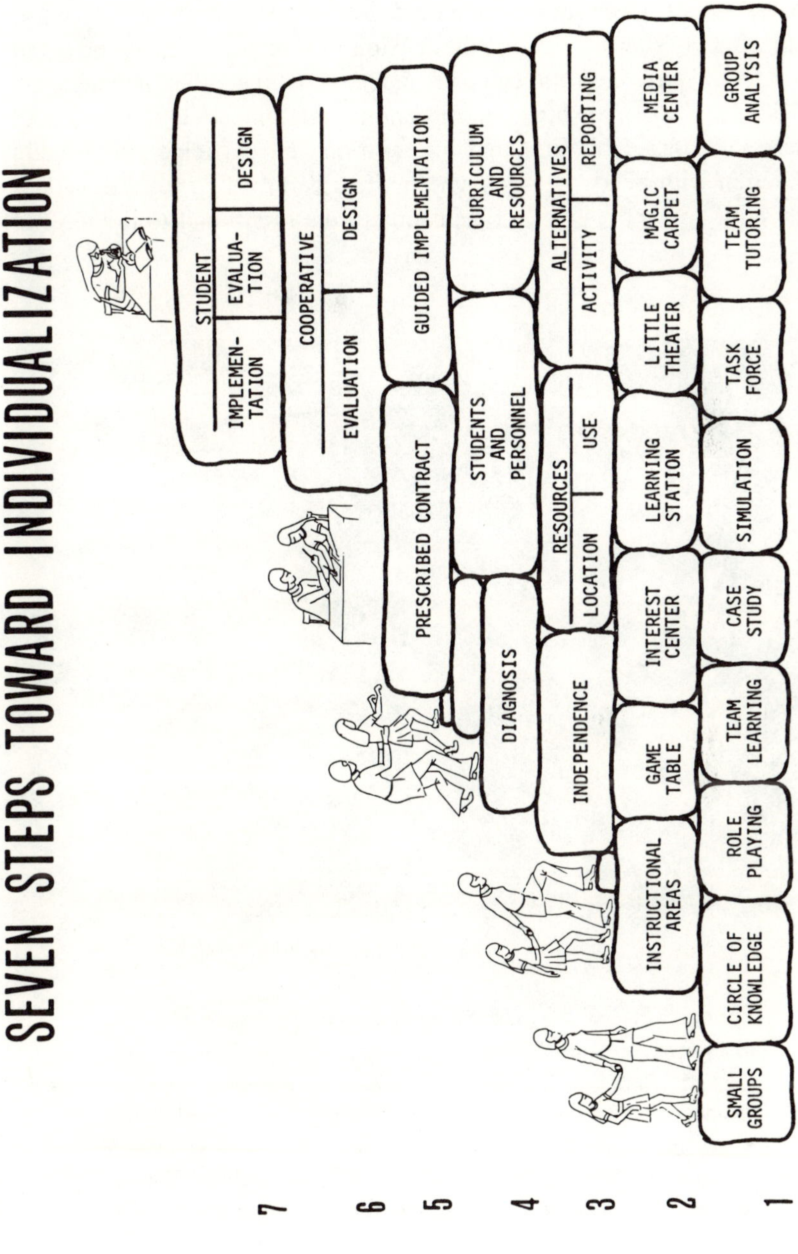

SEVEN STEPS TOWARD INDIVIDUALIZATION

		STUDENT	
7		IMPLEMEN-TATION	EVALUA-TION	DESIGN

	COOPERATIVE
6	EVALUATION	DESIGN

5	GUIDED IMPLEMENTATION

4	CURRICULUM AND RESOURCES
	PRESCRIBED CONTRACT

	STUDENTS AND PERSONNEL
3	ALTERNATIVES
	ACTIVITY	REPORTING
	DIAGNOSIS

	RESOURCES
	LOCATION	USE
	INDEPENDENCE

2	INSTRUCTIONAL AREAS	GAME TABLE	INTEREST CENTER	LEARNING STATION	LITTLE THEATER	MAGIC CARPET	MEDIA CENTER
1	CIRCLE OF KNOWLEDGE	ROLE PLAYING	TEAM LEARNING	CASE STUDY	SIMULATION	TASK FORCE	TEAM TUTORING	GROUP ANALYSIS

SMALL GROUPS

Figure 2-1

ing occurs through cooperative small-group effort without the teacher serving as a constant guide or fountain of knowledge.

The small-group interactions also permit youngsters to solve problems in cooperation with other students so that they need not fear failure or embarrassment. Even if errors are made, sharing the responsibility with a group of peers sharply reduces the tension or trauma. Further, the small-group techniques help students to understand how other people reach decisions and work toward solutions and permit the development of additional skills based on firsthand observation and participation. Finally, interaction with peers creates sounding boards on which to reflect ideas, build solutions and suggest conclusions to the group and to the teacher.

Photos 2-5, 2-6, 2-7, 2-8. Sharon Sussman (eight years of teaching experience) distributes many magazine advertisements. She asks each group to identify the propaganda techniques used and to analyze their effectiveness by recognizing the merchandise from which the brand name has been removed. The students' analysis skills increase rapidly through this small-group strategy. (Photographs courtesy of Merrick Avenue Junior High School, Bellmore-Merrick, New York.)

Photo 2-6

Photo 2-7

Photo 2-8

Step 2: Establishing Instructional Areas

Once students can learn effectively together by using at least three or
four of the small-group techniques, the teacher should establish a variety of
instructional areas such as learning stations, interest centers, game tables,
little theaters, magic carpets and media corners[2] so that youngsters may
begin to work independently or with partners at defined learning spaces.
Each instructional area serves a specific purpose and thus attracts pupils
with different objectives and interests at varying times.

Separating the learning environment into multi-instructional areas
encourages students to examine their objectives carefully, to determine the
resources through which they will attempt to achieve their objectives, to
select the means they will use to determine how much they have accomplished and how much more they still must complete, and to evaluate
their own progress. A student must proceed through this structured process
in order to determine (a) which instructional area he will work in, (b)
what he will find there or need to take with him, (c) when to move on to
another area, and (d) when to request assistance or guidance. In addition,
each of the instructional areas should provide multiple options so that the
student is required to make some choices as he progresses and, at some
point, evaluate the selections he has made. Once a youngster is able to

begin working independently (or with a friend or two) at two or three instructional areas, he is ready for the next step.

Step 3: Developing Pupil Self-Reliance

As the students begin to use the instructional areas, they will need to be taught how to (a) locate and use the resources available to them, (b) make selections, and (c) evaluate their own and their peers' progress. These skills are preparation for functioning in any of the individualized methods of programed learning, instructional packages, contracts, or work-study and community experiences. It is at this point, when they actually are (a) using the materials and depending upon their own ability to assess the task correctly, (b) locating information and resources, (c) recording what they need to remember, (d) selecting ways of demonstrating accomplished skills, and (e) evaluating and defending their own progress, that students will learn best.

Photos 2-9, 2-10. Elizabeth Horton, teaching for three years, limits the number of children using an instructional area at one time. Her kindergarteners indicate their preferences by removing a color-coded ring from the keyboard. When there are no more keys for a selected activity, choices must be made from among remaining options. Children who are painting or cooking wear colored headbands so that at any time Elizabeth can look around the room and know where they belong. The use of headbands prevents the removal of paints and ingredients from appropriate areas. (Photographs courtesy of the Westorchard School, Chappaqua, New York.)

Photo 2-10

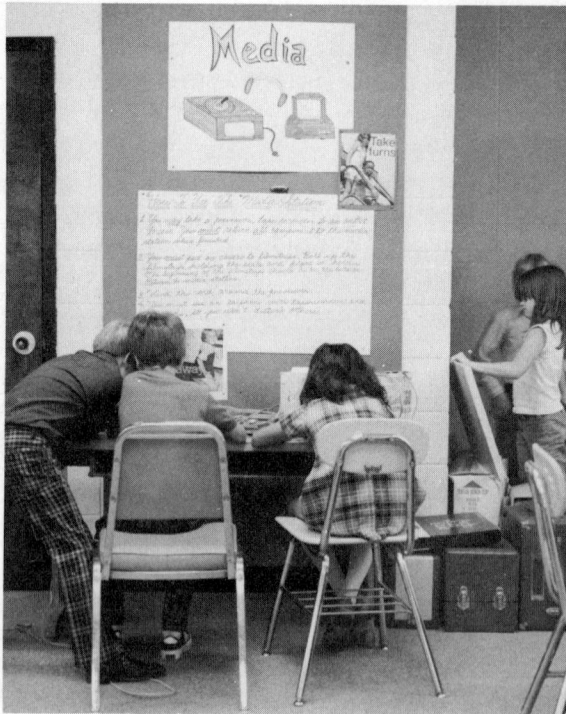

Photo 2-11. Media should be placed at a central location for easy access and used as shown in this media center. (Photograph courtesy of the Floral Park-Bellerose Elementary School, Floral Park, New York.)

The teacher should recognize that not all students go through identical readiness phases at the same point in time. Therefore, when a student needs to use a catalog, he should be taught how. When a student can't use a filmstrip because it is torn, he should be taught how to repair it. Moreover, many students require tightly structured and directed programs longer than others. It is important to build self-reliance in those youngsters slowly and effectively.

The teacher need not go through the same task repeatedly, but should instead train two or three students at one time and then appoint them as a cadre of assistants for that specific task. They, in turn, should teach other students the necessary skill when the other youngsters need to learn it.

Step 4: Strengthening Teacher Diagnostic Skills

Shortly after the teacher begins to guide students into effective use of the small-group techniques, she should carefully begin to observe the youngsters and to record their obvious strengths, interests, and learning styles. These should form the basis of the prescription that is eventually

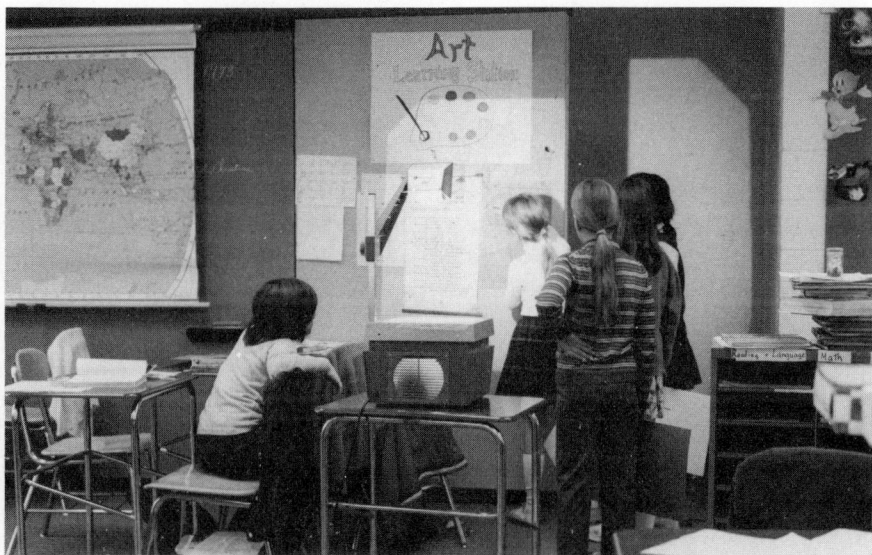

Photo 2-12. Media may be moved, however, when needed at another area. Students in this art learning station are using an overhead projector to enlarge a map transparency on a wall. Many students may now use the projection at one time, each for a different purpose. One girl is developing a three-dimensional diorama of clay; two are reproducing the map on cardboard in order to create a puzzle. A third is using the map as a cover for a scrapbook. (Photograph courtesy of the Floral Park-Bellerose Elementary School, Floral Park, New York.)

Photo 2-13

Photos 2-13, 2-14. A magic carpet area is a quiet corner of the room where children may go to read in private. Nancy Cox, a student teacher from St. John's University, uses it to read to a small group of youngsters in the class where she serves as a full-time assistant teacher. (Photographs courtesy of the Seaford Manor Elementary School, Seaford, New York.)

Photos 2-15, 2-16. A little theater is a place in the room where youngsters can write, dramatize, produce costumes, design scenery, and engage in many theater-related arts. (Photographs courtesy of the Roaring Brook School, Chappaqua, New York.)

developed for that pupil. The instructor should also assess the available resources and personnel and plan how to use them in the instructional setting.

A teacher who is just beginning the individualization process should select only one curriculum area in which to begin. That area should be the one that she likes most and in which she believes herself to be most proficient. The curriculum to be introduced should be analyzed to determine exactly what (a) all students will be required to learn, (b) all students may choose to learn, (c) interested students may choose to learn, and (d) selected students may be assigned to learn. These curriculum concepts, facts, or skills should then be written as "behavioral"[3] or "performance" objectives so that each student knows precisely what he will be responsible for learning, how he may show that he has learned it when he has, and the degree of proficiency which will be expected of him.

Teachers will also find that it is necessary to provide students with multisensory materials through which to learn all of their required objectives. Diagnosis of his perceptual strengths and learning style will enhance a student's chance to achieve. If these diagnoses require more time or skill than is available, a variety of multimedia resources on many ability levels will achieve the same result if students are permitted to self-select the resources through which they learn. After some initial experimentation with varied sensory materials, students tend to return to those resources through which they learn most easily. These invariably are the resources that complement their perceptual strengths. If students err in their first selections they quickly face difficulties and then seek alternative materials.

Step 5: Designing Prescriptions for Students

When the teacher believes that selected students may be able to begin self-instruction, she should assign to them relatively simple but interesting curriculum prescriptions. The first or second prescription may require extensive teacher guidance through the various stages; the third should produce a relatively independent student learner who maintains the option of working with a friend or small group of friends throughout the process.

When working on an individualized prescription, students will need to know how to (a) use their time wisely and efficiently, (b) work with others to achieve certain goals, (c) evaluate their own progress, (d) record those things that they cannot easily commit to memory, and (e) test themselves to determine how much of what they are required to learn they already know and how much remains to be achieved. Students should also learn how, when and from whom to obtain assistance and how to wait patiently until they can receive help.

Step 6: Achieving Joint Student-Teacher Evaluation and Design

Ideally, the student will progress along the individualization continuum, gradually becoming increasingly confident and able to work independently and well. Eventually he should be able to evaluate his growth in terms of accepted objectives without too much dependence on the teacher. Finally, he may be able to design for himself subsequent prescriptions that include (a) clearly stated objectives, (b) alternative resources, (c) activity and reporting options, (d) a self-assessment instrument, and (e) a terminal assessment through either written, oral, or performance means. This latter stage may be reached quickly by a few, within a reasonable amount of time by many, and perhaps never by some.

Step 7: Building Greater Student Independence

As the student's independence and ability to teach himself increases, he will assume additional responsibility for prescription completion, evaluation, and design. When this occurs he may be totally independent of even the prescription structure, and should be encouraged to construct an instructional process and environment that is uniquely his own. Indeed, as has been mentioned before, teaching is one of the best ways to learn, and he will undoubtedly become a teaching assistant for others as well as himself. Total individualization of teaching and learning will have been achieved for this student.

ORGANIZING AN INDIVIDUALIZED PROGRAM

Before organizing an individualized program it is necessary to determine which of the five basic methods you wish to use. All of the methods are described in Chapter 1 and each is matched on the following chart (Figure 2-2) with the appropriate sequential steps required to move toward sound individualized instruction.

Once you have identified the method to be used (or currently in use), an experienced teacher, supervisor, or administrator will be able to observe and to evaluate the program and to identify which steps require strengthening. Planning and further improvement can be designed by measuring the existing program against the progressive stages of the chart.

To use the chart, find the column that best describes the method you have selected. Then note the appropriate step at which to begin this method by reading the parallel box in the columns under "Methods." Then read vertically downward in the first column to determine how far the program has progressed to date and which steps require introduction.

Process	Methods				
	Contracts	Programed Learning	Instructional Packages	Work-Study Experiences	Community Contribution Experiences
1. Provide small-group interactions.	Begin				
2. Design instructional areas	Step 2	Begin	Begin		
3. Develop independence	Step 3	Step 2	Step 2	Begin	Begin
4. Diagnose	Step 4	Step 3	Step 3	Step 2	Step 2
5. Prescribe and guide	Step 5	Step 4	Step 4	Step 3	Step 3
6. Cooperatively evaluate and design	Step 6	Step 5	Step 5	Step 4	Step 4
7. Student-implemented evaluation and design	Step 7	Step 6	Step 6	Step 5	Step 5

Figure 2-2

As indicated in Chapter 1 under the description of each of the five basic methods of individualizing instruction, small-group techniques are an integral part of the contract method only. Programed learning and instructional packages each tend to isolate the student in the learning environment, although it is possible for teachers to design team learnings, circles of knowledge, case studies, group analysis situations and any of the other small-group techniques to complement programed materials.

Work-study and community contribution programs usually center outside the school building and, because of their involvement with the community, rarely require frequent meetings of students who are each involved with the completion of their own prescription-related objectives. For this reason it is not feasible to build the small-group techniques into these highly diversified programs where students, unless they are engaged in the identical project, rarely meet with each other.

Similarly, although it is necessary to establish varied instructional areas in the learning environment to facilitate the smooth functioning of contracts, programed learning, and instructional packages, this facet of the program is usually bypassed for the secondary students enrolled in work-study or community contribution programs because the learning environment is separated from the school facilities.

Therefore, the five methods of individualizing instruction share in common only steps three through seven.

DEVELOPING STUDENT READINESS
FOR INDIVIDUALIZATION

Whether working with primary, elementary, middle, or high school youngsters, the process by which student independence is developed is essentially similar; only the language and the degree of reinforcement will vary.

Students, whatever their ages, should be prepared for the new method of learning. They will need to have a simple but precise explanation of what they will be doing, what is expected of them, and how they will be evaluated.

Students will need to comprehend the value of objectives, alternative resources, activities, self-evaluation, and small-group techniques. With young children the exposure to independent learning should be gradual and slow. With older students, only a session or two of preplanning may be necessary.

Student independence will be developed over a varying time span. Students will need to have many opportunities to use objectives in the ways

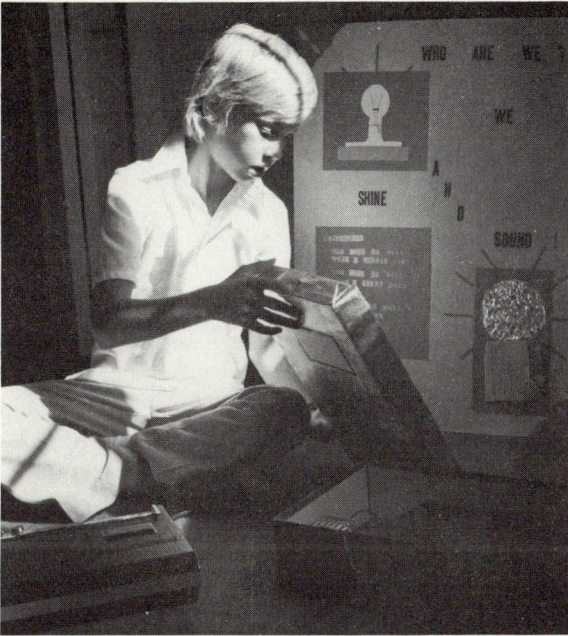

Photos 2-17, 2-18, 2-19. Instructional packages develop students' abilities to follow directions, complete tasks, self-assess themselves, and learn independently. (Photographs courtesy of the Department of Curriculum and Teaching, St. John's University, New York.)

Photo 2-18

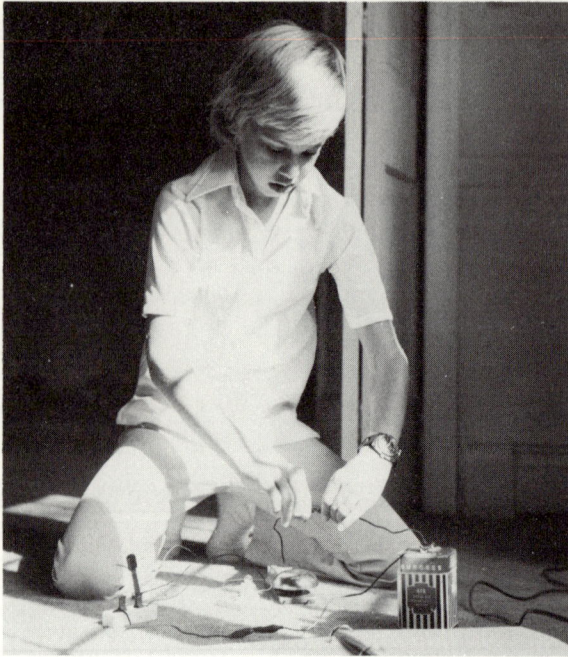

Photo 2-19

demanded by an individualized setting. They will require repeated opportunities to make selections (initially from among approved alternatives), to
test themselves, to evaluate their own progress, and to both share and seek
reactions with their peers. Confidence will grow as experience and success
increase. Initially, students often feel uncomfortable and overworked in an
individualized program. It will take some of the students time to adjust their
learning styles, their pacing, and their motivation, and to overcome insecurity while pursuing this different process. Independence can best
flourish in an environment where many options are available, where
opportunities exist for experimenting with resources, where one may seek
alternative ways of studying and learning, where self-evaluation can pre-
cede teacher evaluation, and where students are not penalized for making
errors—as long as they learn from their mistakes.[4]

Understandably, the implementation of these procedures will tend to
produce the beginning of an informal atmosphere—the kind of environment which is a natural outgrowth of individualization.

Unfortunately, many teachers, in attempting to institute informality,
accomplish the task without developing an appropriate program. Visits to
many school districts often verify that students do ''enjoy'' coming to

school, but are, simultaneously, limited in the amount of learning or academic progress that they can achieve.

A pleasant, tension-free atmosphere is to be applauded if those students who need pressure and who require structure are provided these ingredients in the new educational environment. If provocation is the only way in which an individual is able to learn, then, unfortunately, the teacher will be required to add that amount of stress that will enable the student to succeed. If you are reacting emotionally to this statement, if you believe that it is better to avoid tension and to permit the student to participate in the instructional activities without achieving at his maximum capacity, you may not be personally in harmony with the concept of total individualization. Individualization, if you refer back to the start of Chapter 1, is the recognition that, for each student, whether child or adult, learning is a pervasive developmental process that varies, often completely.

As an educator you must make a decision! Will you help students learn through their learning style or are you going to insist that they learn through your own preconceived mental image of what an appropriate (acceptable) learning style should be? If you are concerned with the student's progress, you should permit him to learn in ways that are most conducive to his successful functioning in the educational environment. What is important is that he learns and that he builds his self-image and love of learning. Indeed, his achievement in a positive and open environment is likely to reinforce a success pattern that will ultimately enable him to learn and to explore in a variety of ways, probably with reduced tension and stress.

A final word of encouragement. Psychiatrists frequently verify that pressure and tension are self-imposed. Few learners react to teachers' admonishments if they do not care. Many students create their own controlled tension as a vital element of their self-motivation. Do not try to alter a youngster's learning style any more than you would attempt to coerce a left-handed student to write with his right hand. What is "natural" to him is probably his best way of learning. Today's teacher needs to diagnose, prescribe, and guide; not play Pygmalion.

- Do not cajole your quiet students into active discussion.
- Do not coerce your active students into quiet submission.
- Do not force your hyperactive students to sit quietly.
- Do not urge your withdrawn students to become peer-involved.
- Do not assign creative activities to your "bread-and-butter" youngsters.
- Do not necessarily require that your creative students respond in written or verbal form (or only in response to behavioral objectives).
- Do not entice the observers into leadership roles.
- Do not squelch the leader because he is overexuberant, very popular, or less conforming than you would like.

Photo 2-20. Increased knowledge, insight, and self-reliance are gained in different ways. Some students of varying ages appear to achieve most comfortably and at a faster rate when they teach themselves. (Photograph courtesy of Briarcliff High School, Briarcliff Manor, New York.)

Photo 2-21. Other youngsters need the social interaction that accompanies the use of small-group techniques, and for these a circle of knowledge provides extremely effective reinforcement. (Photograph courtesy of the Westorchard School, Chappaqua, New York.)

In short, the purpose of individualization is to provide students with increased knowledge, insight, and self-reliance, and thus free them to:

> . . . be nobody but themselves in a world which is doing its best, night and day, to make them everybody else. . .[5]

TEAM LEARNING EXERCISE ON ORGANIZING FOR INDIVIDUALIZED INSTRUCTION

Directions

As in the previous chapter, you may use the following exercise to either assess yourself or to join a group to learn and/or to corroborate the answers to the questions. If you prefer studying with others, follow the procedures for team learning that were given in the Directions for the Self-Assessment Instrument in Chapter 1.

When the questions have all been completed, compare your answers, or the group's answers, with those given here.

TEAM LEARNING: THE SEVEN-STEP PROCESS TOWARD INDIVIDUALIZING INSTRUCTION

Team Members

1. _____ 4. _____
2. _____ 5. _____
3. _____ 6. _____

Recorder: _____

Criterion Referenced Assessment

A. List each of the seven steps through which a teacher should guide children to gradually develop their ability to function effectively in an individualized program.

1. _____
2. _____
3. _____
4. _____
5. _____
6. _____
7. _____

B. Explain why each of these steps is necessary:

Step   *Why Necessary*

1   _____
2   _____
3   _____
4   _____
5   _____
6   _____
7   _____

Comparing Answers to the Self-Instruction Guide—
The Seven-Step Process Toward Individualizing Instruction

A. *Seven-Step Process*[6]   B. *Why Necessary*

1. Use of at least three or four of the *small group techniques*.	To transfer dependence on the teacher to peers; to provide increased opportunity for independence; to promote discussion of studies; to expose students to other children's critical thinking processes.
2. Use of at least two or three different *instructional areas*.	To provide experiences in working independently, making decisions, recognizing problems, and seeking solutions.
3. Locating, selecting, using, repairing and returning of resources and making selections from among alternatives.	To further increase independence of both teacher and peers and to provide additional experience in decision-making and problem-solving.
4. Comprehending each of the tasks involved in *completing an accepted prescription* (or assignment) and recognizing where to obtain assistance and resources when needed.	To develop ability in students to become increasingly responsible for their own progress.
5. Accepting the responsibility for independently *proceeding through the first prescription with the teacher's help*.	To demonstrate personal competence and to increase self-image.

6. *Cooperatively evaluating one's progress* and helping to design the next prescription.

To recognize achievement and provide opportunity for self-selection of goals, resources, activities, and self-teaching methods.

7. *Completing prescription, evaluating progress, and designing new program independently.*

To demonstrate ability to achieve, determine direction, and succeed independently and also to increase motivation and self-esteem.

THREE

Identifying Individual
Learning Styles

Behavioral Objectives for Chapter 3

1. Identify (a) each of the four basic stimulants that affect a student's learning style and (b) a minimum of twelve related elements.
2. Use the Learning Style Questionnaire to identify your own learning style.

. . . .

DEFINING LEARNING STYLE

One of the key procedures in developing a successful individualized instructional program is the effective use of each student's learning style.[1]

As early as 1892[2] experiments were conducted to determine whether oral or visual teaching appeared to be more effective for students. At that time, and as recently as 1965, researchers tried to identify the "best" methods, not realizing that there are no panaceas; that there are only best methods for individuals, and that what is a valuable teaching technique for one student may be ineffective for another.

What is "learning style"?

It is the manner in which at least 18 different elements of four basic stimuli affect a person's ability to absorb and to retain information, values, facts or concepts. The combinations and variances in these elements suggest, perhaps, that no two people in the entire world learn in exactly the same way, just as no two people think *exactly* alike.

For centuries, scholars and professors have tried to impart their wisdom and knowledge to students, rarely recognizing that, unless they introduced the material to their charges through a variety of methods, the likelihood was that only a percentage of each group would retain what was taught in a given lesson. An early experimenter, Kirkpatrick, reported on a study that compared visual, auditory, and motor impressions and revealed that concrete objects were better remembered than written names, and that the latter (the visual) were better than the spoken (oral) names.[3] As remarkably advanced as this conclusion was for 1894, the focus was on "better for everyone," or "better for students," with no awareness of better for whom and under what circumstances, a basic mistake that persisted into the 1960's.

Indeed, many educators still believe that the stimulating teacher or relevant instructional topics, materials or procedures will result in learning. While it is true that a dramatic teacher, an exciting presentation, or an assignment in the "real" world may enhance learning in a given instance or for an even longer period on occasion, how much more successful that teacher and those materials or assignments would be if individual learning styles were consciously used. The responsive chords of learning style are struck too infrequently through an occasional insight by a sensitive, caring teacher. Motivation, relating to peer work groups, positive structure, perceptual strengths, and each of the other 18 elements of learning style may be diagnosed and used to profile and to work with students as individuals.

Moreover, most researchers have been concerned with identifying the one perception that produced increased learning and/or retention;[4] few hypothesized or explored any of the aspects of learning style other than perceptual (or sensory) strengths. Today, the Frostig, Slingerland, and Wu tests clearly indicate perceptual handicaps and relative strengths, and materials can be provided to eliminate or ameliorate deficiencies. As indicated, however, there are at least 17 other identifiable elements of learning style in addition to one's senses of hearing, sight, touch, whole-body involvement and smell.

The Diagnosing Learning Style Chart (Figure 3-1) suggests that four basic stimulants affect the elements that determine how a person learns, these being one's (a) immediate environment, (b) emotional makeup, (c) sociological reaction to people, and (d) physical being.

ANALYZING THE BASIC ELEMENTS OF LEARNING STYLE: ENVIRONMENTAL, EMOTIONAL, SOCIOLOGICAL AND PHYSICAL

Before you are able to diagnose how students learn in a given situation, it is important to understand the definitions and implications of each of the elements that affect learning style.

The Environmental Elements of Learning Style

Sound[5] *in the Environment.* Some proponents of "open education" are fond of saying that children can work easily with noise; that they can

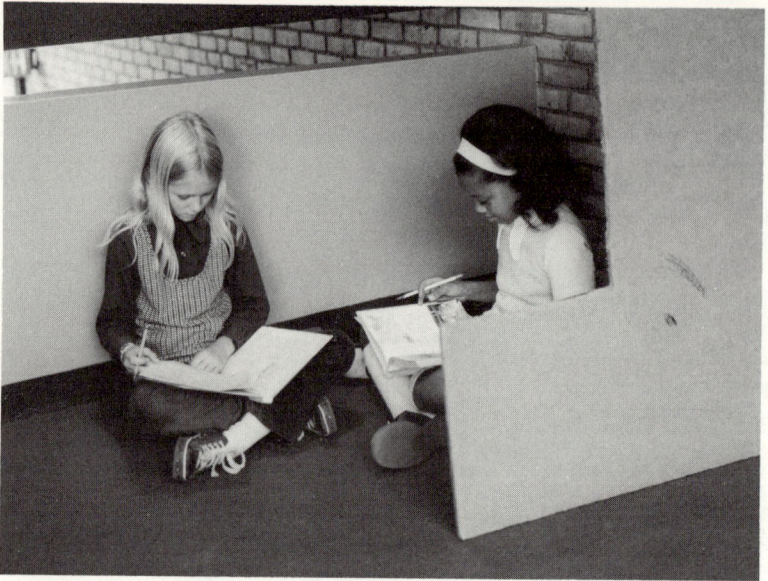

Photo 3-1. Although they are seated near each other, these youngsters are working independently on different objectives. When asked why they were in the corridor outside their room, they responded that they wanted a quiet corner where they could read "alone." They brought a sheet of cardboard with them, apparently to provide a sense of privacy. (Photograph courtesy of the Westorchard School, Chappaqua, New York.)

"block out" sound or ignore it. Not so. *Some* children can block out sound, and so can *some* grownups. *Some* students must be in a relatively quiet environment, and others require a completely silent area to achieve total concentration.

Analyze yourself. When you are concentrating on a term paper for a graduate course, a report for the community, the superintendent or the board, or a document which will be scrutinized by your peers, where can you work best? In an environment where other people are conversing noisily? (Can you block out sound?) In a relatively quiet area? Or do you need absolute silence to concentrate?

Whatever your response, do not think that everyone else will react as you did. In any group of 30 or more persons, some always insist that they can function cognitively despite noise; others can tolerate a small amount of noise; others must have complete silence; some will specify the type of noise preferred.

This is true of students of all ages. Some can function in one way, others in the exact opposite mode in order to progress academically.

DIAGNOSING LEARNING STYLE

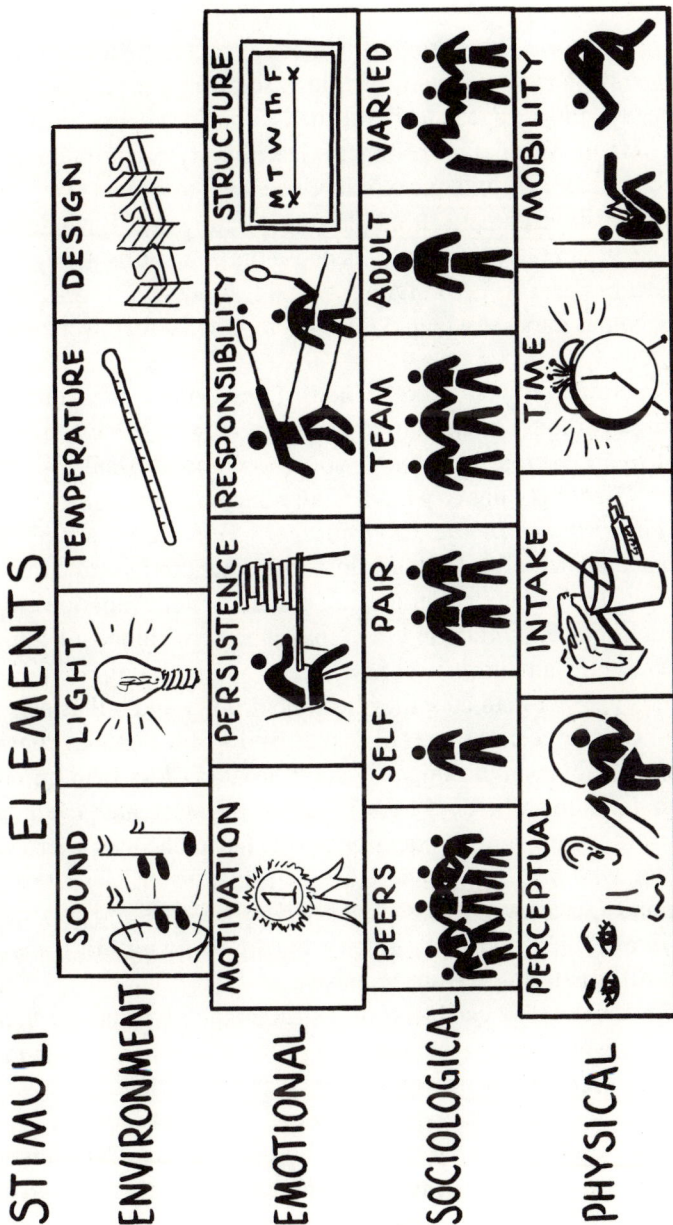

Figure 3-1

Knowing this, you can see how necessary it is to design an instructional environment that includes areas and sections in which students may talk, interact and share, and areas where others may work alone, because both types of students usually comprise any randomly selected group.

Light[6] in the Environment. Light appears to be a factor that affects fewer people than does sound. Although some people are light-sensitive or light-needy, most appear to be virtually unaffected by normal variation ranges of light. When pilot-testing the learning style instrument reproduced in this chapter, we found one or two youngsters in almost every group who intensely disliked camera flashlight units, sitting near a window (because of the bright light), or beaches ("because the glare hurts my eyes"). Many youngsters appear to be oblivious to light, however, unless the environment becomes dark, at which point they miss what they were not aware of previously.

Nevertheless, you may be one of the people who either needs a tremendous amount of light to concentrate or who cannot tolerate a very well-lit room or area. If you are, you know how difficult it is for you to function effectively under what actually becomes adverse circumstances.

Temperature[7] in the Environment. Most of us are aware of the cartoons that depict a husband lowering the thermostat after his wife elevates it. Temperature tolerance, of course, is not a function of sex; it is a function of our individual physical makeup. Some men and some women can focus their attention better when the environment is cool (or cold); when it is warmer than cool they become drowsy and fall asleep or have a difficult time concentrating. Other men and women cannot conceptualize easily when their environment is cool; anything less than an embryonic warmth (and the degree varies!) causes physical and even emotional discomfort and prevents productive effort. Differences in tolerance to heat vary, but who sets the temperature in a classroom? The teacher? The custodian? Certainly not the students who are required to study and to learn. Even if they could, in a given group of 30 youngsters there would be several different temperature requests.

If you intend to establish an instructional environment that permits youngsters with many varied learning styles to function well, bear in mind that the area should provide cooler and warmer sections for those students who need such differences to learn more effectively.

If you are beginning to question how one small classroom can incorporate enough varied areas to accommodate students who need (a) verbal interaction and silence, (b) intense light and little light, (c) coolness and warmth, do not despair. When people say, "It can't be done," they only mean, "I don't know how to do it." Chapter 4 will suggest very low cost

Photo 3-2. Teachers frequently notice students who wear a jacket, a hat, a neckerchief or a sweater when others are warm. Conversely, there are always youngsters who slip out of shoes whenever they sit, or who refuse jackets or sweaters when others bundle up. The youngster at the left is a fifth grader who feels comfortable in a hat. (Photograph courtesy of the Roaring Brook School, Chappaqua, New York.)

Photo 3-3. The youngster at the right is an eighth grader with the same inclination. (Photograph courtesy of Briarcliff Middle School, Briarcliff Manor, New York.)

means of redesigning classrooms to provide for students with varied learning needs.

Casualness or Structure[8] in the Environmental Design. When you decide to write a paper or report that requires concentration, do you begin your work while lounging on a soft couch, chair, or bed? Or do you sprawl on the carpeting? If you tend to follow this pattern, you may be a person who requires an informal, unstructured physical design in which to function effectively.

Conversely, you may be one who cannot work in informal facilities; these may prevent you from producing, may make you drowsy and unable to achieve. Some people must actually sit at a library or kitchen-like table on a hard chair to maintain their cognitive involvement with the task at hand. For others, a tightly designed structure suppresses motivation and creative thought processes. There are some people, of course, for whom design is no problem, or for whom design needs vary with the type of motivation they feel toward the task. Which type are you?

At any rate, this problem is transferable to a classroom where, for years, students were required to be seated for lengthy periods of time at small school desks. For youngsters whose learning style did not complement a structured design, it was difficult (often impossible) to remain passive and conformist and to learn. These students were often inappropriately chastised and called "discipline problems" or pupils with "short attention spans." This nomenclature may have suited them, but frequently the structured requirements of "school" contrasted with the youngsters' learning style and actually *caused* them to behave in a disruptive fashion.

Educators sometimes respond that "school is not for everyone." One of the implications of the statement is that youngsters who are unable to conform to the requirements of a structured classroom should not be required to attend. Compulsory education defeats that argument, for as long as boys and girls legally must be present, educators are morally responsible to provide an environment in which students can function effectively. Beyond this responsibility, students who find it difficult to "sit," "be quiet," "listen," "wait," "raise your hand," "don't call out" or "do your work now!" are probably able to learn in other, less structured patterns. What is important is that the student learns, not the specific method used.

This concept has immediate application to the classroom, which should include areas where youngsters may learn casually and sections that provide desks and chairs for students who function effectively in a structured environment.

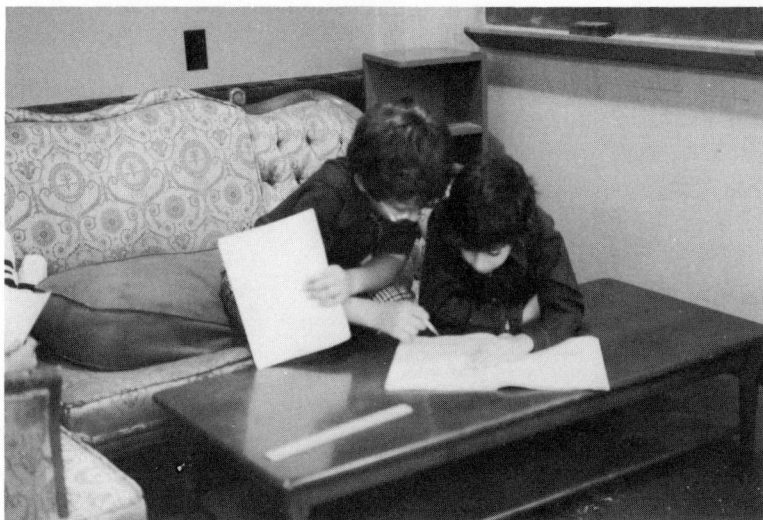

Photo 3-4. Free to study for this activity anywhere in the instructional environment, these two boys elected to complete their objectives in a corner section that houses some comfortable but discarded furniture donated by a local citizen. (Photograph courtesy of the Westorchard School, Chappaqua, New York.)

Photo 3-5. This youngster has chosen to seclude herself behind an easel where she appears to be enjoying both privacy and the game that she is using. Notice that she is following the game's instructions by listening to a tape that her teacher made to help her to become an independent learner. (Photograph courtesy of the Floral Park-Bellerose Elementary School, Floral Park, New York.)

The Emotional Elements of Learning Style

Motivation[9] *as a Function of Emotion.* We all know that some students come to us with a zeal for learning that is unquenchable; everything that they are exposed to becomes interesting, relevant and worthwhile to them! These represent our "motivated" students, the ones who require only a person or resource that can provide information and something new to master!

Conversely, we also recognize the "unmotivated" youngster. No matter what we do, it is difficult to involve this child in learning. Dramatics, "free-time," rewards, and a variety of activities tend to attract him for only a limited amount of time. This student is assumed to have a short attention span in all matters except sports, socialization, or a particular item of interest to him (or her).

At any point along the spectrum, except at the extreme ends, are the youngsters in our schools who are neither motivated nor unmotivated; if "turned on" they will learn, if not, they are bored, restless, or at best, tolerably conformist. Indeed, these youngsters probably represent the majority.

Whether a student is motivated, not easily categorized, or unmotivated determines, to a great extent, how much independence he can be given in an individualized setting. It is important, however, to remember that a student who is not motivated to learn in a fairly conventional environment may become extremely interested in learning and may be able to function responsibly when given many opportunities to (a) make choices, (b) vary the way that he functions to complement his learning style, (c) form social learning groups, and (d) self-test and self-evaluate himself.

Persistence[10] *as a Function of Emotion.* Given a task to complete, some youngsters will pursue the objectives until they have been mastered; others will wander into often unrelated areas or activities within a relatively short while. The element of persistence is a vital factor in diagnosing and prescribing for students.

Just as students should be offered varied objectives based partially on their interest and ability levels, so should the length and type of prescription vary for the individual, based on the teacher's observation of the youngster's ability to "stay with" a task. Students who find it difficult to sustain attention to a given task for 20 or 30 minutes will bear a double burden—that of learning and of learning within a time span that taxes their emotions and ability to function. This is one example where the aspect of "self-pacing" can be employed.

Students should be given their objectives and a time interval in which to complete them, with a clear understanding that although they need not continue learning in an uninterrupted continuum they do need to complete the learning tasks. The students who need frequent relaxation periods and who are not made to feel delinquent or guilty about taking them (as long as they return to the task and complete it) may be emotionally able to acquire the prescribed or selected knowledges and skills, but in their own way, in a flexible time period, and in accordance with their total learning style.

This is an area in which the teacher will need to experiment. Some students will require a few, simple tasks of relatively short duration to function adequately on an independent basis; others will be able to cope with longer tasks of varied complexity. An observation period in which the students begin with relatively few objectives and proceed toward tasks of increasing complexity, difficulty, and duration may be the most effective way of assessing a student's persistence quotient. It is suggested, therefore, that any first prescription (contract, assignment, topic, objectives, package, etc.) be a short one to provide student security in the process, and teacher opportunities for observation of how the youngster functions independently.

Responsibility[11] *as a Function of Emotion.* Some students may be assigned almost any task; they will follow through and complete it to the best of their ability. Others are not able to assume the responsibility for anything without direct supervision.

As with the elements of motivation and persistence, a student's ability to assume responsibility should be taken into account when forming prescriptions for him.

If in doubt about a youngster's ability to work independently and to achieve, assign short, relatively simple tasks for a first prescription. Be certain that he clearly understands (a) what he must achieve, (b) how he may achieve, (c) the time interval to be allotted (always a minimum and maximum amount of time), (d) how he may test himself to note his progress, and (e) how he may show you he has achieved the task (objectives or assignments) when he has done so. It is critical to build expectations for completion of tasks through teacher and peer reminders of deadlines, joint assessment of work, and progress reports and conferences.

As students begin to function with increased confidence, prescriptions may be expanded, lengthened, or made increasingly difficult for those who demonstrate their ability to work independently and successfully.

Photo 3-6. Motivated and persistent youngsters may be diagnosed, given a prescription (contract, package, assignment, objectives, etc.), and permitted to proceed independently without the imposition of constant supervision. (Photograph courtesy of the Roaring Brook School, Chappaqua, New York.)

Structure*[12] *as a Function of Emotion. As students begin to work independently on relatively easy miniprescriptions, the amount of structure required for individuals will become immediately apparent. Some students need frequent supervision and guidance in the learning process. "Structure" often implies imposed pressure and tight, inflexible scheduling.

The motivated, persistent, responsible student frequently requires little and far less supervision structure than his opposite. These youngsters may, with relative ease, proceed through a first miniprescription (contract, assignment, topic, objectives, package, etc.) to successful completion. Other youngsters, particularly on the first prescription or two, will frequently request confirmation of procedures or goals, assistance, directions, and reassurance.

A good technique for teachers of early childhood or elementary classes to use when beginning the individualization process is the "I Need

Photo 3-7. Other equally bright youngsters will require frequent direct involvement with the teacher. (Photograph courtesy of the Roaring Brook School, Chappaqua, New York.)

You'' listing. The children should be told that when the teacher is talking with either other youngsters or adults, interruptions (except for emergency matters) are not permitted. A child in need of assistance, direction or clarification should walk to a given section of the room (the chalkboard, a chart, a folder, etc.) and write his name under a column on which the teacher has written ''I Need You.'' The first student in need of help writes his name directly under the heading, the second writes his name under the first child's name, and so on. As the teacher completes her discussion with the youngster with whom she has been working, she will look up at the board and ''visit'' the child whose name is first on the list. In the meantime, while waiting, the youngster should be encouraged to seek a solution to his problem by himself, get help from another student, occupy himself with another task or wait patiently and quietly. Many young children have been motivated to begin problem-solving by themselves when the teacher responds positively to the fact that his name *was* on the list but that he no longer needs assistance. Building self-reliance begins with a youngster's finding the answer or ''solving the problem'' by himself.

When students fail to respond favorably to working independently after the first or second miniprescription, the teacher will need to organize

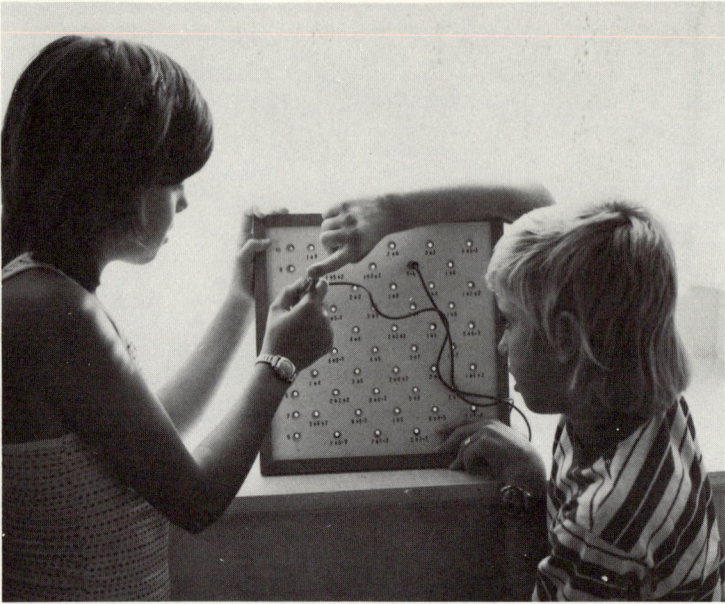

Photo 3-8. There are times when youngsters enjoy learning from their peers or from older students. This fifth grader is demonstrating the use of a self-corrective electroboard to a younger pupil just learning to use math tables. (Photograph courtesy of the Roaring Brook School, Chappaqua, New York.)

the prescription process for that student into tasks or objectives of relatively short duration. That student should have his procedures and achievements checked frequently and carefully, and new tasks should be assigned only after the completion of subsequent ones. It may be that this is the youngster for whom the process releases the teacher to provide stringent supervision for this student on an ongoing basis.

The Sociological[13] Elements of Learning Style

Proponents of ''open education'' classes often say that children learn better from other children than they do from their teachers. This is a broad generalization that is frequently untrue. Some children learn well from other children, and some children love teaching other children.[14] The reverse is also true. Some students cannot learn from their peers[15] and resent being placed in a position where they are required to do so, and some learners have little desire to teach other students.

The truth is that students learn in a variety of sociological patterns that include working alone,[16] with one or two friends,[17] with a small group or

Photo 3-9. Other children learn more easily from adults. For this reason, Imogene St. Paul, principal of a K-5 elementary school, sets aside time in her daily schedule to be with children who appear to respond to direct interaction with her. (Photograph courtesy of the Westorchard School, Chappaqua, New York.)

Photo 3-10. Most children can learn in a small group, particularly when the teacher assists in the learning process. When 4-8 children study together under the teacher's direction there is time and opportunity for questioning, numerous individual responses, positive social experience, and the development of a sense of personal worth. Large groups tend to diminish the effectiveness of instruction and reduce the amount of interaction among the participants. (Photograph courtesy of the Roaring Brook School, Chappaqua, New York.)

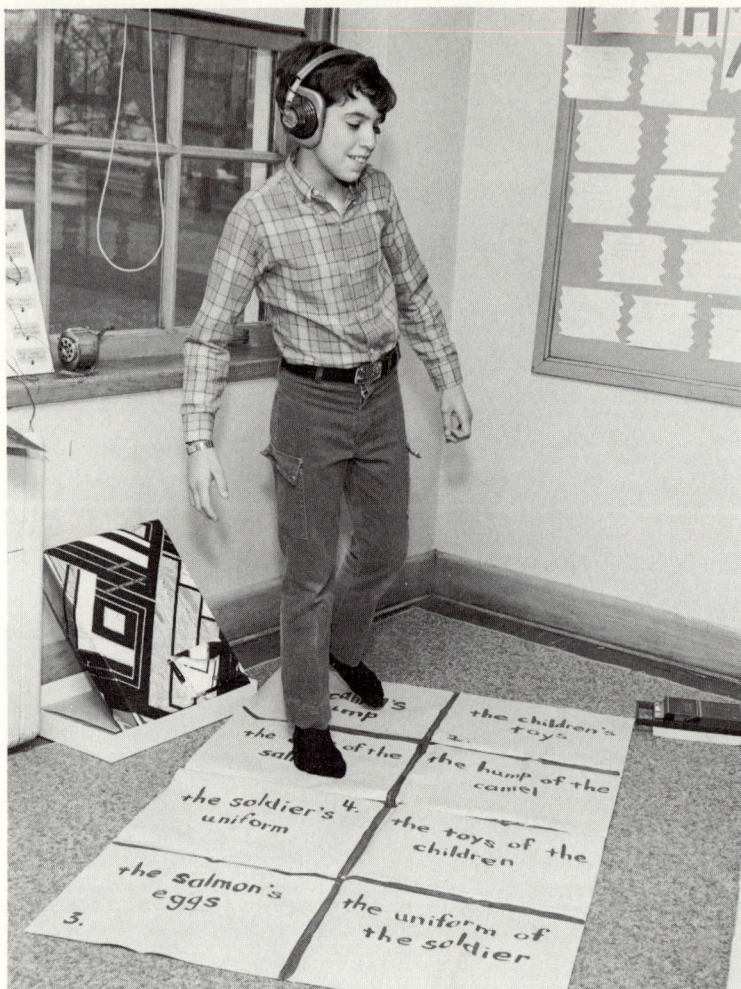

Photo 3-11. This youngster is engaged in a kinesthetic activity that reinforces his understanding of possessives and his ability to use them. The tape, which he hears through earphones to avoid disturbing other similarly involved classmates, explains how to play this "game" and permits self-correction as each of the four sensory tasks in the package is completed. (Photograph courtesy of the Sunrise Park Elementary School, Wantagh, New York, Photograph by Edward Igoe.)

as part of a team,[18] with adults, or in any variation thereof. It is also true that some students can learn best from an adult;[19] they view an older person as a source of wisdom, strength and authority and wish to interact only with this person.

How a student learns sociologically is an easily recognizable factor when youngsters are permitted to select the manner in which they may achieve their objectives. Of course some students will elect to work with friends with whom their level of social interaction actually precludes achievement of objectives. In such cases the teacher will need to speak with the student on a one-to-one basis and indicate that unless the pair (group, team) approaches the task soberly and can show achievement, the members will be reassigned and prevented from working together. When such a warning fails, the students should be stopped from working together if their interaction does not produce growth[20] toward prescribed or approved objectives.

The Physical Elements of Learning Style

Perceptual Strengths as an Element of Physical Needs. Some people tend to remember what they have been exposed to when they are introduced to the material through their auditory (hearing) perception. Others tend to retain most easily when they have seen the information (visual). Still others must be taught tactually (through their sense of touch), while a smaller segment of the population appears to absorb or retain most easily when they are involved in kinesthetic (whole body) learning.

Many function best when a combination of senses are involved in learning. *How* people learn is partially a function of their physical selves, and although some people may learn through several senses, materials should be introduced through each individual's strongest perceptual sense and reinforced through supplementary ones.

There are many tests available for diagnosing a student's perceptual strengths and weaknesses, notably the Frostig, the Slingerland, and the Wu materials. Perceptual weaknesses can be ameliorated through the use of proper techniques, but insisting that a youngster learn through a weak sense is similar to requiring a left-handed student to write with his right hand. He may be able to master the skill, but the loss in efficiency or the impact on his emotional state may be sharp.

If a teacher lectures to a student who learns most easily by seeing, the student becomes handicapped in the instructional environment. The converse is also true; a student who learns by listening may elicit little information through reading books or viewing a filmstrip. Our slower, or "disadvantaged," students frequently experience difficulty when trying to learn because they do not speak the same way that teachers do and thus do not "hear" what is intended. They also do not "see" what they are shown because they cannot extract what is suggested from the visuals due to an existing interpretation gap. The slow learner frequently requires tactual

Photo 3-12. Some youngsters can absorb information by reading, but others must be read to so that they can hear what they need to learn. (Photograph courtesy of the Floral Park-Bellerose Elementary School, Floral Park, New York.)

and/or kinesthetic involvement with information, skills, attitudes or values before he can even begin to understand through either a visual or auditory exposure.

Unfortunately, our teachers have not been trained to teach everything of considered importance through at least three or four senses. Often multisensory resources for a topic are unavailable and, again, teachers have not been taught how to develop these easily while in the classroom with their charges. The development of multisensory resources is not difficult; it merely takes know-how and numerous cassettes, a tape recorder, blank film, transparencies, grease pencils, acetate, a filmstrip viewer and projector and an overhead projector. With this hardware and developed software an excellent multisensory program can be developed through which most children, given appropriate prescriptions, can achieve.

Intake as an Element of Physical Need. When you and I went to school we were taught that chewing gum or nibbling on a cookie during class was disrespectful (and certainly unacceptable!). In later years specific times were set aside during which younger students could have snacks and older students could have "breaks."

Photo 3-13. Some youngsters require intake as they focus on a task because they physically need either an activity that releases tension or the renewed energy supplied by the intake. These two students were seriously engaged in academic studies as one nibbled on an apple and the other ate potato chips. (Photograph courtesy of the Floral Park-Bellerose Elementary School, Floral Park, New York.)

There are some people who, when they concentrate on an assigned task, constantly move back and forth from their place of work or study to the refrigerator. If they do not eat, they smoke, chew gum, or drink. These people require intake as they focus on a task because physically either they need the activity that releases the tension that is built up by their energy output, or they need the renewed energy generated by the intake.

Conversely, other people cannot eat, chew, smoke or drink while they are engaged in a concentrated effort. These people must complete their tasks and only afterwards are they able to relax and indulge in food or drink.

If it is true that some people must counteract their nervous reactions by eating whereas others must complete their objectives and then relax through intake, it becomes necessary to provide students with an instructional environment that permits some intake while learning for those who need it, and some intake after learning for the students who function best without food or drink.

Educators are relatively unfamiliar with the concept that would permit students to eat or drink as long as they completed their objectives successfully. Professional teachers often react negatively to such a suggestion for, unless they have developed an environment in which individualization can occur, instructors do not perceive how students could function with randomized eating while they or others are involved in learning. Chapter 4 will explain how the learning environment can be designed to facilitate maximum incorporation of student learning styles without infringing on either the sobriety of the instructional setting or the effective functioning of peers.

Time[21] *as an Element of Physical Needs.* The proverbial night owls and eager-beaver, early risers are diametrically opposite in their learning styles; one comes alive late at night and the other functions at maximum capacity early in the morning. This is true of students of all ages too. Some people can perform at maximum capacity at one time of day and others achieve most effectively at the extreme opposite time. Which are you? Or do you fall into the group that functions best neither early in the morning nor late at night? Are you a mid-morning bright star? Is it after lunch that your head appears to be most clear? Or is it late in the afternoon that things of concern become clearest to you?

Years ago, education professors told their students, ''Teach reading and math early in the morning, for that's when students are most alert.'' Nonsense! Some youngsters perform at maximum capacity very early in the morning while others really do not seem to awaken until late morning or noon; their most efficient functioning may vary greatly from early morning to late at night. Can the instructional environment be arranged to permit such a wide diversity of time functioning? Absolutely, particularly with middle and high school students where an open campus[22] approach may be introduced.

Mobility[23] *as an Element of Physical Needs.* Frequently those youngsters who receive the most discipline are the ones who are the least capable of reacting positively to it. Teachers assume that restless students require regimentation. They do not realize that some students need a great deal of mobility in the learning environment and cannot function well unless permitted to vary their stance, posture, and location frequently. Other youngsters are able to complete a task while in one physical position for a comparatively long period of time. The desire for mobility is a conglomerate function of one's physical, emotional, and environmental reactions, but most students cannot easily control their need to move while learning.

Students who require extensive mobility should be permitted to function in an informal setting where the frequent changes of position and setting will not tend to interfere with the instructional methods to which others are being exposed. This, too, is a feature that may be incorporated into an individualized environment if the program provided for the students permits academic progress through the personal learning style of each student. Practical approaches to redesigning learning space to permit a flexible environment are described in Chapter 4.

DIAGNOSING LEARNING STYLE

The following pages include what the authors believe to be the first comprehensive approach to the diagnosis of an individual's learning style. This instrument can be a useful initial step toward analyzing the conditions under which a student is most likely to learn. Additional materials such as the Frostig and Slingerland tests should be used to identify specific perceptual strengths and weaknesses, and the Julia Wu manipulative materials being developed at Hunter College in New York City would be effective supplementary diagnoses in this regard. In addition, direct observation of students engaged in the learning process will reveal more information concerning the conditions under which students appear to learn most easily. Former teachers and their recorded comments aid in this diagnosis. Finally, parents can add valuable input regarding attitudes, growth and learning patterns at home.

It should be noted that many of the questions in the instrument are highly subjective and relative. That, of course, is precisely why they contribute to an understanding of how each student learns in ways that differ from his peers'.

Since each youngster's learning style is based on a complex set of reactions to varied stimuli, feelings, and previously established patterns that tend to repeat similarly when the person concentrates, the words "work," "study" and "homework" are used interchangeably throughout the questionnaire and it is not necessary for the student to differentiate among their meanings. Comparisons of answers to questions that include these three words and to others that seem to ask the same things in varied ways permit verification of consistency in the pattern of responses.

The questionnaire does not measure underlying psychological motivation, value systems, or the quality of attitudes. Rather, it yields information concerned with the patterns through which learning occurs. It therefore reveals *how* a student learns, not *why*.

In-depth questions concerned with hostility levels, "middle class" goals based on deferred rewards, and instant gratification attitudes are not within the province of this instrument. Psychological explorations of this type may be necessary only in difficult cases where the diagnosis and prescription evolving from this assessment does not appear to be effective.

Finally, the instrument does not diagnose the finer aspects of work-study skills, such as the ability to outline planned procedures, to organize work, to classify, or to analyze. Again, it evidences how a student learns and not the skills that he uses to do so.

This questionnaire has been used on a sample of over 700 students in nine school districts to determine whether they could understand and respond adequately to each of the items on the instrument. It was also used to compare the perceptions of the students with those of their teachers concerning how these youngsters seemed to prefer to learn. The questionnaire and the procedures associated with its use were also field tested so that decisions could be made in the area of standardization on items such as usefulness, clarity of directions, ease of scoring and transference onto the profile sheet based on pilot data.

The instrument has already obtained a high degree of consensual validity from the school administrators and university faculty involved in its administration, examination, and evaluation. However, to date, construct and empirical validity have not been systematically evaluated. Additional item analyses, the selection and testing of a normative sample population, the determination of both construct and empirical validity levels and the establishment of sharply defined reliability levels of the questionnaire summarize the activities that have to be completed. Nevertheless, the instrument has proved operationally successful in screening individual students for gross learning style patterns and profiles, essential ingredients for diagnostic and prescriptive teaching.

ADMINISTERING THE LEARNING STYLE INSTRUMENT

Students may be given this questionnaire in writing, on tape, or orally. All of the "true" and "false" questions should be answered. There are questions that, if thought about in detail, would cause many modifications, limitations, and exceptions in responses. Students should be encouraged to give immediate reactions to each question on a "feeling" basis. The entire questionnaire need not be completed in only one sitting, but may be responded to at intervals that are convenient to both the student and the teacher or interviewer.

In cases where students do not read fluently, or where they have experienced learning difficulties, it is valuable to administer this instrument through a personal interview. The one-to-one relationship that develops as the adult questions the youngster about his preferences often provides new insights into a student's thinking that may not be afforded otherwise.

When the questionnaire has been completed, all of the "true" and "false" answers in each category should be checked against the Consistency Key and added. The total number of each category's set of responses should then be placed above the line on top of the numeral under either "true" or "false" in that category's column under the section called "Totals." A preponderance of answers in any one column, or pair of columns in a category, will indicate the probable type of learning style for that element.

When answers are divided among several columns in one element the indication may be that there is no predisposition toward any one category. That element, therefore, may not be a factor in that student's learning style. In some cases, answers that are divided among several categories in an element may indicate that the student has no major preferences and can function effectively under a number of varied situations, such as during many hours of the day or with peers, adults, and alone.

Comments based on the highest ratios in each category should be noted on the learning style profile sheet found at the end of the questionnaire and should be used to individualize the student's prescription. Every student, and certainly those with learning problems, should be diagnosed to identify his or her learning style, particularly since the research verifies that students are able to identify how they learn.

Learning Style Questionnaire

Name_____ Teacher_____

Class_____Date_____Counselor_____

Directions: (To the Student)—Answer *True* or *False* to each of the following questions.

I. Environmental Stimuli
   A. Sound

		True	False
1.	I study best when it is quiet.	___	___
2.	I can work with a little noise.	___	___
3.	I can block out noise when I work.	___	___
4.	Noise usually keeps me from concentrating.	___	___
5.	Most of the time I like to work with soft music.	___	___
6.	I can work with any kind of music.	___	___
7.	I often like to work with rock music playing.	___	___
8.	Music makes it difficult for me to work.	___	___
9.	I can work if people talk quietly.	___	___
10.	I can study when people talk.	___	___
11.	I can block out most sound when I study.	___	___
12.	It's difficult to block out TV when I work.	___	___
13.	Noise bothers me when I am studying.	___	___

Totals: (To be completed by the teacher)

Needs Quiet		Sound Is Acceptable	
True	False	True	False
7	7	8	5

Consistency Key: (For the teacher)

Needs Silent or Quiet Areas		Sound Is Acceptable or Desirable	
True	False	True	False
1			1
2		2	
	3	3	
4			4
5	5	5	
	6	6	
	7	7	
8			8
	9	9	
	10	10	
	11	11	
12			12
13			13

Directions:

Total the number of trues and falses for each column. Fill in the top half of the fraction. Follow these instructions for all categories.

B. Light

True False

1. I like studying with lots of light.   ___ ___
2. I study best when the lights are low.   ___ ___
3. I like to read outdoors.   ___ ___
4. I can study for a short time if the lights are low. ___ ___
5. When I study I put all the lights on.   ___ ___
6. I often read in dim light.   ___ ___
7. I usually study under a shaded lamp while the rest
   of the room is dim.   ___ ___

Totals:

Requires a Great Deal of Light	Requires Low Light	Light Not a Factor	
True	True	True	False
4	3	6	6

Consistency Key:

Requires a Great Deal of Light	Requires Low Light	Light Not a Factor
True	True	
1	2	Light is probably
3	6	not a factor if six
4	7	or seven questions
5		are marked either
		all true or all false.

C. Temperature

	True	False
1. I can concentrate if I'm warm.	___	___
2. I can concentrate if I'm cold.	___	___
3. I usually feel colder than most people.	___	___
4. I usually feel warmer than most people.	___	___
5. I like the summer.	___	___
6. When it's cold outside I like to stay in.	___	___
7. When it's hot outside I like to stay in.	___	___
8. When it's hot outside I go out to play.	___	___
9. When it's cold outside I go out to play.	___	___
10. I find extreme heat or cold uncomfortable.	___	___
11. I like the winter.	___	___

Totals:

Needs Cool Environment	Needs Warm Environment	Temperature Not a Factor
True	True	True
___	___	___
5	5	5

Consistency Key:

Needs Cool Environment	Needs Warm Environment	Only Temperature Extremes Are a Factor
True	True	True
2	1	3-4
4	3	6-7
7	5	10
9	6	
11	8	

(Divided or paired [3 and 4; 6 and 7] answers may indicate that temperature is not a factor.)

D. Design

True False

1. When I study I like to sit on the floor. ____ ____
2. When I study I like to sit on a soft chair or couch. ____ ____
3. When I study I feel sleepy unless I sit on a hard chair. ____ ____
4. I find it difficult to study at school. ____ ____
5. I finish all my homework at home. ____ ____
6. I always study for tests at home. ____ ____
7. I finish all my homework in school. ____ ____
8. I find it difficult to concentrate on my studies at home. ____ ____
9. I work best in a library. ____ ____
10. I can study almost anywhere. ____ ____
11. I like to study in bed. ____ ____
12. I like to study on carpeting or rugs. ____ ____
13. I can study on the floor, in a chair, on a couch, and at my desk. ____ ____
14. I often study in the bathroom. ____ ____

Totals:

Requires Formal Design	Requires Informal Design	Design Not Important
True	True	True
4	9	2

Consistency Key:

Requires Formality	Requires Informality	Design Not Important
True	True	True
3	1	10
7	2	13
8	4	
9	5	
	6	
	10	
	11	
	12	
	14	

II. Emotional Stimuli

A. Motivation Toward School Work

		True	False
1.	I feel good when I do well in school.	___	___
2.	I feel good making my mother or father proud of me when I do well in school.	___	___
3.	My teacher feels good when I do well in school.	___	___
4.	Grown-ups are pleased if I bring home good reports.	___	___
5.	Grown-ups are pleased when I do well in school.	___	___
6.	I like making someone feel proud of me.	___	___
7.	I am embarrassed when my grades are poor.	___	___
8.	It is more important to me to do well in things that happen out of school than in my school work.	___	___
9.	I like making my teacher proud of me.	___	___
10.	Nobody really cares if I do well in school.	___	___
11.	My teacher cares about me.	___	___
12.	My mother cares about my grades.	___	___
13.	My father cares about my grades.	___	___
14.	My teacher cares about my grades.	___	___

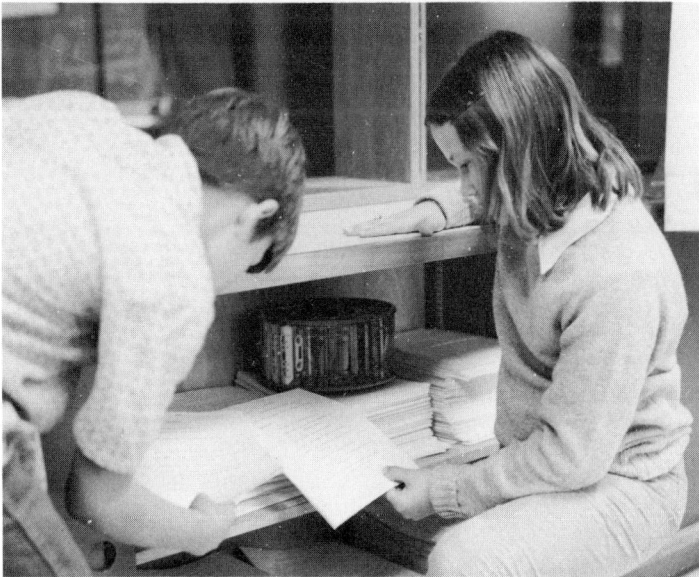

Photo 3-14. Well-organized, multilevel resources facilitate the development of self-directing students. (Photograph courtesy of the Robert E. Bell Middle School, Chappaqua, New York.)

15. Somebody cares about my grades in school. ____ ____
16. I want to get good grades for me! ____ ____
17. I am happy when I do well in school. ____ ____
18. I feel bad and work less when my grades are bad. ____ ____
19. I feel happy and proud when my marks are good. ____ ____
20. There are many things I like doing better than going to school. ____ ____
21. I love to learn new things. ____ ____
22. A good education will help me to get a good job. ____ ____

Totals:

Self-Motivated	Adult-Motivated	Teacher-Motivated	Unmotivated
True	True	True	True
6	8	7	4

Consistency Key:

Self-Motivated	Adult-Motivated	Teacher-Motivated	Relatively Less School-Motivated
True	True	True	True
1	2	3	8
16	4	6	10
17	5	7	18
19	6	9	20
21	7	11	
22	12	14	
	13	15	
	15		

B.   Persistence

True False

1. I try to finish what I start. ____ ____
2. I usually finish what I start. ____ ____
3. I sometimes lose interest in things I began to do and then stop doing them. ____ ____
4. I rarely finish things that I start. ____ ____
5. I usually remember to finish my homework. ____ ____
6. I often have to be reminded to do my homework. ____ ____
7. I often forget to do or finish my homework. ____ ____
8. I often get tired of doing things and want to start something new. ____ ____

9. I usually like to finish things that I start. _____ _____
10. My teacher is always telling me to finish what I'm supposed to do. _____ _____
11. My parent(s) remind me to finish things I have been told to do. _____ _____
12. Other grown-ups tell me to finish things that I have started. _____ _____
13. Somebody's always reminding me to do something! _____ _____
14. I often get tired of doing things. _____ _____
15. I often want help in finishing things. _____ _____
16. I like getting things done! _____ _____
17. I like to get things done so I can start something new. _____ _____
18. I remember on my own to get things done. _____ _____

Totals:

Persistent	Not Persistent
True	True
7	11

Consistency Key:

Persistent	Not Persistent
True	True
1	3
2	4
5	6
9	8
16	10
17	11
18	12
	13
	14
	15

C. Responsibility

True False

1. I think I am responsible. _____ _____
2. People tell me that I am responsible. _____ _____
3. I always do what I promise to do. _____ _____
4. People say that I do what I said I would do. _____ _____
5. I do keep my promises most of the time. _____ _____

Photo 3-15. This youngster responsibly completes assigned task and then self-corrects her answers with the teacher's guide. (Photograph courtesy of the Robert E. Bell Middle School, Chappaqua, New York.)

6. I have to be reminded over and over again to do the things I've been told to do.   ____ ____
7. If my teacher tells me to do something I try to do it.   ____ ____
8. I keep forgetting to do the things I've been told to do.   ____ ____
9. I remember to do what I'm told.   ____ ____
10. People keep reminding me to do things.   ____ ____
11. I like doing what I'm supposed to do.   ____ ____
12. Promises have to be kept.   ____ ____
13. I have to be reminded often to do something.   ____ ____

Totals:

Responsible	Not Very Responsible
True	True
9	4

Consistency Key:

Responsible	Not Very Responsible
True	True
1	6
2	8
3	10
4	13
5	
7	
9	
11	
12	

D. Structure

	True	False
1. I like to be told exactly what to do.	___	___
2. I like to be able to do things in my own way.	___	___
3. I like to be given choices of how I can do things.	___	___
4. I like to be able to work things out for myself.	___	___
5. I like other people to tell me how to do things.	___	___
6. I do better if I know my work is going to be checked.	___	___
7. I do the best I can whether or not the teacher will check my work.	___	___
8. I hate working hard on something that isn't checked by the teacher.	___	___
9. I like to be given clear directions when starting new projects.	___	___

Totals:

Needs Structure	Needs Little Structure
True	True
___	___
5	5

Consistency Key:

Needs Structure	Needs Little Structure
True	True
1	2
5	3
6	4
8	7
9	8

(Four or five answers in both columns may indicate that structure or the lack of it is not necessarily a factor.)

III. Sociological Stimuli

                                                                    True False

A. When I really have a lot of studying to do:
   1. I like to work alone.   ____ ____
   2. I like to work with my good friend.   ____ ____
   3. I like to work with a couple of my friends.   ____ ____
   4. I like to work in a group of five or six classmates.   ____ ____
   5. I like to work with an adult.   ____ ____
   6. I like to work with a friend but to have an adult
      nearby.   ____ ____
   7. I like to work with a couple of friends but have an
      adult nearby.   ____ ____
   8. I like adults nearby when I'm working alone or
      with a friend.   ____ ____
   9. I like adults to stay away until my friends and I
      complete our work.   ____ ____

B. The thing I like doing best, I do:
   1. alone.   ____ ____
   2. with one friend.   ____ ____
   3. with a couple of friends.   ____ ____
   4. with a group of friends.   ____ ____
   5. with a grown-up.   ____ ____
   6. with several grown-ups.   ____ ____
   7. with friends and grown-ups.   ____ ____
   8. with a member of my family who is not a grown-
      up.   ____ ____

Totals: Prefers Learning, Working, Studying or Doing

Alone	One Peer	Two Peers	Several Peers	With Adults	Combined
True	True	True	True	True	True
3	4	3	3	3	4

Consistency Key: Prefers Learning, Working, Studying or Doing

Alone	One Peer	Two Peers	Several Peers	With Adults	Combined
True	True	True	True	True	True
A1	A2	A3	A4	A5	A6
A8	B2	B3	B4	B5	B7

Alone	One Peer	Two Peers	Several Peers	With Adults	Combined
True	True	True	True	True	True
B1	A8	A9	A9	B6	A7
	B8				A8

IV. Physical

True False

A. Perceptual Preferences
 1. If I have to learn something new, I like to learn about it by:
  a. reading a book.
  b. hearing a record.
  c. hearing a tape.
  d. seeing a filmstrip.
  e. seeing and hearing a movie.
  f. looking at pictures and having someone explain them.
  g. hearing my teacher tell me.
  h. playing games.
  i. going someplace and seeing for myself.
  j. having someone show me.
 2. The things I remember best are the things:
  a. my teacher tells me.
  b. someone other than my teacher tells me.
  c. someone shows me.
  d. I learned about on trips.
  e. I read.
  f. I heard on records.
  g. I heard on the radio.
  h. I saw on television.
  i. I wrote stories about.
  j. I saw in a movie.
  k. I tried or worked on.
  l. my friends and I talked about.
 3. I really like to:
  a. read books, magazines, or newspapers.
  b. see movies.
  c. listen to records.
  d. make tapes on a tape recorder.
  e. draw.
  f. look at pictures.
  g. play games.
  h. talk to people.
  i. listen to people talk.

j. listen to the radio.   _____ _____
k. watch television.   _____ _____
l. go on trips.   _____ _____
m. learn new things.   _____ _____
n. study with friends.   _____ _____
o. build things.   _____ _____
p. do experiments.   _____ _____
q. take pictures or movies.   _____ _____
r. use typewriters, computers, calculators or
    other machines.   _____ _____
s. go to the library.   _____ _____
t. trace things in sand.   _____ _____
u. mold things with my hands.   _____ _____

Totals:

Auditory	Visual	Tactile	Kinesthetic
True	True	True	True
16	15	6	9

Consistency Key:

Auditory	Visual	Tactile	Kinesthetic
True	True	True	True
1b	1a	1h	1i
1c	1d	2i	2d
1e	1e	3e	2k
1f	1f	3o	3g
1g	1h	3t	3d
2a	1j	3u	3l
2b	2c		3p
2f	2e		3q
2g	2h		3r
2h	2j		
2i	3a		
3c	3f		
3h	3b		
3l	3k		
3j	3s		
3n			

B. Intake

	True	False
1. I like to eat or drink, or chew while I study.	___	___
2. I dislike eating or drinking, or chewing while I study.	___	___
3. While I'm studying I like to:		
a. eat.	___	___
b. drink.	___	___
c. chew gum.	___	___
d. nibble on snacks.	___	___
e. suck on candy.	___	___
4. I can eat, drink, or chew only after I finish studying.	___	___
5. I usually eat or drink when I'm nervous or upset.	___	___
6. I hardly ever eat when I'm nervous or upset.	___	___
7. I could study better if I could eat while I'm learning.	___	___
8. While I'm learning, eating something would distract me.	___	___
9. I often catch myself chewing on a pencil as I study.	___	___

Totals:

Requires Intake	Does Not Require Intake
True	True
9	4

Consistency Key:

Requires Intake	Does Not Require Intake
True	True
1	2
3a-e	4
5	6
7	8
9	

C. Time

	True	False
1. I hate to get up in the morning.	___	___
2. I hate to go to sleep at night.	___	___

3. I could sleep all morning.   _____ _____
4. I stay awake for a long time after I get into bed.   _____ _____
5. I feel wide awake after 10:00 in the morning.   _____ _____
6. If I stay up very late at night I get too sleepy to
    remember anything.   _____ _____
7. I feel sleepy after lunch.   _____ _____
8. When I have homework to do, I like to get up
    early in the morning to do it.   _____ _____
9. When I can, I do my homework in the afternoon.   _____ _____
10. I usually start my homework after dinner.   _____ _____
11. I could stay up all night.   _____ _____
12. I wish school would start near lunch time.   _____ _____
13. I wish I could stay home during the day and go to
    school at night.   _____ _____
14. I like going to school in the morning.   _____ _____
15. I can remember things when I study them:
    a. in the morning.   _____ _____
    b. at lunchtime.   _____ _____
    c. in the afternoon.   _____ _____
    d. before dinner.   _____ _____
    e. after dinner.   _____ _____
    f. late at night.   _____ _____

Totals: Functions Best

Early Morning		Late Morning		Afternoon		Evening	
True	False	True	False	True	False	True	False
3	7	3	7	6	5	8	3

Consistency Key: Preferred Functioning Time

Early Morning		Late Morning		Afternoon		Evening	
True	False	True	False	True	False	True	False
8	1	5	3	3	7	2	6
14	3	12	8	5	8	4	8
15a	5	15b	9	9	11	5	14
	10		10	12	13	10	
	11		11	15c	14	11	
	12		13	15d		13	
	13		14			15e	
						15f	

(A fairly equal distribution among all four categories
usually indicates that the time of day or night is not an
important factor.)

D. Mobility   True False
1. When I study I often get up to do something (like take a drink, get a cookie, etc.) and then return to work. ___ ___
2. When I study I stay with it until I am finished and then I get up. ___ ___
3. It's difficult for me to sit in one place for a long time. ___ ___
4. I often change my position when I work. ___ ___
5. I can sit in one place for a long time. ___ ___
6. I constantly change position in my chair. ___ ___
7. I can work best for short amounts of time with breaks in between. ___ ___
8. I like getting my work done and over with. ___ ___
9. I like to work a little, stop, return to the work, stop, return to it again, and so forth. ___ ___
10. I like to stick to a job and finish it in one sitting if I can. ___ ___
11. I leave most jobs for the last minute and then have to work on them from beginning to end. ___ ___
12. I do most of my jobs a little at a time and eventually get them done. ___ ___
13. I enjoy doing something over and over again when I know how to do it well. ___ ___
14. I like familiar friends and places. ___ ___
15. New jobs and subjects make me nervous. ___ ___

Totals:

Needs Mobility	Does Not Need Mobility
True	True
7	8

Consistency Key:

Needs Mobility	Does Not Need Mobility
True	True
1	2
3	5
4	8
6	10
7	11
9	13
12	14
	15

Learning Style Profile

Name_____ Teacher_____School_____
Grade_____ Counselor_____Date_____

Comments Based on Highest Ratios Noted on Questionnaire

    I. *Environmental*   Sound_____
                             Light_____
                             Temperature_____
                             Design_____

    II. *Emotional*   Motivation_____
                             Persistence_____
                             Responsibility_____
                             Structure_____

    III. *Sociological*   Appears to Work Best With:
                             1. _____
                             2. _____
                             3. _____

    IV. *Physical*   Perceptual Preferences_____
                             Nutritional Intake_____
                             Time_____
                             Mobility_____

                                Checked by_____

Team Learning Exercise

Directions

    You may use the following exercise to reinforce your developing knowledge of learning styles and to compare your own assessment of your learning style with the data revealed by the Questionnaire. If you prefer studying with others, follow the procedures that were given at the end of Chapter 1 for the team learning exercise. If you prefer, you may proceed independently.

Team Members:

1._____   4. _____
2._____   5. _____
3._____   6. _____

Recorder:

Criterion-Referenced Assessment

A. Identify each of the four basic stimulants that affect a student's learning style and at least 12 of their related elements.

When you have completed Question A, compare your answers with those in Figure 3-1.

B. Test yourself on the Learning Style Questionnaire (pages 95 to top of 110) and try to identify your own learning style. Compare the test results with your own perceptions of how you learn best.

When you have completed the Questionnaire, use each of the element's consistency keys to determine what the instrument reveals about your learning style.

Test your answers against reality by evaluating your own results and by asking someone who knows your work habits to verify or challenge your own assessment of your learning style.

FOUR

Redesigning the Physical Environment to Accommodate Individual Learning Styles

Behavioral Objective for Chapter 4

1. Given a student's learning style, you will be able to redesign the instructional environment to capitalize on his or her learning strengths.

. . . .

MOVING FROM THE TRADITIONAL TO A TRANSITIONAL ENVIRONMENT

Years ago almost every classroom contained between 30 and 40 student desks and seats that were neatly arranged in rows that dominated the center of the room and accounted for approximately 80 percent of the floor space. Wide aisles usually were formed around the perimeter, and the teacher's desk was placed so that he could either face the youngsters as they looked toward the blackboard wall or view their behaviors from behind their backs. Each student was assigned his own desk for storage and was expected to remain at it at all times except when given permission to recite, approach the teacher, or go to or from the clothing closet, the lavatory or on an errand.

This interior design may be described as authoritarian and rigid. It certainly is not one that is conducive to permitting youngsters with a variety of learning styles to function effectively.

As teachers began to experiment with varied and more informal instructional procedures they realized that if youngsters are to be encouraged to complete their assignments as they are able to and to use varied multimedia resources that had not previously existed, it would be necessary for students to begin to work somewhat independently and to move

Illustration 4-1. A traditional classroom with student seats arranged in rows all facing the same direction. (Photograph courtesy of The Bettmann Archives, Inc.)

from one instructional area of the room to another, as appropriate to the learning task. Teachers then began to develop different kinds of "centers," "stations," "areas," "corners," "tables," or "labs" and to educate students to use them appropriately and effectively.[1]

Once the room began to be subdivided into varied instructional areas,[2] student desks and chairs could no longer occupy the major portion of the space and some consolidation of seating resulted in the development of new kinds of designs.

RECOGNIZING THE "IN-BETWEEN STAGE" OF ROOM DESIGN

When it became necessary to move desks and chairs into different types of arrangements to provide for varied instructional areas, teachers began grouping youngsters so that several of them sat together, often with their desks immediately adjacent to and touching each other's. This resulted in an inordinate rush to establish "partnership teams"—particularly at the elementary level. The room then began to resemble any one or combination of the alternative environments shown in Figures 4-1 to 4-4.

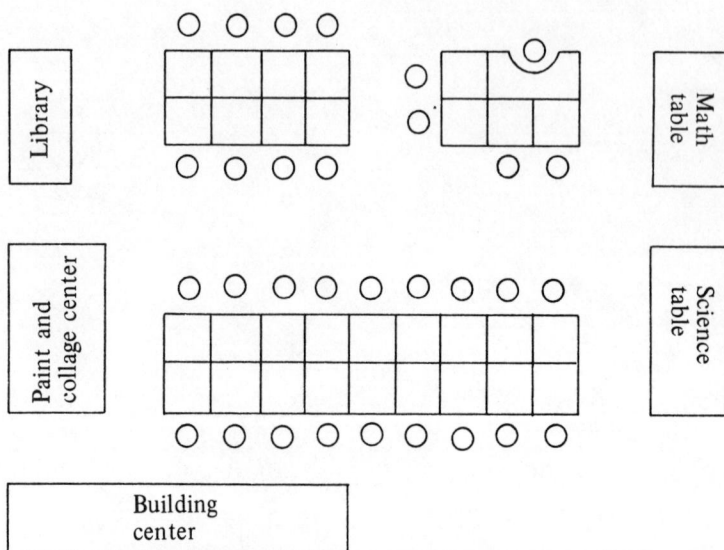

Figure 4-1.[3] This design depicts a classroom that provides for one large (19) and two small (eight and five) group seating arrangements. Students may work individually, in pairs, or in teams at the various instructional areas that form the periphery.

It was during this "transitional" period that effective small-group instruction emerged and that teachers recognized many of the advantages of using interaction techniques[4] such as team learning, circles of knowledge, group analysis, brainstorming, role playing, simulations, team task forces, etc. Group seating plans also emerged based on the philosophy of peer teaching.

Observation of the side-by-side group seating arrangements in operation reveals that youngsters with a strong tolerance for sound, movement, and working with peers appear to function well in such a plan. But what of the student who usually, or even occasionally, requires an essentially quiet area in which to work? Particularly one with little distraction? Is such a youngster able to work with people on either side of him while others face him and still others walk around all about him as they pursue their own objectives? We think not.

Conversely, many of us have seen photographs of students deeply involved in their studies while sitting in isolation in a carrel (see Illustration 4-2), their earphones glued to their heads while a filmstrip viewer completely absorbs their attention. Do youngsters work well this way for

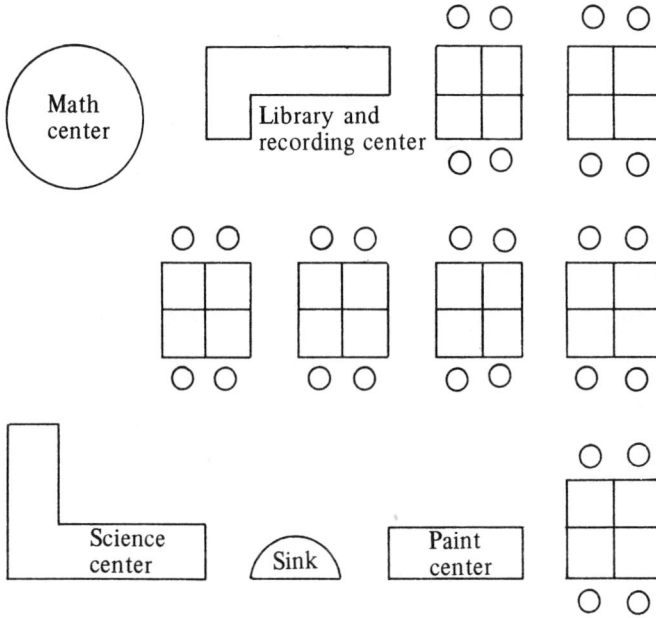

Figure 4-2.[5] This arrangement permits small clusters of four students each to work together when at their desks. Utilization of the centers may be by choice or direction.

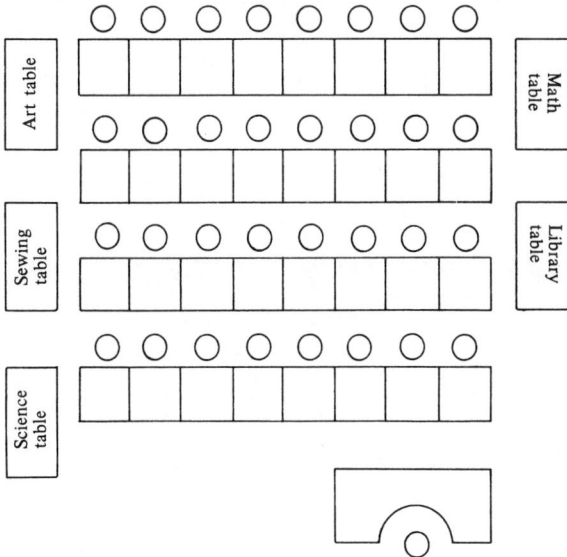

Figure 4-3.[6] In this classroom the traditional row is used horizontally rather than vertically. Varied instructional areas have been placed at both sides of the room while the teacher's desk continues to occupy the front to facilitate large-group instruction.

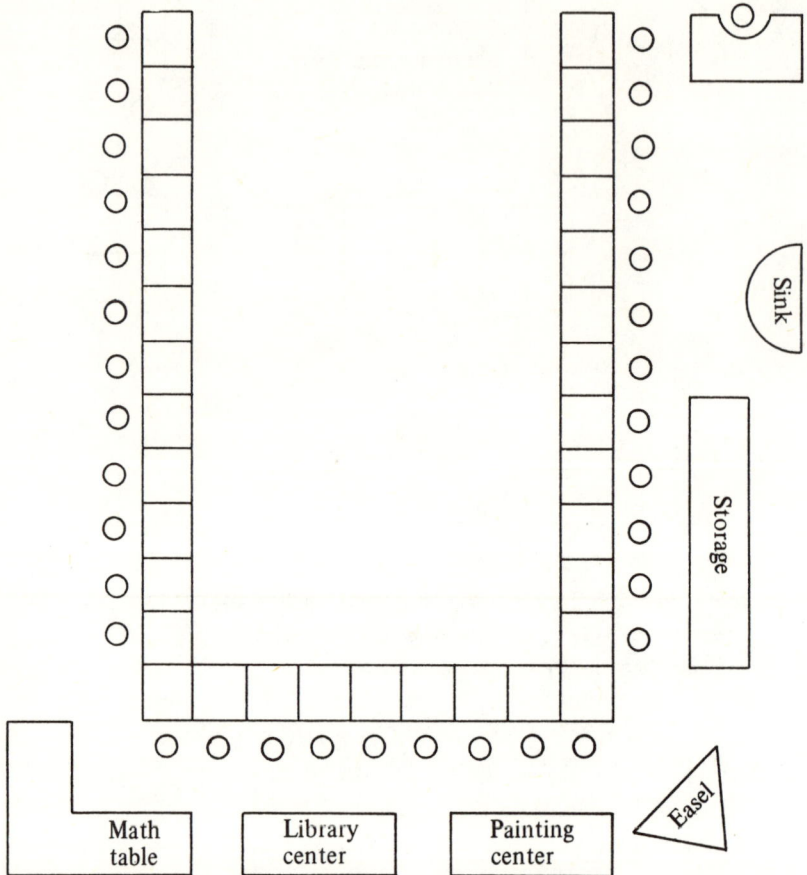

Figure 4-4.[7] This "horseshoe" arrangement varies the seating placement but tends to promote extensive large-group instruction. The math table, library center and painting section may be used by individuals or small groups.

an extensive time interval when devoid of peer group interaction? The answer, of course, is that some do, while others quickly begin to feel themselves alienated in the instructional environment when they do not work directly with other students or with adults. Further, continuous or repetitious procedures with programed materials, or even media, can cause apathy or lack of motivation.

The clustering of four to eight students into small groups with desks and seats placed side by side may be appropriate for students who have verified that they are able to concentrate when in close proximity to others. For youngsters who prefer working alone or who, at various times, have preferences that range from working independently *away* from others to sharing in small- and/or large-group studies, combinations of seating arrangements should be provided.

Illustration 4-2. Students working in isolation in study carrels. (Photograph courtesy of West Hartford Public Schools, West Hartford, Connecticut; Robert L. May, photographer.)

ANALYZING THE REQUIREMENTS FOR AN EFFECTIVE INDIVIDUALIZED LEARNING ENVIRONMENT

If a classroom, or any educational space, is to provide for the many differences in the ways students learn, it should combine all of the following elements. Some of these statements may seem diametrically opposed in approach but they will provide needed alternatives so that student self-selected options become part of the learning process.

- places where several students may work together and discuss what they are doing

- essentially quiet and screened study areas for individuals and pairs

- well-lit reading areas

- darker sections for media viewing, photography, or dramatizations

- warmer areas

- cooler areas

- hard tables and chairs

- carpeted and/or lounge sections

- short prescriptions for students with short attention spans

- longer prescriptions for the persistent

- independence for responsible students

- close supervision for the less responsible

- consistent structure for students who do not follow through
- less structure for those who can function without it

- schedules for youngsters who need sequenced assignments
- time flexibility for youngsters who complete assignments when permitted to determine their own schedules

- whole-body activities for the kinesthetic learners
- manipulative materials for the tactile learners

- tapes, records, television, and sound films for the auditory learners
- films, pictures, study prints, television, filmstrips, transparencies, books and many other visuals for the visual learners

- opportunities for all students to determine whether they will work alone, with a friend or two, in a small group, as part of a team, with an adult, or any combination thereof, provided they show academic progress.

- intake (preferably raw vegetables and fruits, cereals, milk and other nutritious foods) to be available as desired for those responsible students who require it to work effectively as long as their method or time of intake does not interfere with the progress of others.

- self-pacing (within appropriate time intervals) for those who are able to progress academically without constant direct supervision.

BEGINNING THE REDESIGN FOR INDIVIDUALIZATION

The basic objective in planning the physical layout of an individualized instructional environment is the provision of all, or most, of the listed ''requirements'' in the preceding section. In general, therefore, options should be provided with dens or alcoves designed to permit privacy for those who need it to concentrate. It is also necessary to design small areas in which from two to four youngsters may work together, talk and interact as they learn, without intruding on those who want to study alone. Finally, a larger area is essential for whole-class or large-group (from 12 to 30 students) meetings for the introduction of new material appropriate to all and for group discussions or sharing.

To divide the room into each of the three types of areas (den, small group, and large group), it is advisable to locate as many items of furniture as possible perpendicular to any existing wall or board space. Such items would include file cabinets, desks, bookcases, tables, shelves, material displays, screens, charts that stand freeform, or cardboard or wooden cartons or boxes that may be attractively painted or decorated.

Because each classroom or open area differs from almost every other room in the amount of space that is available, the placement of stationary items such as windows, chalkboards, closet areas, etc., must be considered. Every area, therefore, should be analyzed to determine (a) usable wall space, (b) movable items that may be used perpendicular to walls, (c) fixed items, and (d) the number of possible options given the physical conditions of available space and furniture.

When moving the furniture and developing the physical environment, it is always wise to do it *with* the students. They should be aware of what is going to be created, why, and that it will take an adjustment period to become acclimated to the change. Their involvement in the development of the design invariably creates a positive attitude of acceptance for the revision and, of greater importance, elicits the input that permits correct placement for students with definite learning needs.

Begin your conversation with the students by explaining that, as in their apartments or homes, the way the furniture is arranged in an area should make sense for the people who live there; that some of the boys and girls who "live" in their room (and it *is* living for four or five hours each school day!) may enjoy the arrangement just as it is, but that others must feel uncomfortable because people are different from each other and some need certain kinds of things that are not currently present.

For example (and here begin to personalize with them), everyone in the present arrangement is seated, in a sense, out in the open, even if there are separations between groups. With many students at close range it must be difficult for some of them to concentrate as they see and hear the door opening, chairs and people moving, materials being used and replaced, etc. Some need a quiet, cozy place to concentrate on their studies, and for those people you would like to create small den or alcove areas where they can be by themselves, or with a friend or two, to complete their work.

You could add that one of the things you would suggest is the establishment of some areas where students (or small groups of students) may literally turn their backs on what is happening in the room and become absorbed in their work. This can be done by facing their chairs toward any available wall space. You may add, "If I told you that you were going to face a wall, you might think, 'who wants to look at a blank space?'; but if I added that each person facing a wall would be facing his own bulletin board on which he could display the things that he likes best—things that are of major interest to him—wouldn't you like that?" Most elementary and middle school students enjoy the prospect of having a bulletin board in their seating area and making it attractive with a personalized decorating scheme; older students vary in their reactions and this could be an optional aspect. Usually high schoolers are required to

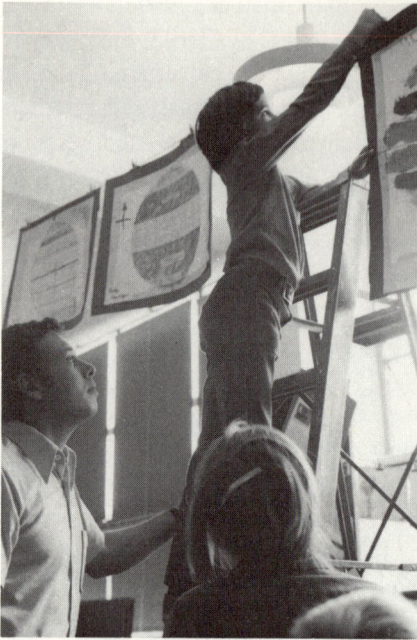

Photo 4-1. Dr. Daniel Schepis, who has taught for 11 years, is a strong believer in encouraging his students to undertake the major responsibility for designing and decorating their learning environments. (Photograph courtesy of the Roaring Brook School, Chappaqua, New York.)

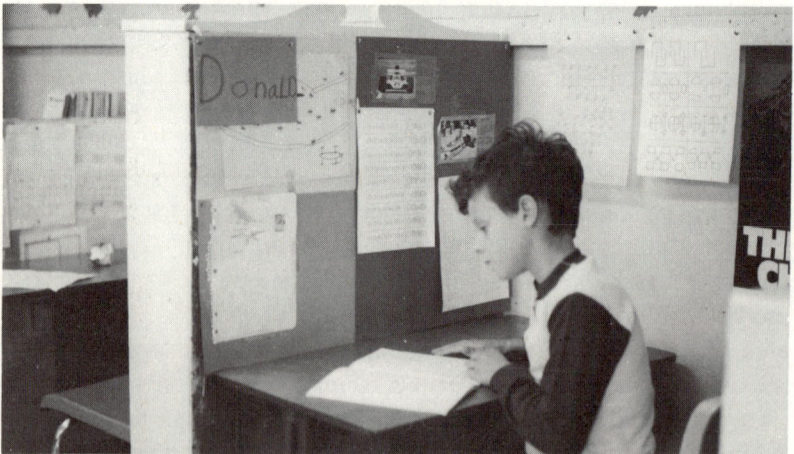

Photos 4-2, 4-3. These students are using the backs of bookcases for their bulletin board areas. They have each covered the surfaces with attractive construction paper on which they have mounted items of interest or achievement. (Photographs courtesy of the Floral Park-Bellerose Elementary School, Floral Park, New York.)

Photo 4-3

move from room to room for sequenced periods and adaptation of this system would not necessarily include the decoration of their seating areas.

To increase "bulletin board" motivation, use sheets of colored construction or drawing paper to form a rectangular wall area as wide as the desk adjacent to it. Scallop a border to complement the paper and vary the colors so that bulletin boards that are next to each other reflect individual decorative preferences. Frequently there is not enough wall space in the room for each student to have a bulletin board and some may not want the responsibility for keeping one attractive and current. Establish rules for what may or may not be displayed but, within the confines of good taste, permit wide variability based on student determinations.

Describe how you plan to clear one section of the room at a time, that you will explain the kind of den it will be (number of students it can hold, light or shady, warm or cool, open or partitioned, etc.), and that if individuals would like to try locating in that area (either alone or with a friend or two—or occasionally three), they should so indicate by any method you suggest (raised hands, quietly spoken words, etc.).

Preface any decisions by clearly explaining that students who shout for recognition, call out "Oooooh!" or in any way behave disruptively, will slow down the process and will have to wait longer for their turn. (Do not confuse excitement with disruptiveness and be prepared to be flexible.)

It is also necessary to explain that they really have to know themselves, that some of them work best alone. These students should not volunteer to sit with their friends, for if they do not complete their work, their seats will have to be changed; it's better to diagnose themselves correctly in the beginning. Conversely, if youngsters promise they will work well with a friend (even if they previously ' played" more than they "worked," and therefore made little academic progress), give them an opportunity of trying to do so. Warn them, however, that if they do not show achievement, their seating arrangements will be altered. Students frequently become extremely motivated when allowed to share a secluded section of the room with a friend or two and will often gradually conform to higher standards of behavior and effort than previously shown.

Mention to your students in this pre-redesign discussion that, just as they are used to the placement of the furniture in their homes, they are currently "at home" with the placement of the various items in their classroom. Explain that it takes time for people to adjust to new things but that the more flexible a person is, the faster he adjusts. (This will encourage many of the pupils to experience positive reactions to the emerging redesign. Many will then assist others to become acclimated to the new arrangement.)

Finally, assure the students that if they do not like the redesigned room you will help them return to the present arrangement; ask them, however, to agree to live with the new placement for at least one week before deciding whether to keep it or to revert to the way the room was arranged before the proposed change.

Once the students indicate a willingness to experiment with the classroom furniture and to remain with the change for at least a one-week trial period, you are ready to actually redesign.

HOW TO CHANGE YOUR OWN CLASSROOM

The major objective of changing the placement of furniture in the classroom is to provide different types of areas to permit students to function through patterns that appear to be natural for them and for their learning styles.

Some students, however, may not know how they work best or where they prefer to sit; they can only try new placements and determine whether or not the arrangement is good or appropriate for them on the basis of how they react after the change. Therefore, rather than asking students where they would like to sit, begin by establishing the areas. Then, one by one, explain the advantages and/or disadvantages of each, describing the responsibilities of those who elect to sit in that den, alcove, corner, or section. Next, request volunteers. Students need only try the area for a one-week period; if they are dissatisfied, or unable to work there, changes can be made on a flexible basis with your approval.

A simple way to begin involves the clearing of a section of the room *other* than a window wall. Then identify all of the movable objects in the room that can be used as perpendicular extensions to break up the linear effect and to provide small areas. If there are few movable items such as bookcases, file cabinets, tables, or chests available, very low-cost dividers can be constructed easily with cardboard.[8]

Photo 4-4. A file cabinet serves as a divider for these two youngsters who asked ". . . to be near each other but separate when we want to work." The sides of the cabinet are used as bulletin boards and reflect the individual personalities of each of the young ladies. (Photograph courtesy of the Floral Park-Bellerose Elementary School, Floral Park, New York.)

The movable objects may be used in a variety of ways in different sections of the room. For example, bookcases of varying lengths and widths may separate pairs of desks to provide privacy and to permit quiet areas (see Figure 4-5). Small groups of desks (3 to 5) may be isolated in a charming little den or alcove that encourages small-group teamwork (see Figure 4-6). The movable objects may also set apart resource instructional areas such as learning stations or media corners so that students may conduct their work out of the mainstream of activity (see Figure 4-7). In addition, dividers may be used to separate the motivated, persistent students from those who do not follow through on their prescriptions and who require constant supervision (see Figure 4-8). The use of furniture to establish areas in each classroom depends on (1) the physical possibilities that are inherent in the room, (2) the number and type of movable objects

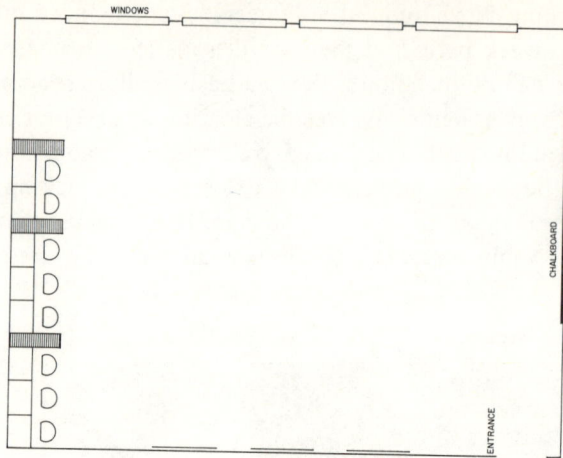

Figure 4-5. Bookcases, file cabinets, extra tables and other movable items may separate desks that have been arranged to face the wall so that students have their backs to the center of the room and can thus turn away from the hub of activity to concentrate on their work. The wall space directly in front of the desk is used for a personal bulletin board. The divider provides privacy for occupants on both sides of it.

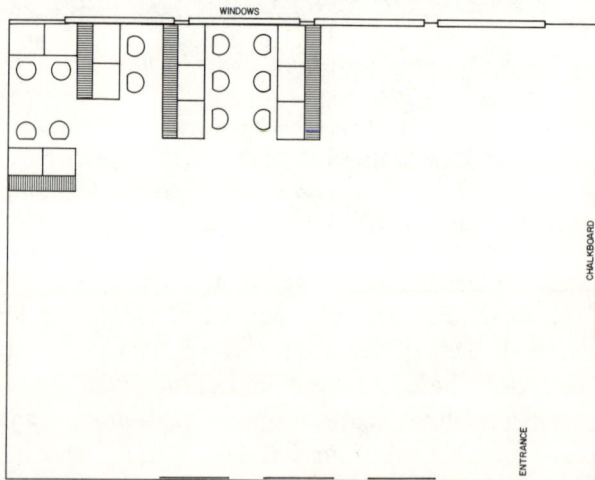

Figure 4-6. To create small den areas for two or more pairs of students (selected by student preferences), separate the desks from adjacent groups by using the movable objects perpendicular to the walls. Face each pair or small group of desks toward the divider so that the paired students have their backs to other pairs. This arrangement is conducive to the development of close peer relationships between the members of each paired group, but not necessarily among the members of the two groups.

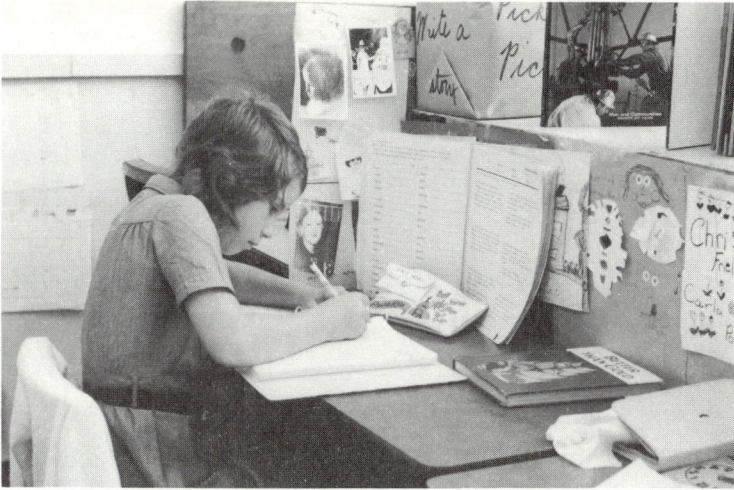

Photo 4-5. This student has extended beyond the bulletin board area provided by the bookcase divider in front of her desk and has moved her papers onto the wall to her left, making the entire section attractive and alive. (Photograph courtesy of the Floral Park-Bellerose Elementary School, Floral Park, New York.)

that are available, (3) the teacher's preferences for whole-class, small-group, or totally individualized instructional strategies, and (4) student preferences for sitting (a) alone, (b) with one or two friends, (c) in a small-group den area, or (d) near the teacher (see Figure 4-17).

When you have cleared the first section of the room, you may begin by saying, ''Here is an area that is far from the windows. The lighting will probably be soft and the temperature may be a little cooler in the summer and in the winter (if that is true). If you think you'd like to work where the lighting is less bright and it's a little less warm than in other areas of the room, you may sit here with one or two friends—if you are certain that you'll work quietly with those friends and learn too. This area, because it is next to the wall, will have a bulletin board space. Remember, if you accept the responsibility of the bulletin board, you'll have to keep it looking attractive, neat, and interesting. Is there anyone who would like to sit here with a friend or two?''

If one youngster volunteers, ask him with whom he would like to sit. If he names one or two friends, ask them if they would like to sit together with the person who nominated them. If so, ask them to each bring their seats and desks to the area.

You may place the first two or three desks side by side against and facing the wall, the chairs on the outside of the desk (as in Figure 4-5).

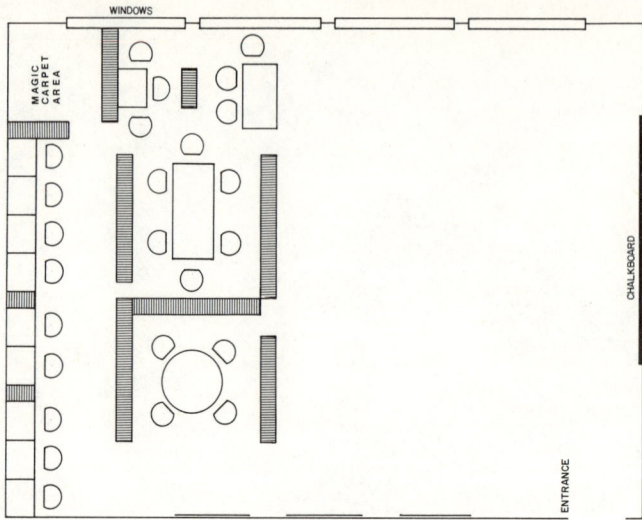

Figure 4-7. Cleverly used dividers can separate the active area of the classroom (which frequently centers around interest centers and learning stations) from the magic carpet corners and other study-reading areas. Such an arrangement provides students with the options of working either in the center with others or studying alone, or with a friend at his desk or den area.

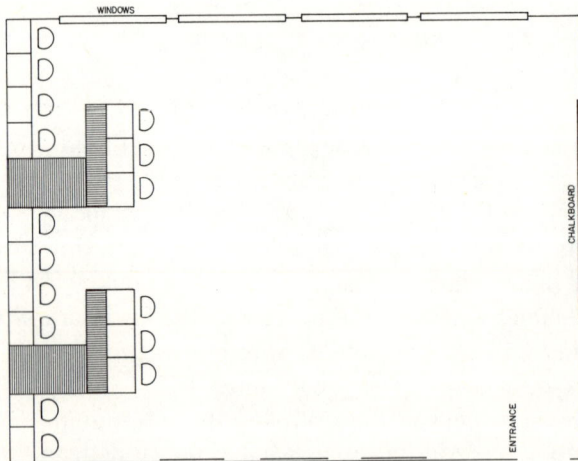

Figure 4-8. Dividers may also be used to separate those students who are capable of working independently from those who need constant supervision. The former are provided den or alcove areas on the periphery while the latter are seated toward the center of the room where the teacher is closer and may work with them more directly.

Show the students the wall section that will hold their bulletin boards and ask them again if they are willing to assume the responsibility for keeping their bulletin boards attractive, up to date, and interesting. If they respond affirmatively, give them an opportunity to try with your approval. They may immediately obtain the construction paper and masking tape (it does not pull off paint when removed) and begin mounting their boards. Move the first object that will be used as a divider and place it perpendicular to the wall at the end of the grouped desks to form the first private section in the room (see Figure 4-9).

Should the first selected student request that three of his friends sit together, you have the choice of either extending the grouping (as in Figure 4-9) to include one additional desk and then placing the divider to establish that group area, or dividing the four students into two pairs and then placing each pair's desks and chairs in the den area back to back, so that two face the wall that parallels the divider and two face the divider (as in Figure 4-10). The two students on the right may have their bulletin boards either on the wall facing their desks or on the wall to their right. The second pair may use the side of the divider that they face as their bulletin board. If that is not feasible (for example, if the divider has open shelves on both sides), they may share the wall space to their left with the

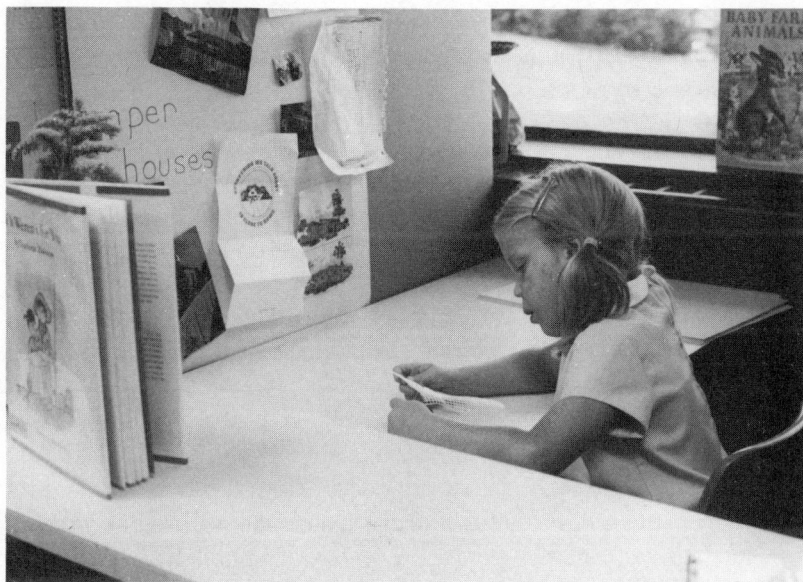

Photo 4-6. A sheet of colored oaktag attached to a standing partition comprises the bulletin board for this very personal, quiet, formal reading area. (Photograph courtesy of the Westorchard School, Chappaqua, New York.)

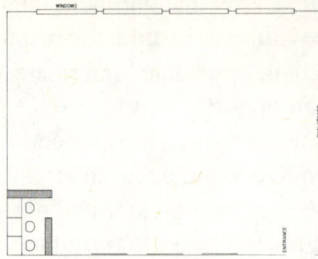

Figure 4-9. The first step in classroom redesign is to divide available wall space into small dens or alcoves to provide privacy and relative quiet for those students who need these elements to function effectively.

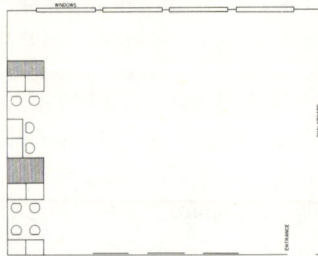

Figure 4-10. An alternative beginning plan where two pairs of students share the same den area.

first pair, or perhaps use the top of the divider as a display case. A third alternative would be to face the first pair so that they face the rear wall, leave enough space for moving in and out of seats, and place the second pair so that they face the divider (as in Figure 4-10).

If the divider that you have used to mark off the first den area is long enough to place two side-by-side desks on the other side, you can begin the second den area by describing that arrangement to the class. This would be an area that would tend to be a little lighter than the first, a little less warm, and would, again, offer a relatively secluded space to its occupants. This section also would contain space for individual bulletin boards. Again, request volunteers and, depending on your and their preferences, place their desks either directly against the wall as in Figure 4-9 or in back-to-back pairs (see Figure 4-10). Combinations of the two designs provide increased interior interest, but some people prefer either one or the other pattern. Exact placement is not of prime importance; what is necessary is that small groups of youngsters each have a place of their own in which to escape the activity and accompanying classroom distraction so that they may work effectively alone, or with a friend or two.

Photo 4-7. This den area is occupied by two boys who enjoy working together. The bulletin board on the wall in front of them is shared. The area is set apart from others by a movable bookcase (to the right) used as a divider. The back of the bookcase is used as a bulletin board for the students in the adjacent alcove. (Photograph courtesy of the Floral Park-Bellerose Elementary School, Floral Park, New York.)

Some dividers, such as a single file cabinet, aid in isolating an individual youngster who prefers to work alone. Explain that this is an area that permits a person to work quietly and independently, and encourage the students to know themselves and to select a placement that will enhance their learning style.

After the second or third den area has been situated, identify two long dividers that can set off a magic carpet (or extremely quiet, casual, reading-meditating) corner of the room where absolutely no discussion is permitted. This should be close to the windows where students may go to relax, to read in silence, or to rest if they feel the need.

The term "magic carpet" is derived from the notion that "magically" the students within the area can withdraw (temporarily) from the noise and activities of the class, thus transforming this corner into the quietest area of the room. It is usually carpeted and/or pillowed. It holds no chairs, desks or hardware—only an unlimited number of interesting

Photo 4-8. These two students preferred sitting together near a sunny window. Cardboard, placed against the windows, serves as a colorful bulletin board and light screen without shutting off all the light. A utility cabinet, placed at a right angle, provides them with desired privacy. (Photograph courtesy of the Floral Park-Bellerose Elementary School, Floral Park, New York.)

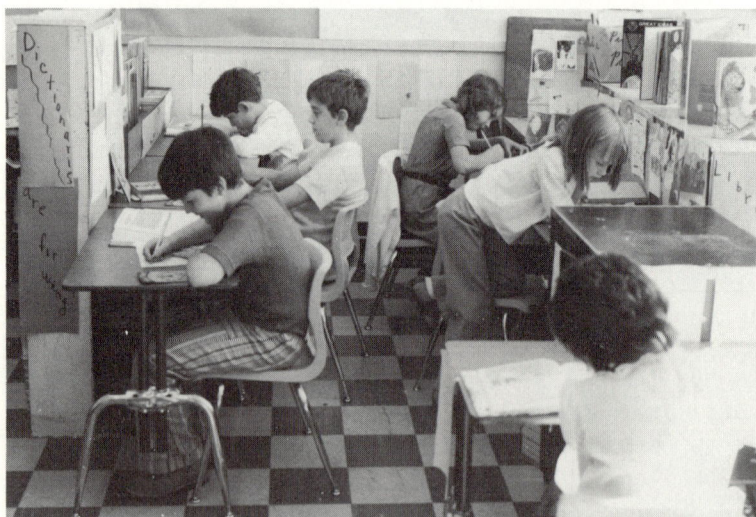

Photo 4-9. This is an alcove area that houses a group of three boys and two girls. The backs of the bookcases faced by each group are used as bulletin board surfaces. Notice that the wall at the rear of the room has been pressed into service as an additional area for mounting student work. (Photograph courtesy of the Floral Park-Bellerose Elementary School, Floral Park, New York.)

books to be read. There are other places in the room (shelves, bookcases, display cases) that also house interesting books of every subject, but those are easily accessible to all students. The magic carpet books are only accessible to the students who are in the area for as long as they choose to remain. The teacher may be flexible, of course, and permit students to take books out of the area to be read elsewhere (perhaps by a pair), but the object of maintaining a current display there is to prevent other students, who may want to browse through or take a book away from the magic carpet area, from intruding on the privacy of the youngsters who are actually in that corner at any given time. The authors therefore suggest that a special group of nonmovable books (that may be duplicated in other sections of the room) be kept in this special area.

To establish the magic carpet area, use two bookcases (or cardboard open-shelf dividers) at right angles to each other in the corner of the room at the other end of the wall on which you began to establish the den areas. This should be a corner near or at a windowed section (to provide light for the readers). Place the two dividers so that each is perpendicular to the two corner walls (as in Figure 4-11), but not touching. Leave room for a small entranceway that should be the only means of access to the magic carpet area. When established, spread a piece of Mystic tape on the floor stretching from the near entrance end of one bookcase to the next entrance end of the second. This suggests the line beyond which shoes are not permitted (to enhance its ''special'' nature and to prevent the carpeting from becoming soiled and undesirable to sit or lie on).

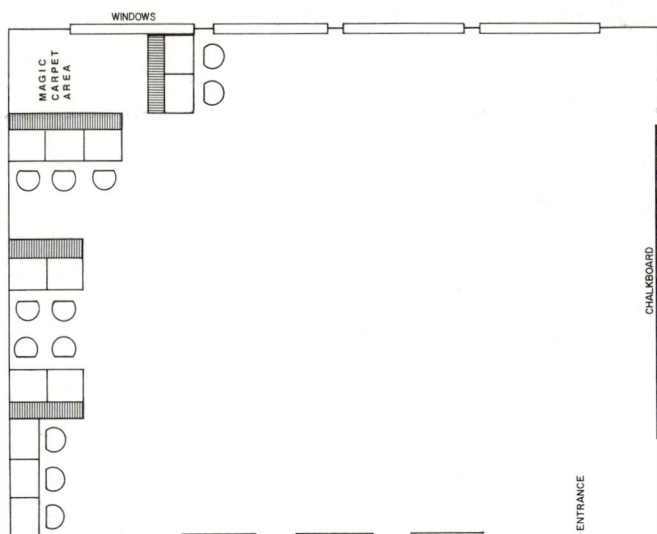

Figure 4-11. The formation of a magic carpet area, a casual, carpeted area where students may read or meditate in silence.

Photo 4-10. The magic carpet area is in the upper right hand corner of the picture. In this room it is a quiet, secluded section where youngsters may go to read or to think without interruption. (Photograph courtesy of the Floral Park-Bellerose Elementary School, Floral Park, New York.)

Merchants who sell carpeting frequently will donate the previous year's samples and remnants. These squares and rectangles then may be placed end to end inside the area to provide a clean, soft, inviting and quiet place.

Explain to the students that shoes may not be brought onto the carpeting; it will then remain clean and pleasant to sit on. Show them how to neatly remove their shoes and to place them side by side directly outside the Mystic-taped entrance. Caution them to place their shoes carefully so that bypassers do not carelessly kick one or the other shoe away from the entrance.

It is wise to establish rules to limit the number of students who may "ride" the magic carpet at one time. The number will vary in accordance with the size of the area, but should rarely be more than six. Explain that the area provides privacy and that the students who are using it should not be disturbed or intruded upon. Tell the youngsters that if they want to use the magic carpet area, there is a good way to determine how many students are currently using it *without* looking directly into the area. First ask them how they might know this. If they cannot identify a method, remind them that only five or six students may use the area at one time. If there is no response ask them about the rule concerning shoes. When they understand that they can count the number of shoes on the outside of the Mystic tape entrance to compute the number of youngsters on the inside, give them a few examples to help them decide whether or not an individual may enter the area.

Photo 4-11. Youngsters in this multi-aged "family grouping" use the magic carpet area to read to each other. The older boy in the corner is reading to the younger one, but the older girl is listening to the two younger ones and is helping them to improve their sight vocabularies. (Photograph courtesy of the Roaring Brook School, Chappaqua, New York.)

You might pose the question, "If I wanted to go inside the magic carpet area and counted (make believe you are really counting with primary and some elementary pupils!) one, two, three, four, five, six shoes, may I go in!" When they respond, ask, "Why?" Explain, if they do not, that six shoes indicate that three children are already using the area and that since as many as six children may use it at one time, three more may still enter.

After one or two additional examples, ask them, "If I counted one, two, three, four, *five* . . . shoes, what might that mean?"

They will offer various solutions, e.g., someone is inside with one shoe on, someone lost a shoe, etc. Respond that it could mean that someone did not place his shoes together, side by side, in the Mystic tape area and that another person accidentally kicked one shoe away from the taped line. Ask them what they could do if that ever happened and add that it would be kind to look for the missing shoe, locate it, and replace it next to the other half of the pair.

Photo 4-12. At certain times students in this class may read to each other in the magic carpet area. At other times they read alone, or to a very special listener—a doll who "loves to be read to because she herself can't." (Photograph courtesy of the Seaford Manor Elementary School, Seaford, New York.)

If you make this preparation for working in the magic carpet area gamelike, the students are likely to remember what they have discussed with you. The area (and the classroom) will then function with fewer crises than might otherwise be anticipated.

Once the magic carpet area has been established, you will be able to determine how many desks may be placed against each of the two dividers that were used to mark off its boundaries. Show the students that you plan to place desks snugly up against each of the dividers to begin the formation of additional dens.

If the back of the divider is solid, place the solid part so that it faces the front (or the inside) of the room. When the desk is pushed up against that surface, the back of the divider (if high enough) becomes a bulletin board for each youngster who faces it. If the divider has only one open side (such as a one-sided bookcase), use the book shelf part on the *inside* of the magic carpet area and the closed shelf part on the *outside* to form a bulletin board surface. If *both* sides of the divider are open, place the books in the divider so that the bindings are easily accessible to the students inside the magic carpet area.

Explain the attributes of each of the two newly created den areas to the students, e.g., "This section is near the windows. It is likely that the light will be brighter than elsewhere in the room. It is also near the heater. If you volunteer for this space be certain that you like warmth. You'll also be near the magic carpet area, so you'll have to be able to avoid socializing with students as they enter and leave that section. *Can* you work quietly only with the friend you select, and can you ignore the traffic going in and out of the area? If so, this may be a good location for you. You'll be responsible for keeping the top of the divider attractive and covered with new books, the bulletin board interesting and current, and so forth. If you would like to sit here with a friend or two, raise your hand."

Once each of the two sections behind the two dividers that border the magic carpet area have been occupied by their new tenants, survey the entire wall area with which you have been working. Do you have room for an additional pair, a single youngster who wants to work alone, another divider to provide even more privacy than we have discussed? Add whatever appeals to you aesthetically and makes sense educationally. Your first wall should be near completion and may look something like one of the models in Figures 4-12 or 4-13. If not, do not be concerned. As long as the students are positive about their seating arrangements and you are willing to try the design, further adjustments may be made as the need for them becomes evident.

Bear in mind that dividers may be 42" by 54" cardboard sections placed horizontally on top of each other and separated by bricks, concrete blocks, wooden or plastic wedges, or any other cast-aside or inexpensive material. Three-ply board is sturdy, durable, and relatively inexpensive,

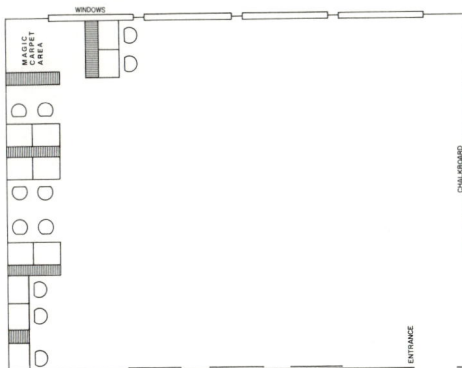

Figure 4-12. This is one plan for the development of small den or alcove areas where two to four students may share their efforts toward completing their individual and/or group prescriptions. On the right, near the window corner, is the magic carpet area.

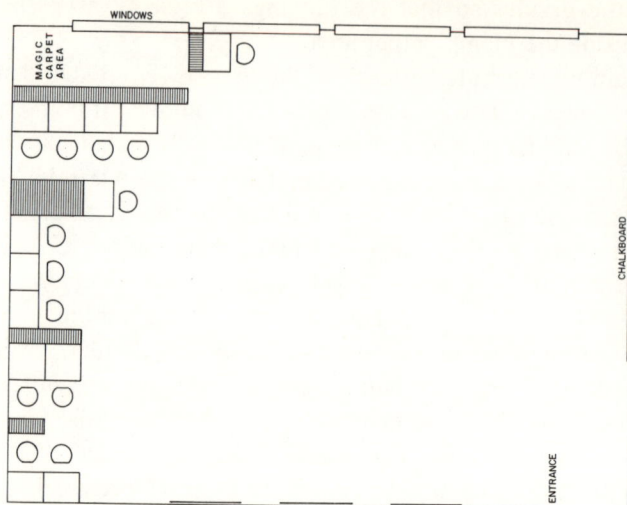

Figure 4-13. An alternative plan for redesigning a far wall in a traditional classroom. This arrangement also features the magic carpet near the windows (to provide light) and on the far, rear wall (to provide quiet).

and may be painted by volunteering parents and students to complement the classroom color scheme.

Once the far wall has been designed to your initial satisfaction, the front wall directly opposite across from the one you have just completed should be redesigned.

Begin with the section of the front wall that is directly opposite the magic carpet area. Establish a den by using two dividers to enclose the corner. Determine if you wish to place two pairs of youngsters, two groups of three students or some other number. The width and depth of the den will depend on the number of desks and chairs you place there.

Once the dividers have each been located perpendicular to the two right-angled corner walls, the students' desks may be placed so that they either face the interior wall (as in Figure 4-14) or face the *back* side of either one or both of the dividers (as in Figures 4-15 and 4-16). The latter placement is directly opposite to the way we used the dividers in the magic carpet area where students needed access to the books from *inside* the area. In this den the students inside do not need to be able to reach whatever will occupy the shelves or drawers of the dividers used to form the den; it will be the students who do *not* share this area who will need to be able to get to the materials housed in the dividers without intruding on the youngsters inside.

There are many possibilities for utilizing each of the den areas, depending on the teacher and the students involved and their determinations of what is aesthetically pleasing and functionally effective to them.

Photos 4-13, 4-14. Veteran teacher Dorothy Haarmann (15 years) establishes den and alcove areas for her students because she believes they are then ". . . less distracted by others, more able to become involved in their own studies, and feel as if it's their own part of the room." Photographs courtesy of Floral Park-Bellerose Elementary School, Floral Park, New York.)

Photo 4-14

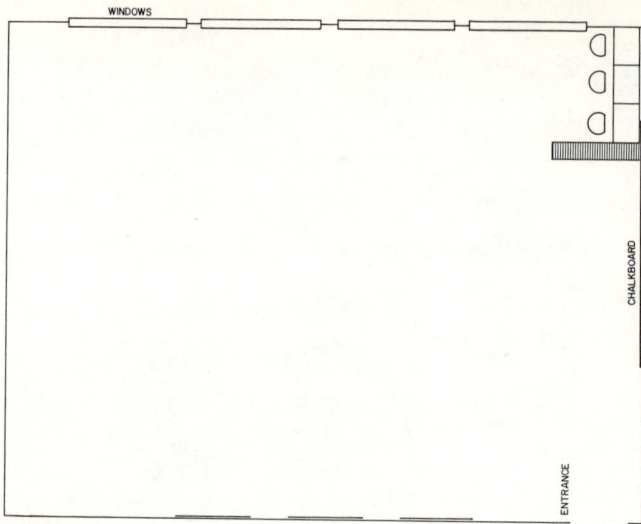

Figure 4-14. Students in this corner den have placed their desks so that they face against the interior wall, which then provides bulletin board space for its occupants.

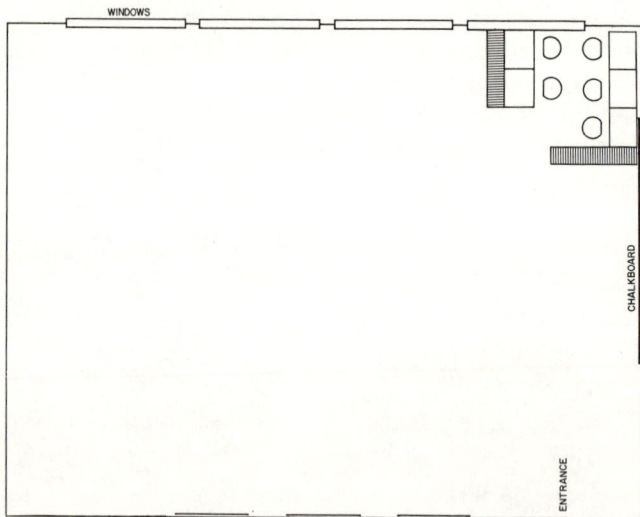

Figure 4-15. In this corner den some of the students' desks face against the back of one of the dividers and others face against the interior wall.

If a bookcase or cabinet is used as a divider on the outside of the corner den, two or three additional students may be placed at right angles to it on the outside of the corner area. These new desks could face the front wall and begin to form the next area. If the divider on the front wall of the corner area has neither side shelf nor side drawer space (such as a file

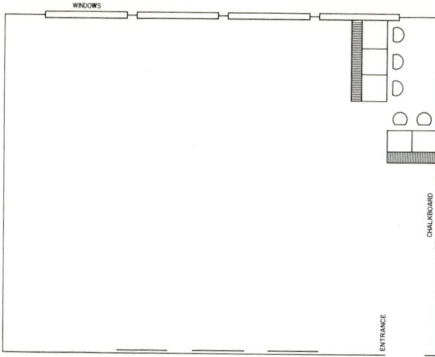

Figure 4-16. In this den all the students' desks have been placed facing against dividers. The wall space on the interior wall may be used as bulletin boards.

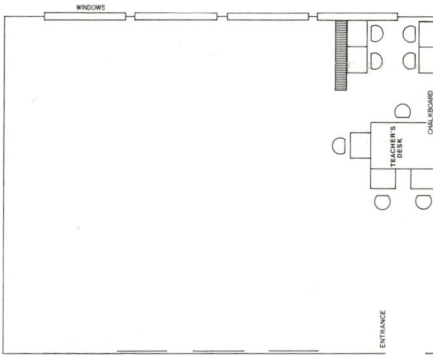

Figure 4-17. In this area the students' desks have been placed so that two youngsters face the interior wall and two face the back of the divider. The teacher's desk has been used as a divider and two (or three) additional pupils' desks may be placed so that they face the teacher (who rarely occupies her seat).

cabinet where the drawers face the center of the room), desks may be placed up against the divider itself. A table may be used as a material resource center and may be flanked on both sides by dividers. This arrangement would permit an additional area where students who do not share a den area may meet to work together during a small-group instructional activity such as a circle of knowledge, simulation, case study, etc. (see Figure 4-18).

Any of the techniques for grouping two to five students may be used to continue the pattern of establishing small den or alcove areas. The section nearest the door lends itself very well to being a material resource section. Dividers may be placed at right angles to the walls near the entrance to provide an open passageway where books and manipulative

WINDOWS

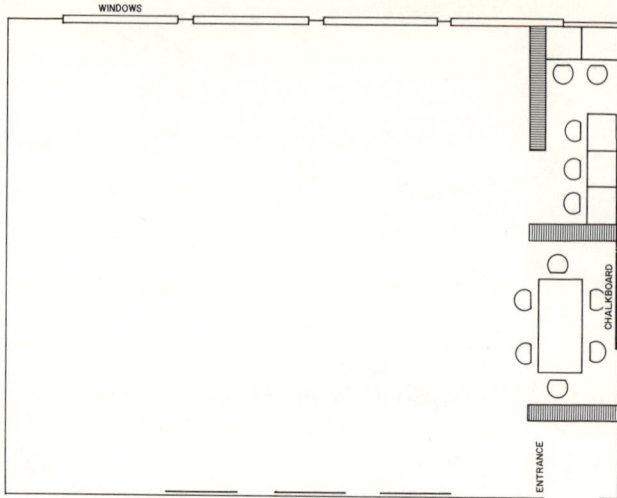

Figure 4-18. A table has been designated as a material resource center (e.g., a place where mathematics or reading materials may be available) and placed between two dividers to facilitate easy access to the materials and privacy when using them. This area can also be used as a small-group center where students who do not share a den may meet to work together.

materials (games, reading and math equipment, etc.) may be selected easily without intruding on others (see Figure 4-19).

Behind the bookcases on the side wall near the door, two or three students' desks may be placed to form another den. When a wall includes a clothing closet, it may be feasible to establish only one den area behind the entranceway bookcase. The remaining section must be free for access to the closet. In older, traditional buildings, closets frequently have some stationary doors. These may be used for individual youngsters who prefer to work alone. Their desks may be placed against the nonmovable doors that may then be used as bulletin boards (see Figure 4-20).

Where large, old-fashioned heating units are exposed to view it is possible to cover the surface with thin sheets of asbestos and to use the units themselves as areas against which one or two desks may be placed, using the portion of the unit above the desk heights as a bulletin board.

When sections of the room appear to be unusable for desk placement (such as long sections of wardrobe walls, built-in bookcase walls, or sink and other "wet" areas), it is attractive to leave an aisle between these sections and a series of horizontally placed dividers. This arrangement creates an attractive resource aisle on the periphery of the room and permits small dens to be established toward the inner part. Access to the materials placed in the dividers does not interfere with students engrossed in their studies outside the area (see Figure 4-19).

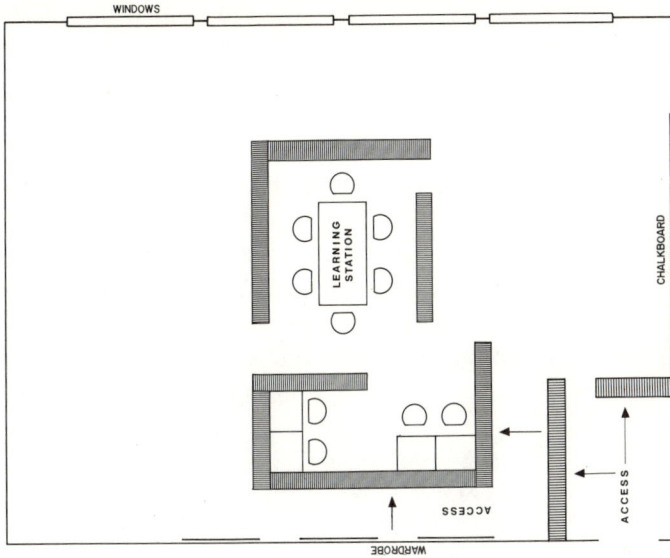

Figure 4-19. The entrance to a room serves effectively as a resource center, providing easy access to learning materials without intrusion on working students. Built-in wardrobes or bookcase walls may be made increasingly functional by placing dividers three to four feet in front of them with access to the materials they house from the part away from the middle of the room. Student desks may then be placed against the dividers on the inside of the room to create new den areas.

The various patterns of separating the rear and front walls of the classroom into small den areas to accommodate between two to five students should be extended all around the outer area of the room with the exception of closets or sinks. If sufficient space is available, it may be possible to establish one or more material resource centers or small-group meeting areas within the total design. The outer sections of the room should be maintained as quiet work areas for independent, paired, or small-group work. The teacher should move from youngster to youngster and from small group to small group to check each student's progress, to respond to questions, to guide youngsters in need of assistance, and to evaluate the quality of what has been completed.

Initially, redesign efforts should be restricted to the outer perimeter of the room. The center should be reserved for areas where students may work together in more gregarious or mobile activities. The den areas that foster privacy and small-group quiet interaction will aid in keeping the noise level down and student concentration high. Youngsters may work alone, in pairs, or in small teams in their dens or in the small-group instructional areas that have been established on the outer edge of the room. For more interactive activities, they may work in the center of the

room. With this method, youngsters involved in their independent prescriptions can literally turn their backs on the activity in the center and
remain with their tasks. Should it be appropriate to join those involved in
the center of the room, at a holiday interest center for example, they need
merely move to the larger area. Basic rules and procedures for moving
from one area to another should be established to promote positive learning activities for all.

The center area might include a learning station or two, an interest
center, or a game table. If the teacher and class prefer, one of the corner
den areas may be used as a ''little theater,'' or a media corner.[9] The room
arrangement may be as creative as the teacher, but much of the practical-
ity of this kind of redesign will not become apparent until experienced by

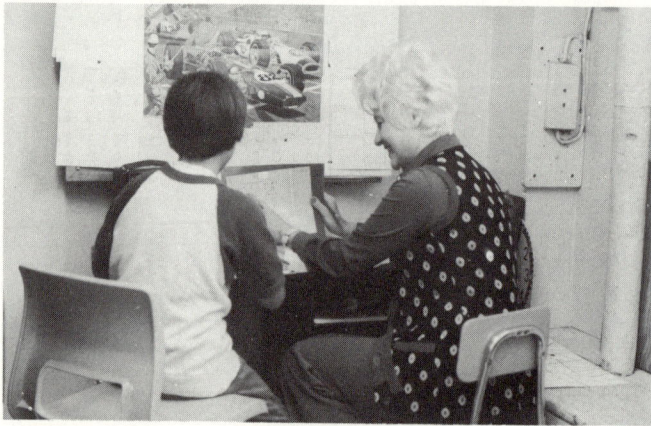

Photos 4-15, 4-16. Dorothy states that students develop a vested
interest in making their areas attractive and sharing them with their
friends. (Photographs courtesy of the Floral Park-Bellerose
Elementary School, Floral Park, New York.)

Photo 4-16

Photo 4-17. Doris Weber, who has taught for 14 years, establishes a language arts learning station in the center of the room so that, as she works with each group, she is able to see everything that is happening at each of the remaining instructional areas. (Photograph courtesy of the Floral Park-Bellerose Elementary School, Floral Park, New York.)

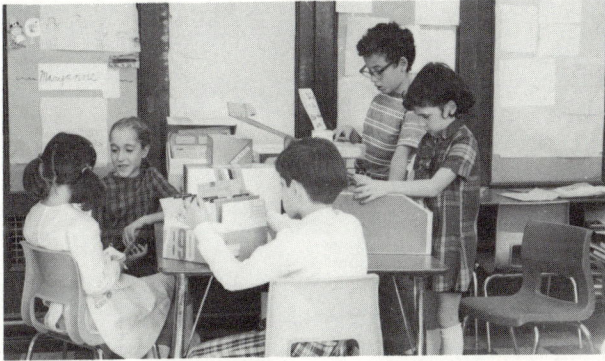

Photo 4-18. As Doris is working with the children at the language arts learning station, another group is deeply involved in self-directed study at the math learning station. (Photograph courtesy of the Floral Park-Bellerose Elementary School, Floral Park, New York.)

the group for a week or more. The room should be revised, especially in the early stages, to meet needs as they emerge.

What should, of necessity, be incorporated into the development of the redesign process is (a) the clear explanation of what each den area offers a youngster, (b) his free choice to volunteer for den placement, and (c) the right to change dens if, after a one-week trial period, the youngster does not seem able to function effectively according to his personal learning style or ease in the environment.

Since each group of 30 or more students contains youngsters with many varied learning styles, the redesign suggested in this chapter provides only a beginning toward the accommodation of individual differences. Once the room has been arranged into smaller and larger areas and students have been permitted to volunteer for their seating placements in dens and alcoves, the teacher will need to observe carefully to ascertain whether, in truth, the youngsters have been able to accurately identify how they learn best. Should the teacher, as she moves from student to student and group to group, recognize that individual boys and girls are not achieving academically, or are not making suitable or appropriate progress, she will need to either diagnose the youngsters by administering the Learning Style Questionnaire suggested in Chapter 3 or experiment with alternate seating-studying arrangements until the proper placement for the student becomes apparent.

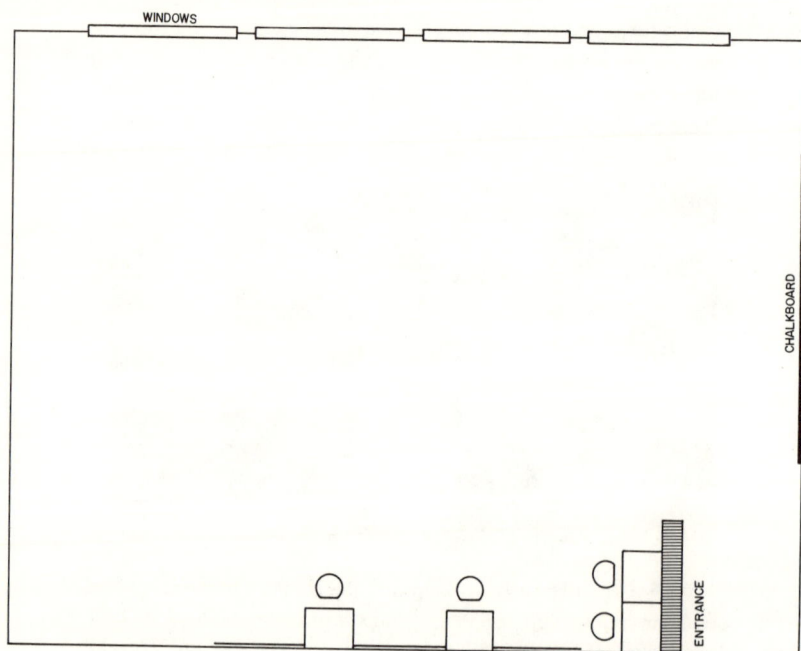

Figure 4-20. Behind the entranceway bookcase is the first side wall den area. If this is a clothing closet wall and the closets include some nonmovable doors, individual youngsters may occupy the spaces directly in front of the stationary doors and may use the doors as bulletin boards. An alternative would be to establish a resource aisle directly in front of the wardrobe area by placing dividers approximately four feet away from the closets and permitting access to materials from the closet side (see Figure 4-19).

Once the instructional area has been redesigned, it is important to teach the students to use it effectively. This necessitates the ability to cooperate with peers, to choose from among appropriate alternatives, to complete assignments or tasks, to locate, use, share, repair, and return resources, and to function independently in an environment that requires increased decision-making and student responsibility. These are the items that are more fully discussed in Chapter 5.

Photo 4-19. Four or five youngsters are absorbed in self-selected readings at the magic carpet area. (Photograph courtesy of the Floral Park-Bellerose Elementary School, Floral Park, New York.)

Parents are interested in the concepts and strategies to which their children are being exposed, especially if they are new. Once the class has become adjusted to the redesigned room, invite parents in to visit and to discuss the rationale of the room or area redesign. Explain the advantages of capitalizing on each youngster's learning style and describe how the students participated in the developing arrangement. Once parents understand why the instructional environment has been altered, they usually are willing to support the effort until sufficient time has elapsed to yield both objective and subjective results such as student responsiveness, teacher reactions, academic progress and increased provision for individual differences and learning styles. Actually the students themselves will "presell" the change with the enthusiasm they express at home about their new "interior decoration." (See Figure 4-21 for a completed model room.)

Photo 4-20. Other students are involved in a variety of educational activities including reading, geography and math contracts. (Photograph courtesy of the Floral Park-Bellerose Elementary School, Floral Park, New York.)

Photos 4-21, 4-22. Kathleen Fontaine begins her room redesign by moving her desk perpendicular to the chalkboard wall, leaving just enough room behind so that she can work quietly with a small group of students without interfering with the learning activities of the larger group. She places two or three desks adjacent to her own so that students who "need" her can be "close." (Photographs courtesy of the Floral Park-Bellerose Elementary School, Floral Park, New York.)

Photo 4-22

Photos 4-23, 4-24. Kathleen, who has taught for four years, divides a long wall section with a filing cabinet and places two pairs of volunteering friends at each side so that they can share the "bulletin board" surfaces. (Photographs courtesy of the Floral Park-Bellerose Elementary School, Floral Park, New York.)

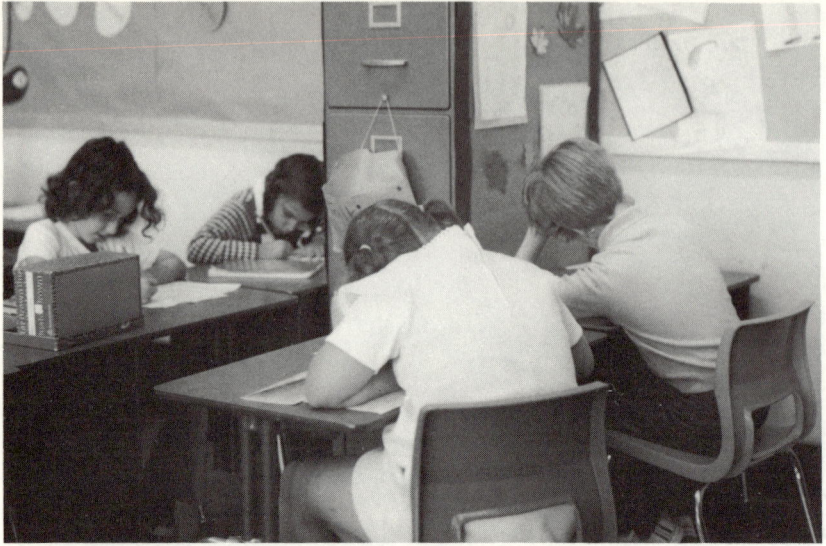

Photo 4-24

Photos 4-25, 4-26. A group of three or four students may form a den area by placing their desks against the far end of the long wall and establishing bulletin boards on the wall they face. One or two students (backs to camera) can form another separate area by forming a new section at right angles to the desks that have been placed perpendicular to the large wall. (Photographs courtesy of the Floral Park-Bellerose Elementary School, Floral Park, New York.)

Photo 4-26

Photo 4-27. Kathy permits students who want to be away from the larger group to work alone or with a friend. (Photograph courtesy of the Floral Park-Bellerose Elementary School, Floral Park, New York.)

Photo 4-28. She also provides for small groups of students to establish their own out-in-the-center areas if they prefer. She then designs the learning stations, interest centers, and various other instructional areas around the outer areas of the room. (Photograph courtesy of the Floral Park-Bellerose Elementary School, Floral Park, New York.)

BRAINSTORMING EXERCISE ON REDESIGNING THE PHYSICAL ENVIRONMENT

Read the following case study description of Brewster King. Following the directions for brainstorming, fill in as much information as you can under each of the brainstorming columns. Then compare your responses with those provided by the authors to determine the type of instructional environment that might be provided for Brewster.

Case Study: Brewster King

The six of them walked into the schoolyard looking as if they planned to attack and conquer at the slightest provocation. Hands in their pockets, chips on their shoulders, and apparently ready for action, they sauntered toward the area where the sixth-grade line should have been forming.

Other students watched them as they meandered across and through the younger children's lines, pushing the boys and girls gently out of their path. Brewster King led the group but, peculiarly, despite the air of authority assumed (and apparently enjoyed), he was clownlike in his appearance. Above the rough exterior were two squinting eyes that teared from the sunlight (which was not really too strong for most people) and caused him to frequently brush dampness away from his face with his sleeve. His neck, too, was wet and showed extreme perspiration, as did his collar. The sight of the group may have been fearful to some youngsters, but professional sociologists would have recognized the scene.

The group had been friends since entering kindergarten; this was the neighborhood's young "old guard." They were jovial, but hard playing. They appeared to tolerate no new intrusions into their midst and remained close together. Except for their casually inconsiderate behavior of younger children and peer-aged girls, they kept mostly to their own activities.

Scholastically they were poor students and, perhaps because they felt unable to compete, they often withdrew from class academics and began in-group games in the room. Their parents had been contacted, but viewed these offenses as trivial. Perhaps if the parents had supported the teachers . . . , but they, too, had not been able to function well academically. Brewster, in particular, always chewing or eating candy, seemed to listen as long as he could understand. When the teacher began to move beyond his ability level he would, in a sense, organize his group and become disruptive. Often it would begin by his changing his seat near the window and saying, "I don't remember what you say, Teach, unless I can hear you." Sometimes, if permitted to move closer to the teacher, he would listen longer, but eventually the wisecracks would begin and the class would be interrupted.

Brewster behaved nicely during sound-track films (particularly when he was permitted to run the machines). The teacher occasionally lamented, "I can't let him watch films all day. When would he learn?"

Filmstrips with printed explanations were not as rewarding for him, perhaps because he did not read at grade level. Tapes worked nicely; he would use the cassettes repeatedly, often needing five or six listening sessions before he could understand fully what the objectives were. With these he progressed academically, although slowly.

Brewster's friends often tried to listen to the tapes or view the filmstrips sitting side by side. When they talked, or began to kid around, Brewster would silence them; he seemed to be interested. However, when other kinds of lessons were given (teacher lecture, question and answer sessions, workbook, etc.), he and his friends in the back of the room invariably became rambunctious. When the teacher separated Brewster from his group, he catcalled and pleaded (out loud, of course!) "Let me go back to my friends!"

Brewster has been recommended for a "special" class. His teacher believes that by separating the group, its members can be disciplined more effectively. She even suggested "leaving the six of them back this year," considering that the shame of being in a sixth-grade class for the second time and with younger children would be "good" for them. Brewster's dad came in a couple of times but said that he did not want to hear about the teacher's troubles; he had plenty of his own! Brewster's mother attends to their meager apartment and five other older youngsters, all of whom experienced poor academic progress when they were in elementary school. The mother works at odd jobs when she can, as do two of the older children.

Brainstorming Exercise

Use the following exercise to literally "storm your brains" in a short but quick effort to draw out your knowledge in response to each question. This may be done alone or with a pair, although the technique is more effective in a group of from five to 30 or more. The rules are simple and require that:

1. Each participant call out his thoughts or reactions as soon as an opening (silence) presents itself after the leader says "begin." If you try the technique by yourself, obviously it is not necessary to verbalize your thoughts; merely jot them down under the correct column heading.
2. Focus or concentrate on the specific questions in each column (one at a time)—*and nothing else*.
3. No analysis, editorial comment, negative criticism or put-downs are permitted. If you are brainstorming by yourself, do not second-guess your immediate ideas; merely jot them down.
4. All suggestions and ideas pertaining to the question should be written in the correct column whether they seem realistic or far out; scrutiny and analysis *follow* the initial brainstorming and recording of thoughts.
5. Use short time intervals, two to three minutes maximum for each column.

If you are brainstorming with a group, a leader facilitates the process by keeping the group on target, synthesizing responses, and asking for clarification when necessary as he records the total group's responses. He may also request repetition or a temporary slowdown if the ideas being called out cannot be recorded as quickly as they flow from the participants.[10]

If you are brainstorming by yourself, set your mind toward coping with each column for approximately a three-minute period. Devote your entire attention to identifying possible answers to each column, one at a time, for that amount of time, and then move onto the next column. Within just eight to ten minutes, you may be able to identify important aspects of Brewster King's learning style and then suggest how to provide him with an instructional environment to complement them. (You may wish to review the elements of learning style, Chapter 3, before you begin.)

1. List all the data you know that relates directly to Brewster's learning style.	2. List all the data you do not know about Brewster's learning style.	3. Considering what you *do* and *do not* know about Brewster's learning style, how would you design his classroom environment?

Comparing Responses to Sample Answers

1. What did the Case Study reveal about Brewster's learning style?	2. What did the Case Study *not* reveal about Brewster's learning style?	3. Considering Columns 1 and 2, how could Brewster's learning style be accommodated?
He may need quiet to concentrate (Brewster would shut them up). Sunlight bothers him (squinting, tearing eyes). He's sensitive to heat (extreme perspiration). He would probably prefer an informal physical design (much movement shown by preference and without permission). Motivation increases with auditory resources and comprehension—he behaves during sound films, when using tapes, and when he understands or is near (can hear) the teacher. He seems to be persistent when using tapes or when able to function on his level of understanding. He is responsible to some extent (likes to operate film projector). He probably needs short prescriptions (assignments, objectives, study plans, etc.) that are frequently supervised. He needs intake available to him (always chewing or eating candy). He functions effectively within his peer group (remained close, wanted to sit with them, could direct them, etc.). He remains with his "in-group" (jostles younger children and girls, avoids relationships with other classmates). He probably needs to be mobile (moves frequently). He is probably an auditory learner (needs to hear teacher, is attentive to auditory resources, etc.). He would probably resent having to learn with younger children (inconsiderate behavior toward them in yard).	Whether, if given auditory resources, he would become a more responsible learner. Whether he is, in fact, an auditory learner, or whether tactile or kinesthetic resources would be more effective for him. Whether he would be willing to learn alone if he could function independently and feel a sense of progress and achievement. Whether he could relate to the teacher if he were progressing academically. Whether, in reality, he might respond positively to varied sociological patterns (peers and teacher). The time of day in which he functions best. His relationship with either his parents or his older siblings.	By his choice, he should be permitted to work alone in a quiet area when he prefers to do so, or with his small group of friends. He should have available a seat away from the window in a cool den where the sun does not intrude. He should be permitted to move from area to area if he is engaged in purposeful work and if progress is evident. He should have some intake available to him (gum, raw vegetables) in the instructional setting. He should have tapes, sound films, records and filmstrips accompanied by tapes. When possible, more able students or the teacher (on tape) could read written material to him. "Grade level" curriculum (if used) should be introduced on his level of comprehension, which requires multilevel resources. He should be given single objective (or very short) assignments that he is able to master to build his confidence, elevate his self-image, increase his independence to help him outgrow his in-group. The teacher should permit him to sit where he can hear well, even on the floor at her feet. He should not be retained for a second year at the sixth grade level, for he would inhibit the smooth functioning of younger students and probably fail to achieve. He should be given some responsibility for sound equipment and opportunities to teach others.

Look at the drawing of a redesigned classroom (Figure 4-21) and place an X on the den area that you would recommend to Brewster based on what you know of his learning style. Check your choice with the correct answer below.

. . . .

Answer to the placement of Brewster King.

Brewster probably would function nicely if placed in the first den area on the left at the entrance to the room. Note the proximity to the multimedia area where he can learn through tapes, the teacher (because he is on the outside of the divider rather than partially concealed behind one), and the distance from the window wall which tends to be sunnier and warmer than other classroom sections.

Another group member's desk could be added to the den if the two occupants strongly desired it. The top of the divider could hold a plastic dish of raw carrots or celery to provide intake when necessary.

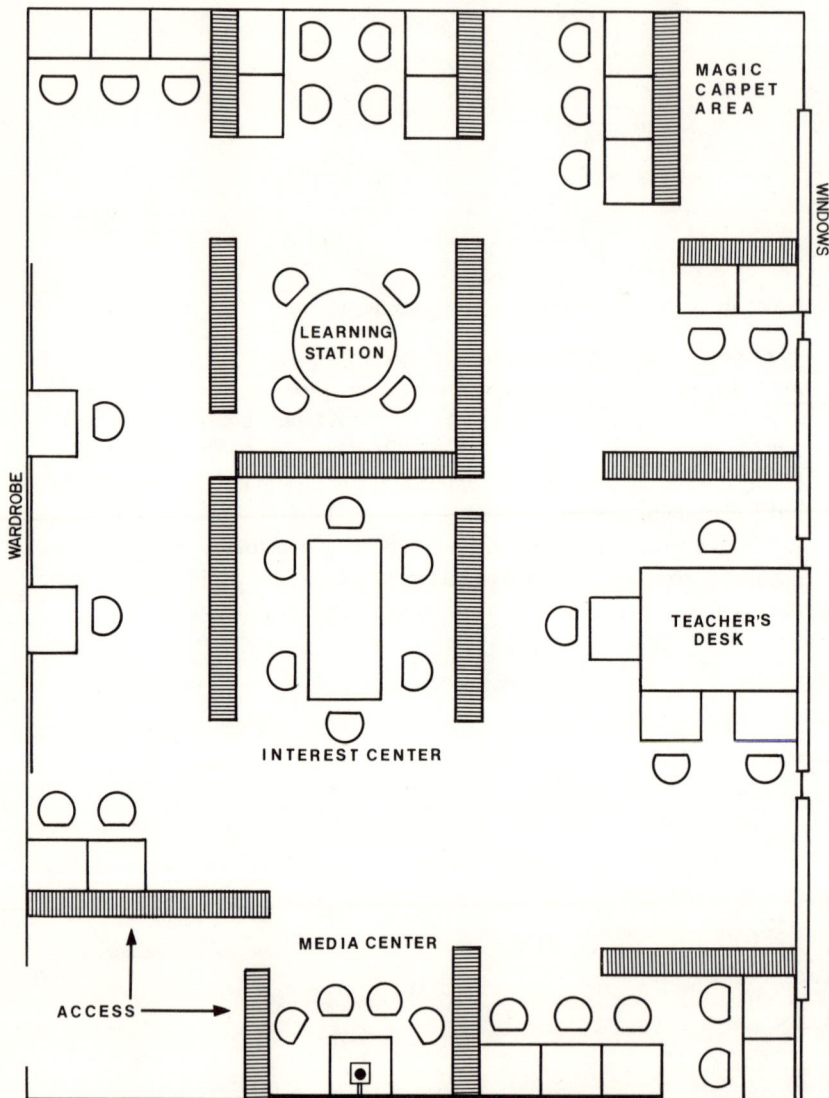

Figure 4-21

FIVE

Developing Student Independence in an Individualized Environment

Behavioral Objectives for Chapter 5

1. You will be able to name at least five skills that students need to function independently in an individualized program.
2. You will be able to name at least five strategies that nurture the development of student independence skills.

. . . .

RECOGNIZING THE NEED FOR POSITIVE STUDENT ATTITUDES AND APPROPRIATE SKILLS

Many teachers who have begun to individualize have been disappointed and frustrated by the lack of total success. These able instructors identified a method that they believed to be appropriate, discussed plans for varying instruction with their students, established some rules for functioning in the new environment, and proceeded to introduce the changeover. To their dismay, their charges often appeared to "take advantage" of the informality of the setting. Discipline occasionally became a problem, particularly with those students who previously had been unmotivated or nonconformist. Some students, unprepared for their new role, resented the responsibilities placed on them by teachers who fully believed that "kids must learn how to learn alone."[1] The concept is correct, but the ability to achieve independently requires appropriate attitudes and skills that many students do not have.

Before students are permitted to function in an informal instructional setting they should be taught how to do so effectively. As they begin to recognize the responsibilities that accompany freedom and choice, they will be able to "do their own thing" in a positive way.

INDENTIFYING THE SKILLS OF INDEPENDENCE

Illich bitterly complains that schooling is "intellectually emasculating" because it confuses teaching with learning and therefore prevents students from "taking control of their own learning."[2] The following chart itemizes what students should be able to *do* if they are to function effectively in an individualized program that, by its very nature, requires youngsters to progress independently. These skills are essential if students are to take additional responsibility for the "control of their own learning."

Desirable Independent Student Behaviors in an Individualized Program

Learners should be able to:	In relation to assigned or selected:	Seeking assistance (if necessary) from:		
		Teacher	Peers	Others
Identify:	Objectives	+		
Select from among approved alter-natives:	Resources		+	Librarian
	Activities	+		
	Reporting choices		+	
Make decisions concerning:	Learning style options	+		Supplementary personnel
	Environmental options		+	
	Sociological		+	
	physical and		+	
	emotional options	+	+	
Locate, use, care for, share, repair, and return:	Multimedia "software" and "hardware"		+	Media personnel, custodians
	Self-assessment instruments	+	+	
	Teacher guides or answer sheets	+	+	
Create personal:	Priorities	+		Parents
	Time schedules	+		
	Demonstrations of competence	+		
Complete:	Objectives	+	+	

PROMOTING INDEPENDENCE THROUGH TASK EXPERIENCES AND THE COMPLETION OF OBJECTIVES

Because one of the best ways to learn is by doing, students can become independent and responsible learners by experiencing many activities in which they are encouraged to achieve objectives[3] on their own. Some may be hesitant and others will be fearful[4] but eventually most, if not all, will begin to feel the wonderful sense of accomplishment that accompanies success. "Nothing succeeds like success" will become a reality for students who were previously unmotivated or apathetic. These youngsters will recognize that they *can* progress academically when permitted to do so at their own rate and through their own selection of learning resources.

For students to achieve successful mastery of their objectives, a few simple guidelines are suggested:

1. Permit the student to select the objective(s) he will work toward from among approved alternatives.[5]

Examples

Complete objectives one (1), four (4), seven (7) and ten (10), and any other three (3) of the remaining six (6).

1. Describe at least five (5) characteristics of the Middle Ages.
2. Explain why a feudal type of government came into existence.
3. Describe life in a medieval manor.
4. Identify at least three (3) changes that took place in the later centuries of the Middle Ages which have affected our way of living.
5. List five (5) effects the barbarian invasions had on Western Europe.
6. Describe the part knighthood and chivalry played in the Middle Ages.
7. a. List at least three (3) of the heroes of knighthood.
    b. Name at least two (2) myths that describe the adventures of a knight.
8. Discover at least five (5) events which brought about the end of the age of feudalism.
9. Reconstruct the daily events of life in a monastery.
10. List at least five (5) contributions of the monasteries.

A partial list of objectives from a contract entitled "Life During the Middle Ages," prepared by Anita D'Onofrio, Woodmere Public Schools, New York.

Complete objective six (6) and any other three (3) of the remaining five (5).

1. You will be able to explain at least five (5) ways in which you and other people throughout the world are alike.
2. Be able to list at least six (6) emotions or feelings that all people experience.
3. Explain at least two (2) ways that people express or communicate the feelings that you have listed in objective two (2).
4. Describe at least five (5) characteristics which make you a special person.
5. Explain six (6) ways in which you might accidentally make someone feel bad at home, in school or at play.
6. List ten (10) things you can say or do to help make someone feel good about himself at home, in school or at play.

A partial list of objectives from a contract entitled "All About Me," prepared by Evelyn Zeidman, New York City Schools.

2.   Encourage the selection of only one or two objectives during the first few attempts at mastery.
3.   Provide relatively easy objectives in the first group of options.[6]
4.   Permit the student to select the resources (books, tapes, films, film-strips, slides, records or other multimedia) through which he will learn.
5.   Permit the student to work at ease within his own learning style (either alone, with a friend or two, in a small group or with an adult; either at a desk or casually on the floor or carpeted area; for longer or shorter time intervals of his choice, etc.).
6.   Require that he *use* the information he has learned in some form of creative activity, such as designing and developing an original tape, filmstrip, skit, diorama, story, etc. (See pages 176 through 201, Activity Alternatives.)
7.   Encourage him to self-assess (test) *before* he decides whether or not he has actually achieved the objectives(s).

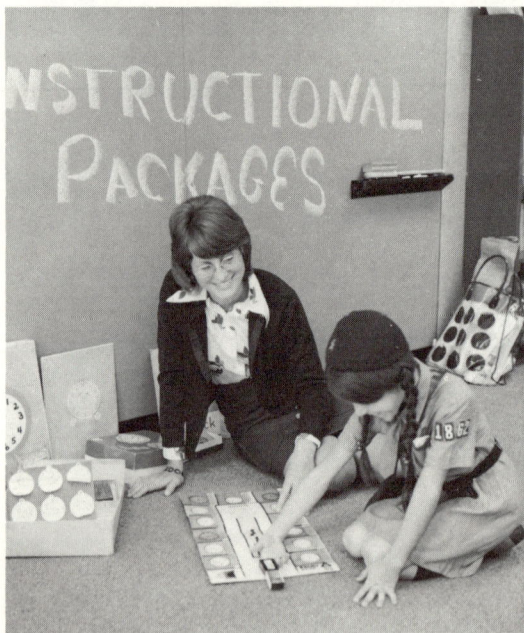

Photo 5-1. Here Karen Plank, who has been teaching five years, introduces one of her students to the correct use of an instructional package on telling time by the half-hour. "Once the youngster is familiar with the procedures of locating the cassette, inserting it properly into the tape recorder and then following its directions, she will be able to use all other packages with ease," she reports. (Photograph courtesy of the Floral Park-Bellerose Elementary School, Floral Park, New York.)

Teaching students to identify, select, and make decisions concerning objectives begins with exposure to small-group techniques.[7] The simplest technique, a circle of knowledge, poses one review question to which there are multiple answers. Obtaining as many correct answers as possible to the question becomes the student's objective. To avoid feelings of insecurity, students are clustered in small groups of between five and eight. The circle as a whole attacks the question and thus the members share both the first objective and success in its mastery. Focusing on this first objective as part of a team enables a student to see how to identify the objective, how to attack it, how to work toward its mastery with others, and how to recognize when it has been achieved.

Once students have learned to function in a circle of knowledge they should be introduced to additional small-group techniques (such as team learning or brainstorming) so that they experience frequent and varied opportunities to identify objectives, to select those they will attempt to

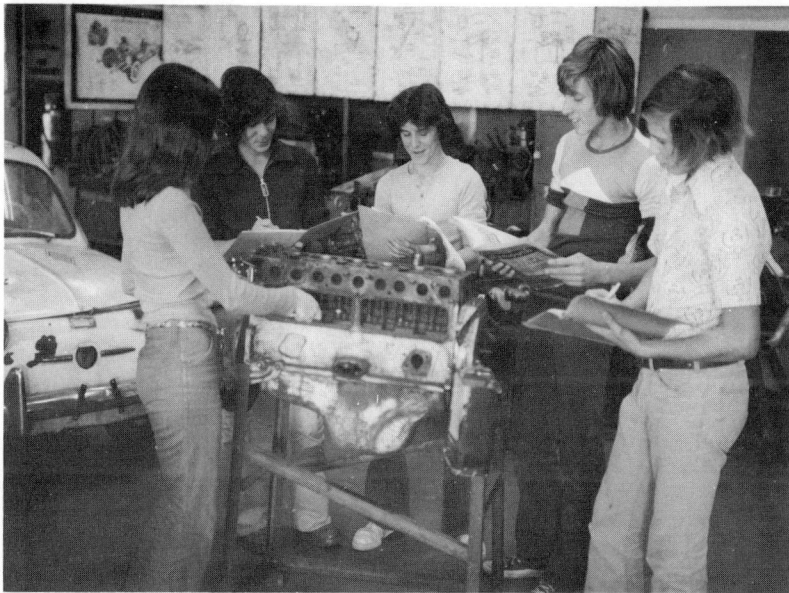

Photos 5-2, 5-3. "For those students who can handle it . . ." Sherman Resnick, with 11 years of teaching experience, uses contract activity packages and/or multisensory instructional packages. Although "all the students enjoyed the uniqueness of both methods," Sherman provides direction for those who do not learn independently. Both groups must demonstrate mastery of the industrial arts objectives under teacher supervision. (Photographs courtesy of the H. Frank Carey High School, Franklin Square, New York.)

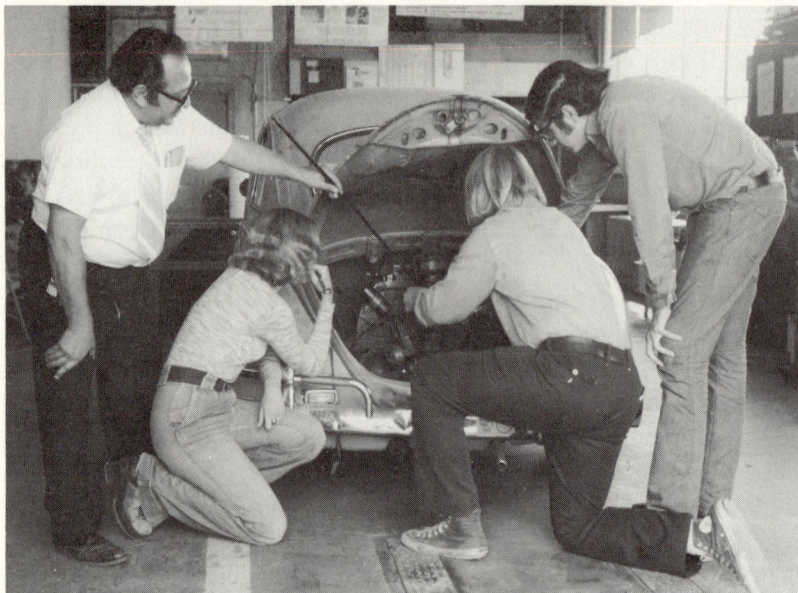

Photo 5-3

Photo 5-4. These kindergarteners are working independently with cut out and labeled geometric forms. By feeling the shapes, tracing them, and copying the names printed on the forms, many five-year olds learn to recognize and identify circles, squares, triangles, rectangles, pentagons, etc. Some of the youngsters even learn to spell the names of the shapes. (Photograph courtesy of the Westorchard School, Chappaqua, New York.)

master, and to decide how they will go about doing so. By developing the necessary skills of independence as part of a group rather than alone, the student has the advantage of seeing how others attack and solve problems and also avoids the tension that may occur when the responsibility for learning is transferred prematurely to him. He eventually recognizes that some of his peers are achieving without constant interaction with the teacher and that, should he require assistance, his peers will also help him.[8]

As soon as four or five students demonstrate that they cooperatively are able to recognize, work toward, and complete their objectives, the

Photo 5-5. One form of self-corrective materials is a series of slab-like rectangular shapes that include a printed numeral and a number of picture objects that are equivalent to it in number. The slabs are divided into two pieces, each having a differently shaped dividing line. Little children can piece together the slabs and begin to recognize the shape of the numeral and identify it with the correct number of objects that it represents. (Photograph courtesy of the Westorchard School, Chappaqua, New York.)

teacher should permit them to compare the group's answers with a check-list of possible responses. This checklist may take the form of a teacher guide, answer sheets, or a listing of correct alternatives that the teacher has developed. The youngsters should be taught how to compare their responses with those supplied by the teacher and how to correct any errors they may have made. Although some teachers, particularly those using a form of programed learning, permit students to compare answers *before* they may have entirely completed their own, this procedure may promote intellectual laziness or apathy in some and is not conducive to the de-velopment of student independence.[9] Therefore, it is suggested that the comparison answer sheets be kept at a specific location and that compari-sons be made *after* the students have made every effort to master the objective.

It is not necessary to be concerned about students copying "correct" answers from the teacher-developed or company-developed lists. Con-sider this exercise a *learning,* rather than a testing experience. As long as the students have tried to think through the possibilities, they should be permitted to see where they have erred and should be encouraged to analyze the reasons they made mistakes.

In a class of 30 students, five or six may be ready to move toward increased independence sooner than the remaining larger group. Do not wait for the others to catch up; they will advance much more quickly than might otherwise be expected if they are motivated by the desire to do something that is only permissible for those youngsters who have demon-strated their ability to achieve and to assume some responsibility for their own progress.

When at least one group of youngsters has learned to work together toward the completion of objectives through three or four small-group techniques, establish the first curriculum-related learning station. Each station should provide at least three activities that yield information and experiences concerning a particular concept or set of data. Attached to each activity should be one or more clearly stated objectives.[10] For exam-ple, next to a box containing many different-sized objects and a scale, a sign attached to the mathematics learning station might read:

1. Select any three items from this box.
2. Write the name of each of the three items on a sheet of paper.
3. Weigh each of the three items.

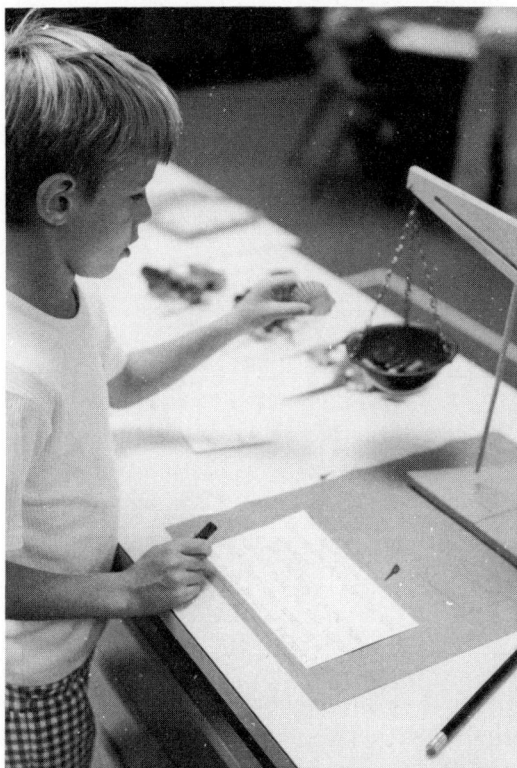

Photo 5-6. This young man is completing objectives that are printed on a task card attached to a scale at a math learning station. When he has recorded the weights of several items he will compare his findings with the answers that are on the back of the card. (Photograph courtesy of the Westorchard School, Chappaqua, New York.)

4. Write the weight of each item next to its name on the sheet of paper.
5. Add the weights of all three items together.
6. Write the combined weight of the three items on the sheet of paper.
7. Look at the answer sheet in the envelope attached to the box and see if your answers are correct.

If your answers are *not* correct, please add your numbers again.

When developing objectives-related experiences for younger children, the teacher might develop a ditto master illustrating each of the items in the mathematics box. Next to each illustration would be the printed name of the item and a space for entering the weight of the item. The objectives, printed on a "task card,"[11] a sheet of colored cardboard, or a 3″ by 5″ file card might read:

OBJECTIVES

1. Weigh any three items in this box.
2. Write the weight of each item next to its picture on the ditto.

A tape that children could play to hear the objectives being read to them might accompany the file card.

A second activity at the mathematics learning station might be a numbers game that could be played by one or more youngsters. Attached to the game would be an objectives card that reads:

OBJECTIVE

1. Play this number game.
2. Count how many times each player has a chance to move.

The third activity at the mathematics learning station might be an instructional package that would teach students to count from one to ten correctly. The objectives for the package would be stated verbally on the tape accompanying the package, but an objectives-related task card could read:

OBJECTIVE

1. **Use this package. It will help you to count from one to ten.**

Photo 5-7. The permanent objectives for this math learning station are creatively hung from the ceiling. Frequently changing objectives are attached to the materials on the table. (Photograph courtesy of the Seaford Manor Elementary School, Seaford, New York.)

Photo 5-8. These young ladies are using a bead frame to solve mathematics problems posed on a series of task cards located at the math learning station. (Photograph courtesy of the Roaring Brook School, Chappaqua, New York.)

Older students should also be given clearly stated objectives so that they know what to learn. Examples of these might be:

OBJECTIVES

1. Be able to define a simple polygon.
2. Recognize and describe all polygons that have up to ten sides.
3. Classify the following polygons* and name their special features, if any.

---

*See Figure 5-1.

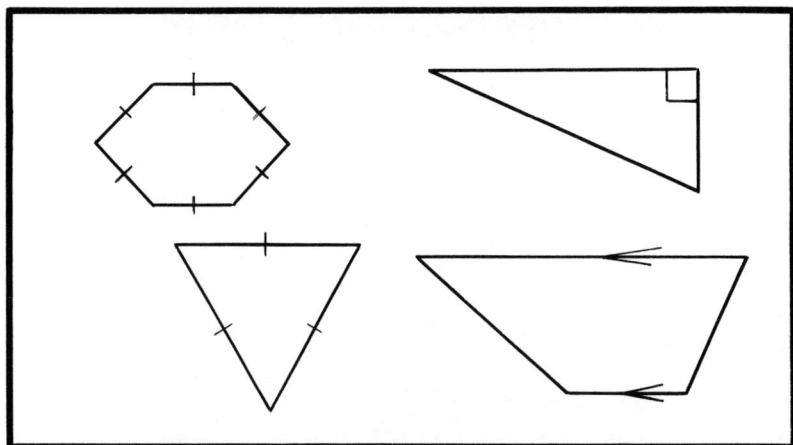

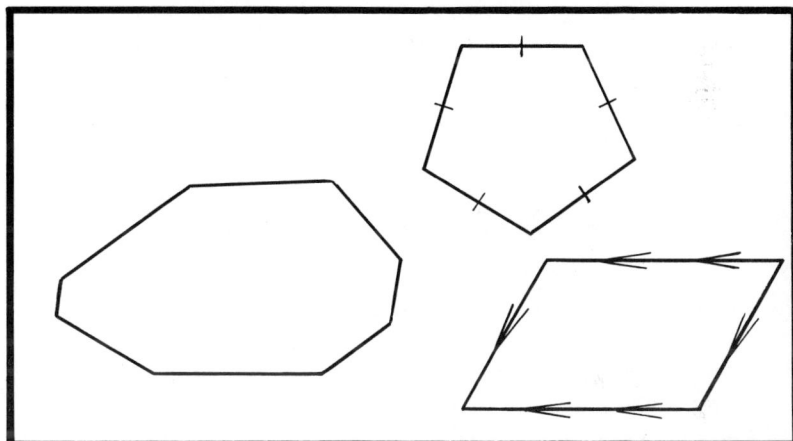

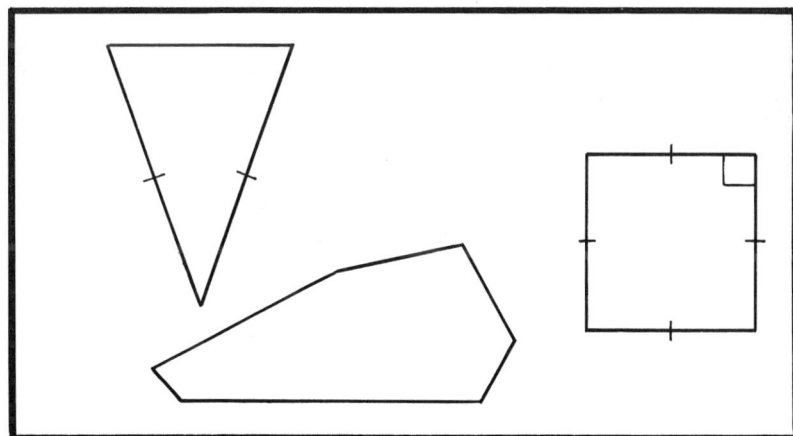

Figure 5-1

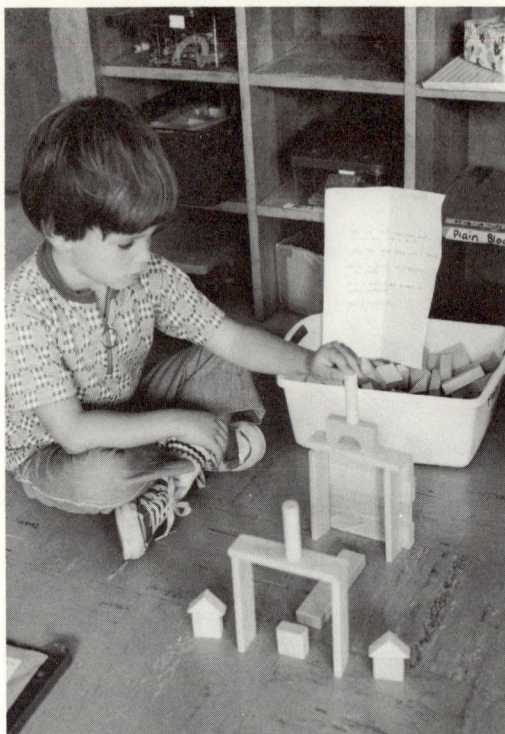

Photo 5-9. This boy is constructing a building by following the directions on a task card attached to the container of blocks. (Photograph courtesy of the Roaring Brook School, Chappaqua, New York.)

The following might also be an activity for older students who are given the freedom of using a mathematics learning station to proceed on their own:

OBJECTIVE

Time yourself. In three minutes, list as many words as you can think of that pertain to finding the area of a polygon.

Even secondary students enjoy learning or reviewing through games. The following objective is popular with students of many ages:

OBJECTIVE

Using all the pieces of multicolored cardboard in the box, form each of the following shapes:

a) a square
b) an equilateral triangle
c) an isosceles trapezoid
d) a hexagon

When selected students are permitted to leave their seats and work independently at a special area of the room designated as an instructional center while the remaining youngsters work at their seats, the freedom of mobility and choice become highly desirable. Students are quickly motivated to demonstrate their ability to progress academically and responsibly when the rewards include increased independence and more options.[12] In addition, when a station or center is attractive and offers many interesting learning options, most youngsters are eager to earn the right to learn there.

The teacher should not use the stations as ways of rewarding or punishing students for any characteristic other than their efforts toward working responsibly, which means that they are able to understand what they should learn and can proceed to use resources to do so. Students may take longer than the teacher believes is necessary; they may need many rest periods if their attention spans are short; but as long as youngsters continue to progress soberly toward the mastery of their objectives (and do not prevent others from achieving), they should be encouraged to begin and to continue to work independently at various instructional areas.[13] Several areas should be available to students so that most youngsters may enjoy the mobility and choice of resources that centers provide.

HELPING STUDENTS TO SELECT APPROPRIATE RESOURCES AND TO MAKE DECISIONS

Students should be free to select the multimedia resources through which they will obtain the information needed to master their objectives. *All youngsters should learn how to read, but it is not necessary to read to*

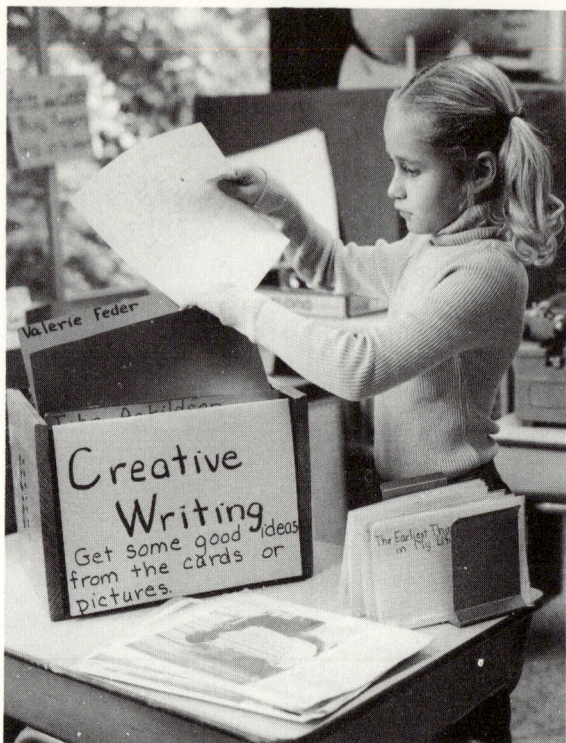

Photo 5-10. When selected students are permitted to work independently at a special area, the freedom of mobility and choice becomes highly desirable. This youngster has learned to follow the directions at the creative writing learning station and is now able to self-pace herself through an extensive series of curriculum objectives. (Photograph courtesy of the Douglas G. Grafflin School, Chappaqua, New York.)

learn. It is permissible for a student to achieve curriculum objectives through tapes, films, filmstrips, interviews, games, records, or any other materials.

Unless a student is not achieving, permit him to self-select his resources. When progress is not evident, be certain that he has been using media that complement his perceptual strengths. If you are not able to make such a determination, refer him to appropriate personnel such as the school physician, nurse or psychologist for testing.

Frequent opportunities to weigh available options, to consider the pros and cons of alternatives, and to determine how to proceed will enhance a student's ability to make choices. Errors in procedural or resource judgment will not cause irreparable harm; an error will only slow progress for a short time. Learning through one's errors (if not repeated) ensures growth, but the teacher should be ever watchful that youngsters

Photo 5-11. These boys are studying the posted objectives related to measurement and will select one or two to complete during this session. (Photograph courtesy of the Roaring Brook School, Chappaqua, New York.)

are not entrusted with too much responsibility before they are able to cope with it.

As soon as students begin to work with objectives, the teacher should list many multimedia resources through which the objectives may be learned. Students should be encouraged to explore many, most, or all of the materials, but *should not be required* to use any one item. Experience with a wide variety of educational resources will increase the pleasure of learning and often cause the retention of informational data that did not previously occur.

To help students to use learned information in a variety of interesting and creative ways, the teacher should also provide a listing of activity and reporting alternatives—stimulating and productive things youngsters can do to apply what they have learned and to demonstrate that they have achieved their objectives.[14] The reporting alternatives will provide reinforcement for both the youngsters who participate in their development and the ones who observe or share in what is being demonstrated.

Completed activities rarely should be demonstrated to an entire class

Photos 5-12, 5-13. One teacher uses plastic bags to form a wall chart into which she places multiple task cards to be selected by students on an optional basis. She also uses a system of individual "mail boxes" for returning completed work. (Photographs courtesy of the Westorchard School, Chappaqua, New York.)

Photo 5-13

Photo 5-14. Another teacher mounts varied objectives near the suggested related activities on a wall chart in groupings related to student ability levels. (Photograph courtesy of the Westorchard School, Chappaqua, New York.)

Photo 5-15. This student is selecting a task card that is housed in a flannel wall pocket chart. The chart remains stationary but the task cards are changed on a regular basis. (Photograph courtesy of the Roaring Brook School, Chappaqua, New York.)

or to a group of more than eight. Rather, they should be shared with individuals, pairs, or small groups. Students who observe can be taught to analyze what has been done in a positive, gracious manner. They can also be permitted to offer suggestions for improvement if some are necessary. In this manner students are taught to evaluate what they see and politely to provide assistance for increasing the effectiveness of a peer. Criticisms should always follow positive and genuine statements of value, e.g.: "All the information was correct, but I had trouble reading your printing. Perhaps if you skipped two lines between each sentence it would be easier to understand."

Students always should be given choices of the activities through which they may demonstrate their mastery or use of what they have learned. Included here are 150 activity and reporting alternatives that may be used to develop options for all students. Teachers may identify those activities that appear to be appropriate for their students, adapt them to the unit, topic, objectives, or prescription, and ask the youngsters to select the one or two they wish to undertake. A choice of two activities from twenty possibilities is more than reasonable.

ACTIVITY AND REPORTING ALTERNATIVES*

Activity Alternatives

1. Make a poster "advertising" the most interesting information you have learned.

2. Make an attractive jacket describing information you have learned for a book on the topic.

3. Make a miniature stage setting with pipe cleaner figures to describe part of the information you learned about this topic.

4. Design costumes for people or characters you have learned about.

Reporting Alternatives

1. Display the poster and give a two-minute talk to three to five classmates explaining why you found the information interesting.

2. Display the jacket and prepare a two-minute talk describing the contents of the book.

3. Display the stage setting and figures and give a two-minute talk explaining them (what they represent, why you selected them, what importance they have, etc.).

4. Describe to a group of classmates (five to eight) how you decided what the costumes should be, how you made them, and the people who would have worn them.

*Many of these alternatives were incorporated into Rita and Kenneth Dunn's "60 Activities That Develop Student Independence." *Learning,* February 1974, Vol. II, No. 6, pp. 73-77. Copyright 1974 by Education Today Company, Inc.

5. Write a "book review" of the topic for a newspaper or a magazine.

5. Ask at least two classmates to read your review and then ask them whether they believe they would like to read the book and whether your review stimulated them to read it. Find out what they would like to know about the book. Add the new information to your review if you believe it will improve it.

6. Make an original illustration describing one of your objectives.

6. Display the illustration and answer questions your classmates may ask about it.

7. Write a movie "script."

7. Ask at least two classmates to divide the script and all of you "read" the parts. Ask your classmates for suggestions for improvement and change the script if you agree with them.

8. Get a group to dramatize some of the information after you have explained it.

8. Either present the dramatization to a group of your classmates or have the group tape record it. Permit each member to take the tape home and play it for members of his family.

9. Prepare a travel lecture.

9. Give the travel lecture before a small group of classmates. You may also tape record it for future use for others who are working on the same topic.

10. Write a book of poems. Tape record several of the verses that best describe important information you found most interesting.

10. Play the tape of your verses for some of your classmates. Permit other students to read your book of poems and discuss it with you.

11. Bring in something you have made describing the information you found most interesting.

11. Answer questions about the display at a simulated "press conference."

12. Write an original story describing the information you most enjoyed learning.

12. Permit others to read your story. Ask them to tell you what they liked best about it. They may write their comments on a separate sheet of paper that you may attach to the end of the story.

Photo 5-16. Lucy Donald, in her thirtieth year of teaching, encourages her junior high school students to share their creative efforts in a variety of ways—through displays, dramatizations, illustrations, discussions, creative or fine arts productions or graphic reviews. Here Lucy observes one group as two others simultaneously present their completed activities. Lucy divides her classtime among the three presentations, moving from one to the other and back again, as appropriate. (Photograph courtesy of Grand Avenue Junior High School, Bellmore-Merrick, New York.)

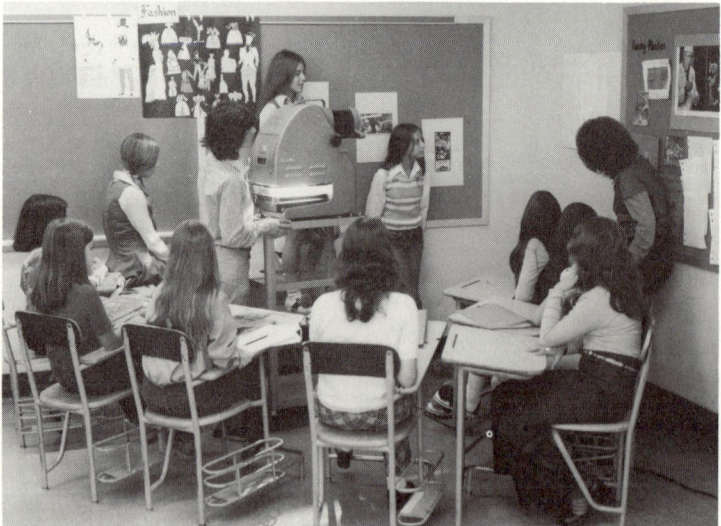

Photo 5-17. Lucy encourages small-group rather than large-group reporting because she believes it develops close peer interaction, a sense of personalization, and frequent opportunities for direct questioning and exchange. (Photograph courtesy of Grand Avenue Junior High School, Bellmore-Merrick, New York.)

13. Tell why you did or did not like learning about this topic.

13. Discuss your reasons either with the teacher or with other students who are working on the same or a similar topic.

14. Explain in graph form how the information you learned could be used in correlation with another curriculum area.

14. Show your graph either to the teacher or to other classmates who are working on the same or a similar contract (or topic).

15. Make a "movie" by drawing a series of pictures on a long sheet of paper fastened to two rollers.

15. Show the movie to one or more small groups of classmates (three to six).

16. Describe an interesting person or character that you learned about and dramatize something he did.

16. If you describe the person or character in writing, ask a few classmates to read what you wrote and to tell you what they think of the human being you portrayed. If you are willing to discuss your thoughts orally, tape record them and permit two or three others to listen and then to tell you how they picture the person. You may even try both methods to compare the results. Which method provides a clearer image of a person—talking or writing?

17. Write or tell a different ending to one of the events you read about.

17. After sharing your thoughts with a classmate or two, ask them to think of other ways the event could have ended.

18. Write or tell one of the following:
    a) Most humorous incident involved in learning the information.
    b) Most exciting happening involved in learning the information.
    c) Most interesting event involved in learning the information.
    d) Part you liked best in learning the information.

18. If you *write* the information, ask a few students to read what you wrote and to tell you whether they have had similar experiences. If you prefer to *discuss* the information, tape record it first and then ask others to listen and to share with you experiences of their own which have been similar to yours.

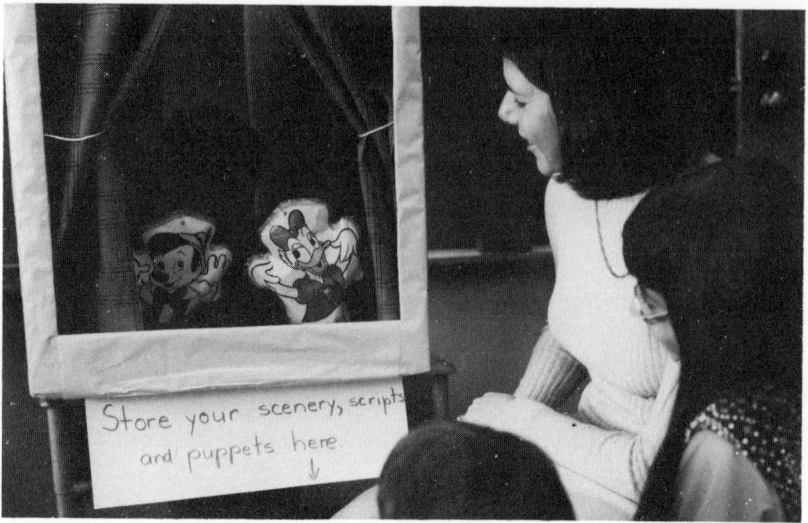

Photo 5-18. This puppet show was presented to a small group of classmates and student teacher. It was photographed as directed in the activity and reporting alternative No. 25 (Chapter 5). (Photograph courtesy of the Seaford Manor Elementary School, Seaford, New York.)

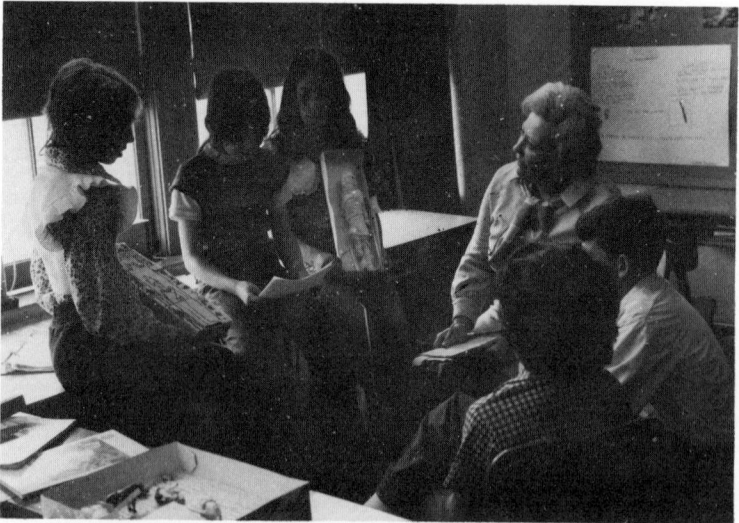

Photo 5-19. Lee Gouthreau, teaching for 26 years, individualizes instruction through contract activity packages and instructional packages. Here she questions a team of three students who have decided to report their completed activities in one presentation. (Photograph courtesy of the Sunrise Park Elementary School, Wantagh, New York.)

e) Saddest part in learning the information.

f) The way life "might have been" if something had been different.

19. Identify beautiful descriptive passages to be read to two to three members of your class for appreciation.

19. Read the passages and ask the others to express their thoughts about the writing.

20. Make a list of new interesting words and expressions to be added to your vocabulary that you learned during this contract (topic).

20. Place the list on an attractively printed chart and display it in the room.

21. Pantomime some information you found very interesting.

21. Let a few others try to guess what you are pantomiming.

22. Write a letter to a friend recommending that he study this topic too, and explain why.

22. Send the letter.

23. Give a synopsis of the information you learned while working on recent objectives.

23. Tape the synopsis and ask two or three others to listen to the recording. Then ask them to tell you what they found most interesting and what they learned.

24. Make a scrapbook suggested by some of the information.

24. Display the scrapbook. Ask at least two classmates to comment on it in writing.

25. Construct puppets and present an interesting part of the information you learned.

25. Have a friend photograph you presenting the information with the puppet(s). Display the pictures and the puppet(s) on a bulletin board or chart.

26. Make a map or chart representing information you have gathered.

26. Display the map or chart and answer questions about it.

27. Have another pupil ask you questions, as in a quiz.

27. Write the quiz questions on a chart. Place the answers on the back. Ask others to quiz themselves or to let you quiz them.

28. Write questions you think everyone should be able to answer on the topic. Organize a panel participation program.

28. Present the panel participation program to a small group in class.

29. Make a list of facts you learned that you will be able to *use* in life.

29. Place the list on an attractive piece of construction paper. Label the chart correctly and display it in class and at home. Ask anyone in your family to comment on it.

30. Dress as one of the people or characters and tell what part you play in the information.

30. Answer questions in an "interview."

31. Broadcast a "book review" of the topic, as if you were a critic.

31. Tape record the review and permit others to listen and tell you if they would now like to read the book, and why.

32. Make a tape recording for a classmate telling why he or she ought to learn more about the topic.

32. Ask one or two classmates to listen to the tape and tell you whether they have become interested in the topic. Ask them to explain *why* in a short paragraph or two.

33. Write a review of the information for another class. Try to encourage other students to want to learn about the topic.

33. Talk to another class and try to stimulate interest in the topic.

34. Outline a biography of one of the authors you read and tell about his writing on tape, in writing, or orally.

34. Use the tape, your written biography, or your own reporting to share the information with three to four students. Ask each to evaluate the biography in a few sentences.

35. Make a clay, soap, or wood model to illustrate a phase of the information.

35. Display the model and answer questions as a lecturer might.

36. Construct a diorama to illustrate the information.

36. Display the diorama and answer questions as an artist might.

37. Dress paper dolls as people or characters in the topic. Prepare a two-minute talk about them.

37. Display the dolls and give the talk for three to five classmates.

38. Prepare a chalk-talk on what you have learned.

39 Make a mural to illustrate the information you consider interesting.

40. Build a sand table setting to represent a part of the topic.

41. Rewrite the information, simplifying the vocabulary for younger children.

42. If it is science information, plan a demonstration for some classmates.

43. If it is historical information, make a time line, listing the dates and event sequences.

44. Make an animated film.

45. If it is biographical information, make a time line, listing the dates and event sequences in the life of the person.

46. Make a tape recording describing the information.

47. Write a song including the information you learned.

48. Make up a crossword puzzle using the information learned.

49. Make up a game including the topic information.

38. Give the chalk-talk to at least three classmates.

39. Display the mural and answer questions that may arise.

40. Explain the sand table setting to others. Ask them to evaluate your effort in a few short sentences.

41. Teach a younger child at least two new vocabulary words and some of the information you learned.

42. Demonstrate the science information for a small group of classmates (five to eight).

43. Display the time line and be prepared to answer questions about it. Ask three to four people to "explain" your time line to *you*.

44. Display the animated film to at least four other students. Ask for their evaluations in writing.

45. Display the time line and answer questions that may arise.

46. Ask two other students who are working on the same topic to listen to the tape.

47. Sing the song (in person or on tape) for a small group of students.

48. Reproduce the crossword puzzle and let other students try to complete it. Check and return their answers to them.

49. Permit others to try to play the game. Play it with them.

50. Make up a quiz to give to your class.

50. Permit several students to take the quiz. Be certain to have the correct answers written on an answer sheet for them. Give them the answer sheet when they have completed the quiz.

51. Prepare an illustrated "weather report" of the area you studied.

51. Give the report to three or four other students. Ask them to compare the weather in your report with their own weather.

52. Write a dramatization or story of one or more historical events you studied.

52. Ask some classmates to read your story and offer suggestions for improvement. Accept those suggestions with which you agree and alter your writing. Whether or not you agree, be polite and appreciative for their thoughts. If you write a dramatization, tape record it creating different voices. Play the tape for your teacher and three classmates.

53. a) Select or develop material suitable for a play, a tableau, a monologue, or a puppet show. Accumulate the props necessary for staging the production.
    b) Participate in all phases of theater production (direction, stage lighting, stagecraft, acting.
    c) Plan this play (tableau, monologue, or puppet show) for a particular age group and present it.

53. Present the puppet show to a small group (five to eight) in your class, a younger group, and, if you like, an older group or parents.

54. Create and stage a comic opera related to your contract (topic).

54. Stage the opera.

55. Direct and participate in creative dramatics and/or choral, speaking about your topic.

55. Present the dramatic or choral creation to a small group (five to eight) of classmates.

56. Write a script for a radio or television program; produce and participate in this program.

56. Produce and present the radio program for a group of classmates.

57. Portray a real person or character role in a monologue without mentioning the person's name.

57. Tape the monologue and ask a few students to listen to it. Ask them to guess who the person is.

58. Tell a story through a sequence of pictures, pantomimes, dances, tableaus, dramatizations, or choral speech presentations.

58. Present the story to one or more groups. Ask someone to photograph the presentation.

59. a) Develop brief reports based on more difficult or advanced reading material than that used by other students.
    b) In presenting the material, use handicrafts such as puppetry, dioramas, stage settings, costumed dolls, shadow screen or feltboard cutouts.

59. Submit the report to your teacher and to one or more students in your class and then present the report to one or more groups of older students that you select.

60. Select, develop, and prepare a story to share orally with another grade group or with part of your class.

60. Share the story orally with a group of five to eight students.

61. Read aloud various types of poetry on your topic with poetic expression.

61. Tape the poetry and share it with two or three others. Ask *them* to read your selections onto tape.

62. Develop commentaries for a silent movie, a filmstrip, or a slide showing. Use photographs you have taken (or slides) as a complementary activity.

62. Present the commentary to a group of students (five to eight).

63. Discuss one of the other student's presentations. Tell how the plot was developed and analyze the character development.

63. Discuss your perceptions with the other student. Be positive and polite.

64. Explain with clarity a technical subject related to your contract (topic), such as a factory operation or some astronomical phenomenon. Use illustrations or models to help explain the main ideas.

64. Make the explanation to a small group of students and the teacher.

Photo 5-20. These fourth graders are participating in a game that resulted from a contract activity alternative. (Photograph courtesy of the Floral Park-Bellerose Elementary School, Floral Park, New York.)

Photos 5-21, 5-22. These high school students are using ". . . different materials than those used by other class members . . ." to learn how to use a micrometer. Their teacher, Sherman Resnick, developed an instructional package that included a tape, a puzzle, a set of directions, and manipulative devices that facilitated independent mastery of the topic. (Photographs courtesy of the H. Frank Carey High School, Franklin Square, New York.)

65. Plan and develop explicit directions for a game, for making an object, for organizing an activity, or for conducting a science experiment on your topic.

65. Place the directions neatly on a chart and ask at least three other students to follow them.

66. Practice public speaking by giving a two-minute impromptu speech on your topic. Develop a file of possible topics related to your contract.

66. Tape the speech and ask two others to listen to it. Place your list of topics on display.

67. Participate in and lead small group discussions on such topics as evaluation of contract learnings, obtaining unusual information, criticisms, group behavior, out-of-school trips, current events as they relate to your topic, or the value of what you have learned.

67. List the group's conclusions on a sheet of paper and give it to the teacher.

68. With others, plan a debate or panel discussion on challenging aspects of your topic.

68. Participate in the debate or discussion.

69. Conduct group analysis and/or team learning sessions. Use parliamentary procedure when suitable. Encourage others to discuss the contract topic knowledgeably.

69. Serve as a ''consultant'' and conduct one of the sessions with a second group.

70. Plan an interview on your topic with an adult or students from upper classes. Ask specific questions.

70. Interview the person and organize the information for presentation to some classmates (five to eight).

71. Prepare appeals before another class on behalf of school or community drives that can be related to your contract.

71. Make the appeals and contribute whatever monies or goods you receive to the proper agency.

72. Make a tape recording of one of your oral presentations to help in self-evaluation and improvement.

72. Evaluate your own recording, erase it, and improve it. Retape it.

73. Use a tape recorder for speeches and reports. Record individually or in a group so that interested

73. Ask at least five students to listen, individually or in a small group, to the recording. Ask

members of the class can listen to it.

74. Develop oral or written reports of concerts, plays, visits to art museums, etc., that you attended which are related to your contract or topic.

75. Write a news story, an editorial, a special column, or advertisement for the school or class newspaper, explaining your views concerning any one aspect of your contract topic.

76. Assemble and edit material for school or class newspapers, scrapbooks, or curriculum topic picture files. Mount the material neatly and attractively.

77. Write letters requesting materials for class use on topics being studied.

78. Correspond with hospitalized children (particularly at holiday seasons). Share interesting information that you have learned.

79. Write a letter to a foreign person (child or adult). Share your learnings through the letter.

80. Prepare a scrapbook of information and materials on your topic to exchange with children from other parts of the country, and from other countries.

81. Design an unusual invitation to a class party or program centered around information on your topic.

82. Write a letter to an imaginary friend about fictitious travels concerned with your topic.

---

them to offer positive suggestions for improvement.

74. Present the reports to a small group (five to eight) of students and the teacher.

75. Submit and display your writing. Ask three students to write "letters to the editor" praising or chastising you as a reporter.

76. Display the materials. Circulate the display, or develop interest in it by asking others to read it, initial it, or comment on it in writing.

77. Send the letters.

78. Mail the letter(s).

79. Send the letter.

80. Try to acquire the name and address of a child who lives in another part of the country. Send a note and the scrapbook to her/him to see. Ask for return of the materials within two weeks.

81. Display the invitation.

82. Mount and display the letter.

83. Imagine yourself in another period or place concerned with your topic and write letters describing the setting.

83. Mount and display the letter(s). You may read the letters and/or materials to one or more classmates.

84. Take a character from a story such as Robin Hood or Cinderella and rewrite the story in a setting suitable to your topic.

84. Mount and display the story.

85. Write an imaginary letter from one story character to another, and tell about something that might have happened had they both lived in relation to your topic (time, place, sequence, etc.).

85. Mount and display the letter.

86. Write and illustrate stories. Use contract topic events, pictures, music, people, or imaginary characters as themes.

86. Mount and display the stories. Read them to one or more classmates. Ask them to make suggestions for improvement. Share them with an adult of your choice.

87. Write unfinished stories on your topic to be completed by others.

87. Ask two or three students to complete the unfinished stories. Display the story (stories) and the varied endings created by your classmates.

88. Create characters for a continued story and episodes on your topic. From time to time add "chapters" about them for a book you will write.

88. Bind the book and display it. Read parts of it to others. Permit interested students to read it and comment. Share it with your teacher and any other adult in your school.

89. Keep a notebook of creative writings you have developed.

89. Permit others to read through the notebook and initial their comments on a separate page.

90. Express, in writing, your feelings about music, paintings, and other art creations concerned with your topic.

90. Bind the writings into a book of your reactions.

91. Look at some objects (tree, landscape, etc.) until you see something not seen before. Then put

91. If you would like others to read this, share it. If you prefer, you may permit the teacher to read it.

your impression on paper and try to relate these to some aspect of your topic. Illustrate these if you can.

92. Take 15 or 20 minutes on several occasions to write whatever you wish, or to write about something (real or imaginary) that happened in relation to your topic or contract.

92. Put these together into a bound ''collection'' and show it to your teacher and at least one classmate.

93. Make up and tell ''tall tales'' about your topic.

93. Either write or tape record at least two of the tales you create. Illustrate them and permit others to react to them.

94. Write plays, poetry, descriptions, biographies, and/or autobiographies related to your contract.

94. Mount what you wrote and display them. Read at least two of your writings to a small group of students. Ask their opinions of the material. Consider what they say and see whether you would like to make some changes.

95. Convert a story you have written into a short play on your topic.

95. Ask a few of your classmates to take parts in the play. Tape record it and present it as a radio program to a group of younger children.

96. Create a poem that you can relate to your topic about a painting seen in a book or gallery.

96. Mount a copy of the painting (or a duplicate of the painting you have made) and your poem on the bulletin board.

97. Write original verses, using interesting forms of poetry such as the Japanese haiku (three lines with five syllables in the first and third lines and seven syllables in the second) and tanka (five lines with five syllables in the first and third lines and seven syllables in the remaining lines) about your topic. Pictures or observations might stimulate ideas.

97. Make a ''book'' of poetry and, if you can, illustrate it. Present the book to your teacher, your principal, and a small group of your classmates.

98. Keep a make-believe diary about your memorable experiences as you lived through the period concerned with your topic.

98. Read a portion of your diary to some of your classmates. See whether they can identify the period concerned with the topic. Add the diary to the resource alternatives available for other people who are studying the topic.

99. Write stories about different phases of your life as they might have happened had you lived in your topic time, place, or sequence. "Important Happenings During My Life," "Important People in My Life," "My Library" (kinds of books I like and why) or "The Most Exciting Thing That Ever Happened to Me" might be some choices.

99. Combine the stories into a "book" entitled "My Autobiography" and show it to your teacher, your parent(s), and a group of your classmates. Add your book to the resource alternatives available for study of your topic.

100. Write a news story on your topic in journalistic style, giving special attention to the lead paragraph.

100. "Publish" (reproduce) the newspaper story and distribute it to your classmates.

101. Make a magazine for the classroom by compiling voluntary contributions on your topic.

101. "Publish" the magazine and distribute it among your classmates.

102. Develop collections of colloquialisms or regional expressions related to your topic.

102. Write the colloquialisms neatly and then mount the paper on attractive construction paper. Display the collection.

103. Collect folklore such as rope-jumping rhymes, counting-out rhymes, legends, or folk songs related to your topic.

103. Write (or type) them neatly and combine them into a "book" of resource materials. List yourself as editor. Use proper credits. If you are uncertain about the format, ask the librarian to show you samples of edited books.

104. Make a collection of poems on the topic you have studied.

104. Make an attractive jacket for the poems and display the booklet. If you would like to tape record several of them you may play the tape for other students.

105. Make a collection of myths, legends, interesting mottoes, and proverbs on the topic.

105. Cover the collection with an attractive jacket and display the booklet as a resource alternative.

106. Try to find old original manuscripts, old page proofs, first editions of books, book jackets, taped interviews with authors or other interesting persons in the community, autographs of authors or any other documentation related to your topic.

106. Bring the material you locate to school and show it to your teacher. She will suggest ways of sharing the information with others. If you can Xerox the material, it can be displayed. Perhaps, if it cannot be brought to school, you and the teacher can organize a small group to visit the place where you found the items.

107. Study the history of books and libraries through the ages and learn how information has been recorded and transmitted through various civilizations. Make a time line to show the history of written communication or make a time line of the events that occurred in the topic sequence.

107. Mount the time line in school. Be prepared to answer questions about it.

108. Study the history or a little of the language connected with the topic you studied.

108. Make a vocabulary list of the words you have memorized and can use. Display the list neatly mounted.

109. Study relationships among different languages.

109. Make a list of the vocabulary words you have memorized in two or more languages. List the words in each (or all) of the languages with which you have become familiar. Example:

Similar Words in Different Languages

English	French	Spanish	Turkish
you	tu	te	sen
very	beaucoup	mucho	cok

Place the list on a sheet of oaktag

and mount it neatly. Be prepared to answer questions concerning the words you have listed.

110. Use different materials than those used by other class members, such as supplemental books on a higher grade level, Landmark Books, Merrill Company Literature Series, encyclopedias, newspapers, current news magazines such as *Time* and *Newsweek,* book sections of Sunday newspapers, editorials, sets of supplemental science books, and such magazines as *Reader's Digest, National Geographic,* and *Popular Mechanics* to learn more about your topic. Summarize your findings on 3 x 5 or 5 x 7 index cards (one for each manuscript).

110. Place the index cards in a small box and make them available as a resource alternative for your topic. Teach one other student in your class how to use these reference resources and you two form a partnership to help others.

111. Learn to use research tools such as the library card catalogs, graphs, charts, tables, maps, the *Reader's Guide,* atlases, encyclopedias, and the *World Almanac* to find more information on your topic.

111. Try to teach one of your class friends how to use them.

112. Learn to take notes from reading or taped lectures. Outline and summarize the information you learned on the topic.

112. Teach one other student in your class how to take notes from reading or a taped lecture.

113. Document some original research you have found on your topic using bibliographies, footnotes, and quotations.

113. Show your work to your teacher.

114. Search the library card catalog and *Periodical Index* and list all the books and articles concerned with your topic.

114. Add the list to the resource alternatives for your topic. Be certain that your teacher gets a copy. Ask her to have it typed for the file or ask for a blank ditto on which you can type or write the information for duplication.

Photo 5-22

Photos 5-23, 5-24. John Soll, who has taught for seven years, uses a contract activity package approach to social studies. He finds that ". . . the activity and reporting alternatives of the contract develop a tremendous sense of student responsibility and provide an excellent outlet for their creative energies." Here John and small groups of students are enjoying the handicraft display developed by his youngsters as part of a cultural fair. (Photographs courtesy of the Baldwin Harbor Junior High School, Baldwin, New York.)

115. Compile bibliographies about subjects of interest related to your topic.

115. Add the bibliographies to the resource alternative file for your topic. Ask the teacher to have the information duplicated onto a ditto.

116. Make constructive evaluations of a TV or other program related to your topic that you have enjoyed.

116. Mount the evaluation (your opinions) on a sheet of construction paper and display it. Discuss your thoughts with someone else in your group who saw the program.

117. Analyze two talks on the same topic and determine why one was more interesting than the other. You may tape record or write.

117. Show this work to your teacher.

118. Make a comparison between getting information by listening or by reading. Compare the devices used in the two media. Which do you like better and why? Write your answers.

118. Compare your findings with those of another student who selected the same activity alternative. Discuss your reasons for selecting one method as being more interesting than the other.

119. a) Become acquainted with the techniques of propaganda. Analyze advertisements and commercials, noting which techniques were used. How might propaganda have influenced the outcome of your topic?

119. a) Discuss your analysis with your teacher.

or

or

b) Make a display showing examples of various propaganda techniques,

b) Mount your display where others can see it.

or

or

c) Learn to distinguish between statements of fact and opinion. By giving supporting evidence, prove that one article is based on fact or the other on opinion.

c) Submit your "proof" to your teacher to see whether she agrees with you.

Photo 5-24

Photo 5-25. In her sixth year of teaching, Mary Ann Cascio and her colleagues designed a wall pocket chart for each student in their interdisciplinary team. When a youngster should be scheduled for a required task, Mary Ann inserts the appropriate task card to indicate that the activity has been scheduled. At other times students may self-schedule their activities and complete their objectives in any preferred sequence. (Photograph courtesy of the Floral Park-Bellerose Elementary School, Floral Park, New York.)

120. Become familiar with elementary logic. Find examples of invalid arguments in reading materials.

120. Show these examples to your teacher. After she has seen them, try to explain the examples to at least two classmates.

121. a) Analyze the ways in which newspapers interest people in a problem and stir them to action. How might newspapers have affected your topic?

   b) Bring in an article in which the author has tried to influence you toward his point of view. Analyze the method used to influence your thinking.

   c) Listen for a week to broadcast by a news reporter and a news commentator to note differences.

121. Report to a small group (five to eight) in the class on a talk that evidenced (showed) bias on the part of the speaker. Give evidence (proof) of the bias. Get one other student to identify (find) bias on the part of the speaker.

122. Study the speeches and written work of a particular public figure, determine his motives and find possible hidden objectives, if any. List any clues that indicate the author's real beliefs.

122. Show your findings to your teacher.

123. View a television program of your choice. Check the facts presented in written materials with those on the program. Draw conclusions. Put them into written form.

123. Share your thoughts or conclusions with your teacher and two other classmates who have seen the same program.

124. Analyze the point of view of an author of a particular book. Read about the author in order to explain why he believes what he does.

124. Tell at least three other classmates something you learned about the author that might account for his point of view in writing the book.

125. a) Recognize words or biased terms that indicate prejudice.

   b) Write an article persuading people to your point of view by using biased words and appropriate propaganda devices.

125. Give your teacher the article and list of words to read. She will give you additional directions if any are necessary.

    c)   Analyze words with similar meanings to differentiate shades of meaning. List at least 20 such words.

126. a)   Study the origin and derivation of words, names, places, persons, flowers, etc.

    b)   Organize a file box for new words, arranging them under headings such as "Descriptive Words" or "Words with More Than One Meaning."

    c)   Compile a list of overused words in class discussions, such as: fantastic, man, great, cool, uptight, beat, and touch. Find substitutes for these words and make a compilation for class references.

126. Add the file box to the resource alternatives for your topic if it is appropriate. If not, show a small group of classmates how you organized the file box and perhaps they can develop a similar file on their topics. Discuss with a small group the words that some people overuse. Show them the substitutes. Should you need guidance, let the teacher help you with this assignment.

127. a)   Compile a reading notebook containing excerpts that are unusually expressive, such as examples of similes, metaphors, alliteration, and onomatopoeia.

    b)   Learn to recognize and use figures of speech. Find examples in reading.

127. Use the figures of speech to describe some aspect of your topic. Explain what you mean to at least two classmates.

128. a)   Develop skill in predicting or guessing the meaning of new, unknown words. Check with the dictionary.

    b)   Create and play language games that involve new words or words with multiple meaning, or games using the dictionary.

    c)   Construct crossword puzzle games that utilize new vocabulary.

128. Play one of the language games (or all, as you choose) with one or more classmates. Give the crossword puzzle on your topic to at least three classmates. Help them to score themselves or to develop a scoring sheet. Duplicate the puzzles on a ditto for others to try.

129. Study the differences in style, vocabulary, etc., of different

129. Discuss your thoughts with either your teacher or your

literary periods or different writers.

teacher and a group of classmates. Tape your findings so that others may learn from your studies.

130. Report on the works and style of a favorite author.

130. You may select whether you would like to report in writing, on tape, or orally. Discuss your thoughts with a small group of classmates.

131. Describe a character in a story. Describe how the author developed the character and influenced the sentiments of the reader.

131. You may decide how you will report (in writing, on tape, or orally). Share your thoughts with at least two or three classmates. Ask for their reactions to your findings.

132. Attempt to understand the behavior of characters in a book by analyzing possible causes. Evaluate the choices made by characters and think through possible alternatives.

132. a) Write a short (one- or two-sentence) description of the character.
b) Write a short description of what the character did in the book (how he or she behaved).
c) Write three possible alternative behaviors the character might have shown. Submit your writings to your teacher.

133. Evaluate children's or young adults' magazines. Establish evaluative criteria and make a recommended list of appropriate articles for your contract topic.

133. Add the list of articles to the topic's alternative resources. See whether you can interest a classmate or two in reading one or more articles on your list.

134. Establish criteria for judging a book. Choose the best books of the year and defend your choices.

134. Tape your defense and ask two or more classmates to listen to the tape and then discuss your reasons for selection. Show them the list of criteria that you established. Get their opinions on the criteria. You may add their thoughts to your list of criteria if you agree with them.

135. Compare the illustrations in different editions of fairy tales, or in various types of books.

135. Draw alternative illustrations for stories you have read (two or three). Label the illustrations as if they were part of the covers of the books.

136. Evaluate varied reading materials such as reference materials for study, or free and inexpensive materials that might be obtained for your contract topic.

136. Make up a list of those materials that you believe would be good resource additions for class use.

137. Read and discuss five pieces of literature related to your topic, interests, or contract.

137. Tape your thoughts and ask your teacher and two classmates to listen to the tape. Ask for their reactions to the tape. Be gracious.

138. Listen to recordings of poetry or prose. List those that are related to your contract topic. Star the best ones.

138. Display the list and answer questions related to it. Play a few of your favorite recordings (related to your topic) for at least two classmates.

139. Chair a committee to discuss a good book that all have read.

139. Visit younger classes and discuss the book to stimulate reading interest.

140. a) Catalog your own books and records or the books and records in the classroom library. (Topic, value, reading levels, etc.).

   b) Plan a personal library. List the books and records related to your topic that you would like to own.

140. Display the attractively mounted list and suggest that others read the books or records that you liked best.

141. a) Develop an up-to-date list relating a favorite hobby or interest.

   b) Compile a bibliography of interesting books and records for the class to use for summer or free choice reading.

141. Ditto the list and distribute copies for your classmates to keep.

142. Arrange displays on your topic for book fairs, for parents, and for other classes in the school. Costumes, book parades, quiz shows, puppet shows, and character sketches are examples of possible programs.

142. Invite another group or class to visit the display or, if possible, you may take the display to them.

143. Plan new and creative ways to

143. Present the creative report to a

present book reports on your topic. These might include dioramas, chalk-talks, slides, overhead transparencies, drawings, the use of tape recordings, or dramatizations. Develop one such report.

144. Organize a Junior Great Books Club. Several students might read the same book and discuss it.

145. Form a poetry club. Members can bring favorite poems to discuss, memorize well-known poems, or compose poems based on contract topics.

146. Create book jackets or play programs using photos of your classmates dressed as characters in the books or plays.

147. Set up a Book Swap Shop for either loans or trades.

148. Check your own reading rate. Use materials designed to improve your rate and chart your progress.

149. Keep an individual account of materials read, with notations.

150. If the class is to read a story with a definite geographic locale or other specialized subject, become a "specialist" on the subject before the class reads the story.

151. Keep records for class activities—committee memberships, a list of jobs to be done, or materials to be used.

152. Design your own activity alternative. (Ask the teacher's approval.)

small group of four or five students of your choice.

144. Present a short written or an edited tape report of the discussion to your teacher.

145. Have the members of the poetry club present a poetry recitation for a large group of students in your own class and either a small or large group in another class.

146. Display the creative book jackets on corridor walls. Hold a contest using student judges.

147. Try to have at least five classmates (or other students) participate in the Book Swap Shop.

148. Show the teacher your progress chart.

149. This should be part of your topic presentation when you report on your readings.

150. Tell the students (as if you were the specialist) some of the things that they will be learning about. Try to whet their appetites for knowledge on the topic.

151. Keep these on an attractive class chart displayed in the room where all may obtain the information if it is necessary or desirable.

152. Demonstrate your new activity alternative to interested students (as well as to the teacher).

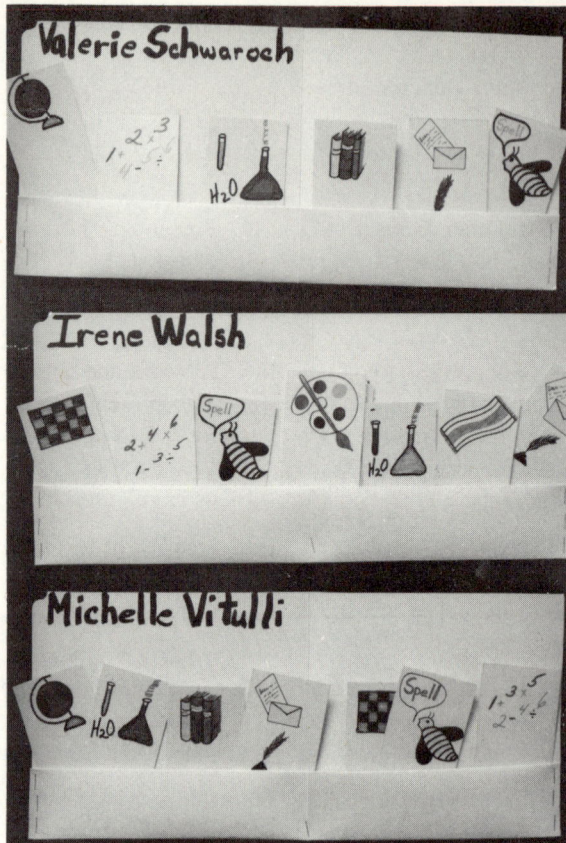

Photo 5-26. The following symbols represent the learning activities: the globe—social studies; the numerals—math; the thermometer and formula—science; the books—reading; the envelopes, stationery and quill—creative writing; the bumblebee and the word "spell"—spelling; the checkerboard—games; the easel—art; masks—little theater; a flying carpet—magic carpet personal reading time. (Photograph courtesy of Floral Park-Bellerose Elementary School, Floral Park, New York.)

These activity and reporting alternatives may be used as part of student assignments, contracts,[15] prescriptions, or free choice activities. They may also be used on task cards placed at a learning station, interest center, little theater or other instructional areas. The ones listed in this chapter for teacher selection are general; they should always be adapted when used with children. For example, Activity #10 reads: "Write a book of poems. Tape record several of the verses that best describe important information on this topic." This statement should be amended to relate the poems to the specific topic that the student is studying. The statement, after translation, could read: "Write a book of poems about the effects of pollution or the energy crisis in the United States. Tape record several of the verses that best describe important information on this topic."

ENCOURAGING LEARNING THROUGH INDIVIDUAL LEARNING STYLES AND STUDENT RESPONSIBILITY

Students always should have the option of learning alone, with a friend or two, in a small group, or with an adult. The only requirements made of them should be that (1) they continue to progress academically, and (2) they do not prevent others from achieving.

The same is true for all aspects of an individual's learning style. Students should be free to take advantage of the environment, food,[16] time, materials, peers, adults, and any educationally supportive resource that is available in ways that appear to be conducive to their comfortable functioning—with the provision that they learn and do not prevent others from doing so. In cases where there is attitudinal or philosophical conflict, the teacher's decision prevails. (Review Chapter 3, this text.) When developing student independence and responsibility, all youngsters should be made aware of the high costs of multimedia materials and the huge amount of work and energy that are devoted to the development of assessment instruments and guides. Part of their training should be devoted to the proper use and care of these valuable items. If some students learn best through auditory resources[17] (tapes, sound films, records, etc.) these should be available and in good repair. This type of software will not survive extensive mistreatment and should be protected from abuse.

One of the best ways to safeguard resources is to train a small cadre of students in their use and care. For example, Ted, Jim, Fran and Sue could be taught to operate the filmstrip projector. A diagram illustrating its use should be placed near the media center or corner and the names of the four-member group should be posted. Anyone wanting to use the filmstrip machine (hardware) must be taught how to use it by one of the four. When the cadre membership is satisfied that a student can operate the projector efficiently, that youngster may use the machine without additional supervision, provided that he continues to demonstrate care and responsibility.

This type of student cadre should be developed for the major pieces of equipment and for sections of software (tapes, films, filmstrips, records, transparencies, study prints, books, etc.).

To assist students in easily locating the various learning resources that are available to them, large, attractively printed signs should indicate where curriculum or topic-related materials are housed. For younger, perhaps nonreading children, the signs may be color or picture-coded.

If students are to function effectively in an informal environment, it is necessary that they independently can find, use, care for, share, repair, and return the materials that permit them and others to achieve without constant need for direction from and interaction with the teacher.

CREATING A FLEXIBLE SCHEDULE FOR INDIVIDUALS WITH DIFFERENT NEEDS

Chapter 2 in this book and Chapters 5, 6 and 7 in *Practical Approaches to Individualizing Instruction* suggest that teachers begin to individualize by teaching the entire class three or four small-group techniques. As one or more groups demonstrate their ability to learn together, they should be given answer sheets to correct their responses. When the teacher observes that the group can focus on its objectives, complete them, self-correct its answers and maintain a semblance of harmony and cohesiveness, she should then permit its members to move out of group situations and begin to function in the sociological patterns they prefer. At this stage, students will begin to select from among approved alternatives and to make decisions. They are then able to begin to function independently rather than as part of a whole. Some of them, however, may prefer to remain in a cluster or as part of a pair or team, and this choice should be respected. Others may wish to vary their pattern and occasionally join a group.

The second step in the process toward helping youngsters to achieve independence would be to alter their instructional environment to provide them with additional freedom and choice. This requires their introduction to varied instructional areas (such as a learning station or interest center) where they may select objectives, resources, and the activity and reporting alternatives on their own. Transition from the small-group process to individual achievement is not difficult for most, but it does take some students longer. Many young people will continue to work closely with selected peers as they move into a situation where increased mobility and scheduling flexibility simultaneously expand their options.

To assist youngsters in designing a time schedule that both complements their learning style and their curriculum requirements, the following alternatives are suggested.

Somewhere in the learning environment, preferably near each student's work area or desk, mount a pocket chart that includes the youngster's name and a series of either task or activity cards that can be slipped in and out of the various pockets by choice. For younger students, the cards may be illustrated to help them remember their tasks.

Students may then be told that they must complete a specific number of activities during the morning (an hour, one day, one week, or any given time interval that appears to be appropriate for the student at this stage of his program), but that the activity he decides to do first, second, etc., is his choice. The student should recognize that he must complete all the *required* activities (tasks, objectives, etc.), but that he may do so in order of his preference. As each task is completed, he should place the corresponding card in the various empty chart pockets so that the teacher, merely by checking his schedule, may know what has been completed and what still remains to be done. The chart also indicates where the youngster is physically and on which task he is currently working.

This system permits youngsters to self-select their schedules. Since this is a privilege extended only to students who have previously demonstrated their developing independence, show them that you are confident that they will soon learn how to schedule their time so that they do complete their requirements but may enjoy some leisure and preference with respect to procedures, timing or new ventures in learning. *Always prescribe fewer activities than they can complete so that they do enjoy some leisure time* or a new topic of their own choice.

Self-scheduling is a system that often motivates those youngsters who have been slow to evidence their developing independence. Youngsters of all levels enjoy the freedom of determining the order of those tasks they will complete. Move additional students into this desirable phase of the program gradually, always selecting the ones who first demonstrate an ability and desire to function independently, regardless of the *rate* of their academic achievement.

Other scheduling devices that teachers have used include varied forms such as those shown in Figures 5-2 through 5-8. These provide spaces for the student to insert those activities that he has completed and, sometimes, comments that he may have concerning them.

When students are permitted to select and schedule their activities, they are moving further along the continuum toward independent learning.

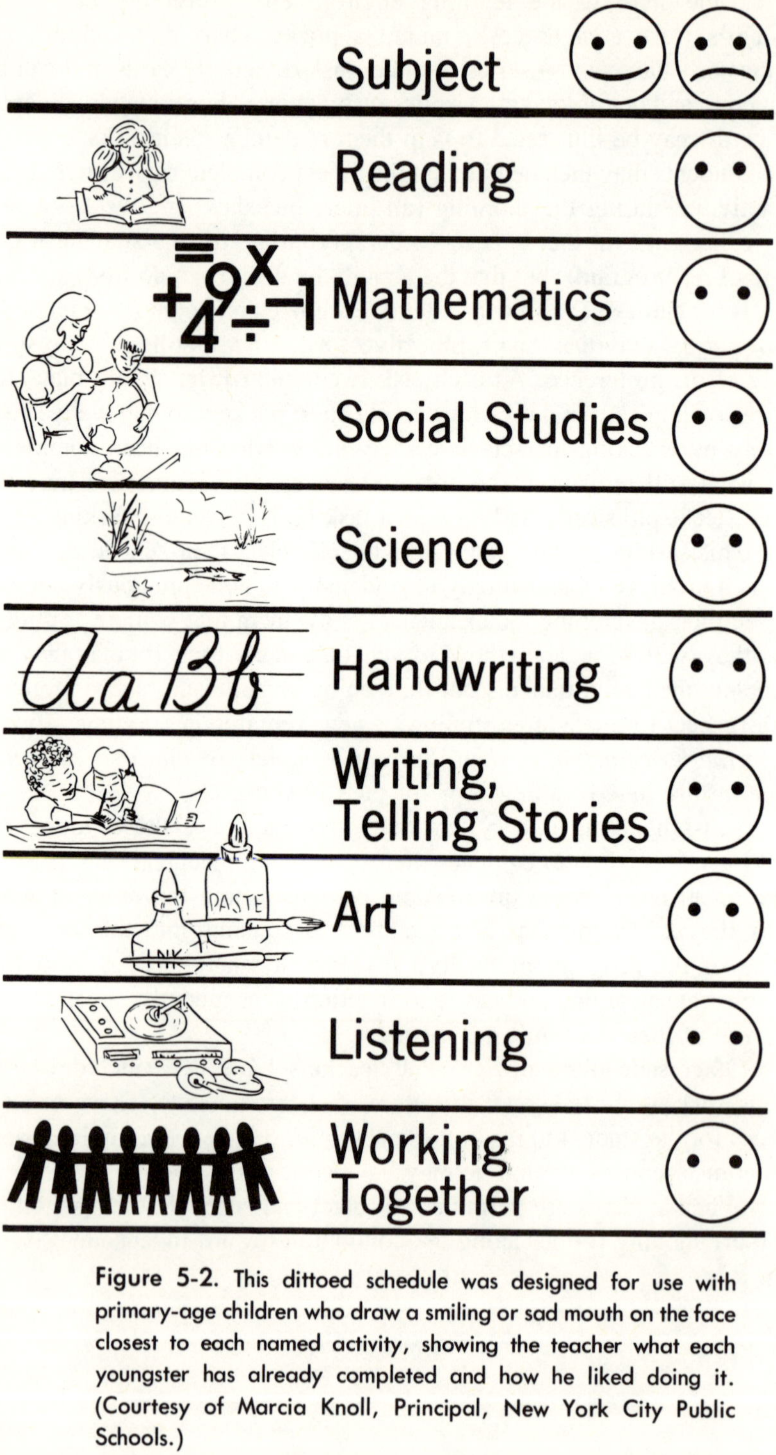

	Subject	😊 😞
	Reading	◯
$+\overset{=}{\underset{4}{9}}\overset{X}{\div}{-1}$	Mathematics	◯
	Social Studies	◯
	Science	◯
$\mathcal{A}a\,\mathcal{B}b$	Handwriting	◯
	Writing, Telling Stories	◯
PASTE	Art	◯
	Listening	◯
	Working Together	◯

Figure 5-2. This dittoed schedule was designed for use with primary-age children who draw a smiling or sad mouth on the face closest to each named activity, showing the teacher what each youngster has already completed and how he liked doing it. (Courtesy of Marcia Knoll, Principal, New York City Public Schools.)

Mon.	Tues.	Wed.	Thurs.	Fri.	Student ELAINE
9:30 Adjectives with Miss Gold (Language Arts Learning Station)		9:30 Circle of Knowledge on *adjectives* with Sue P., Mark, Tim, Donna and Joanne (self-correct)	Mr. Case will have three different experiments available concerned with wind as a force. Schedule yourself into the Science Center sometime today.	Tape record your new spelling words.	*Reading:* Select at least two stories of your choice. Read them and answer questions at the end of each. Place your completed answers (signed) in the "To Be Corrected" tray. *Spelling:* Learn to spell correctly any ten new words that you find in the two reading stories you select. Write all the new words you learned at the bottom of your completed story answers. *Social Studies:* Continue your contract. Complete at least five more objectives. *Math:* Continue subtraction series from ditto forms 30, 31 and 32. Self-correct your work and then place it in the "Completed Work" tray.
	10:30 Mr. Matte would like to meet with students who plan to visit the planetarium on Mar. 6. *Sign out if you go to his office.* 11:15 Music Lesson Room 7			10:30 Review subtraction with Miss Gold at her desk.	
1:00 Circle of Knowledge. *Subtraction* with Sue P., Mark, Tim, Donna and Joanne (self-correct)		Afternoon: Science-Art interest project with students you select who are available at Science Center			
2:00 Team Learning on SS Contract with Robert, Marcia, Tim, Donna, Ava, and Fred (self-correct)			2:00 Circle of Knowledge on SS contract with Robert, Marcia, Tim, Donna, Ava, and Fred (self-correct)	1:00-2:30 Select Resource Center of your choice for independent contract work.	

Figure 5-3. This simple, partially completed sample form used with elementary students provides an opportunity for the teacher to write in those activities that she requires for the youngster. It also permits the learner to fill in every space that was left empty with activities of his choice.

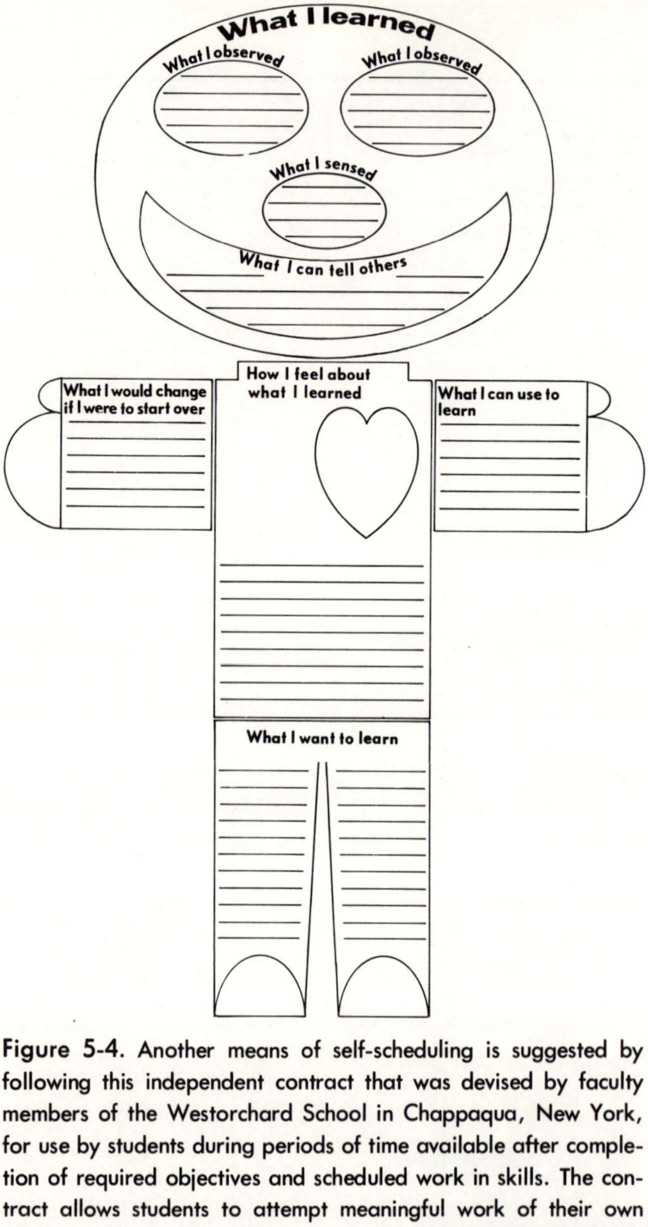

Figure 5-4. Another means of self-scheduling is suggested by following this independent contract that was devised by faculty members of the Westorchard School in Chappaqua, New York, for use by students during periods of time available after completion of required objectives and scheduled work in skills. The contract allows students to attempt meaningful work of their own selection during independent time and provides teachers with a written reference to check and to assist students in new areas of endeavor.

Youngsters call this contract the "man" or "clown" because of its shape when filled in, colored and joined together on a bulletin board. The finished product also builds confidence and a sense of accomplishment in the youngsters. (Courtesy of faculty and Imogene St. Paul, Principal, Chappaqua Public Schools.)

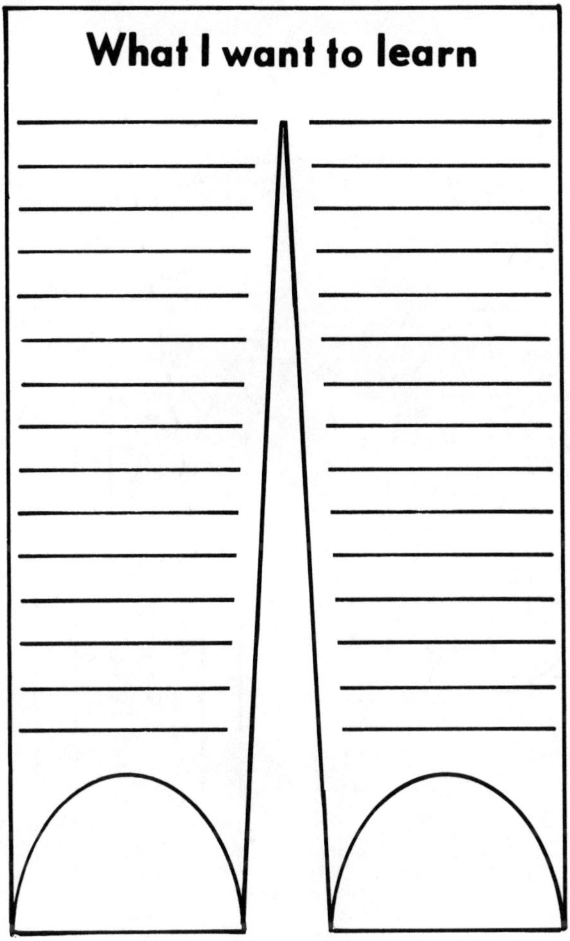

What I want to learn

Figure 5-4(a)

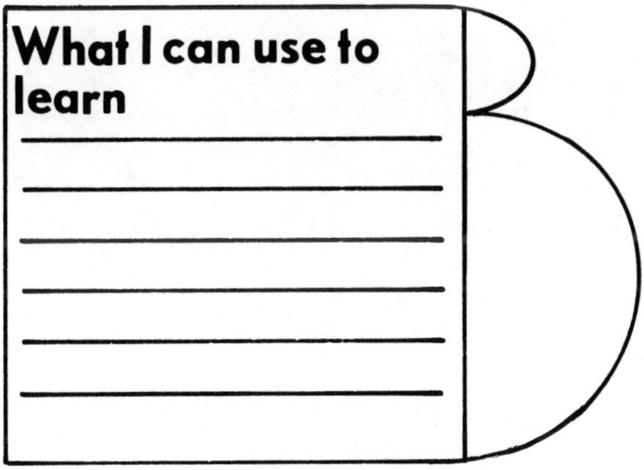

What I can use to learn

Figure 5-4(b)

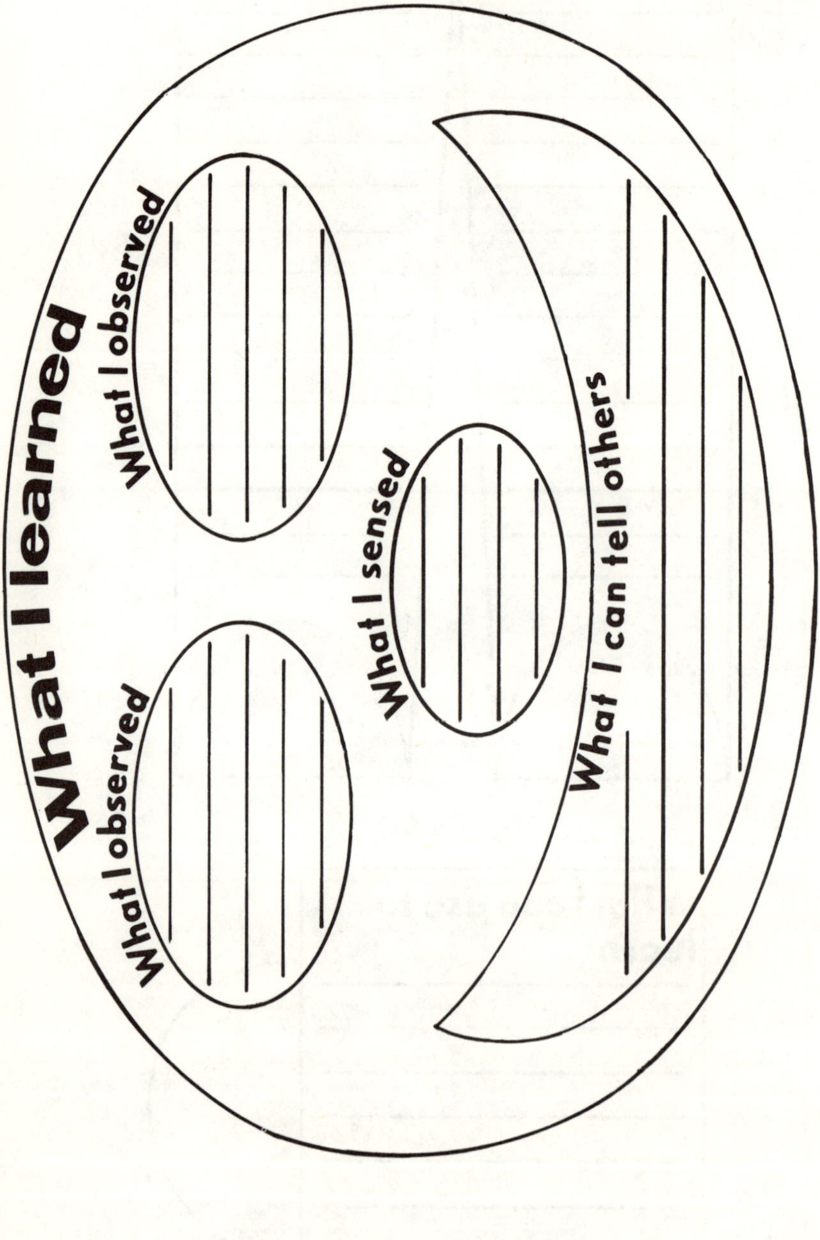
What I learned
What I observed
What I observed
What I sensed
What I can tell others

Figure 5-4(c)

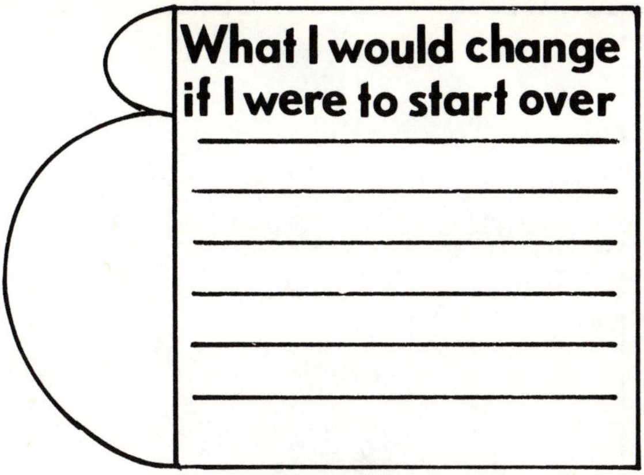

What I would change if I were to start over

Figure 5-4(d)

How I feel about what I learned

Figure 5-4(e)

NAME

CLASS

DATE	A.M. or P.M.	WHAT ACTIVITY: I DID	WHAT EVALUATION: I LEARNED

Figure 5-5. This form has been used with elementary students who have been given a series of activities to complete within a one-week period. Each individually selected schedule is posted in the instructional area and may be overviewed by the teacher at any time. (Courtesy of Marcia Knoll, Principal, New York City Schools.)

MY WEEKLY SCHEDULE

NAME _____ CLASS _____ DATE _____

	READING	MATH	LANGUAGE	SOCIAL STUDIES	SCIENCE	OTHER
MON.						
TUES.						
WED.						
THURS.						
FRI.						

Figure 5-6. This form was designed for upper elementary school children who are encouraged to pencil in their plans on Monday morning to gain an overall perspective. As each activity is completed it is recorded in pen or colored crayon. The teacher reviews the schedule on Friday afternoon and pencils into the following week's plan only those assignments or activities that she believes are necessary for the individual.

NAME: _____ CONTRACT: _____

OBJECTIVES	DATE COMPLETED	ACTIVITIES COMPLETED	GROUP TECHNIQUES COMPLETED
# 1.			
# 2.			
# 3.			
# 4.			
# 5.			
# 6.			
# 7.			
# 8.			
# 9.			
#10.			
#11.			
#12.			
#13.			
#14.			
#15.			
#16.			

Figure 5-7. This form provides an overview of a middle school student's progress and is used with the contract system where students select their objectives from a list of enumerated options.

```
┌─────────────────────────────────────────────────┐
│                                                   │
│  CONTRACT               DATE _____              │
│                                                   │
│  My Tasks For The Day                             │
│  ─────────────────────────────────────────────── │
│     1. Reading _____╫───────────────   │
│     2. Math _____╫───────────────   │
│     3. _____╫───────────────  │
│     4. _____╫───────────────  │
│     5. _____╫───────────────  │
│                                                   │
│  My Choice For The Day                            │
│     1. _____                  │
│     2. _____╫───────────────  │
│     3. _____╫───────────────  │
│     4. _____╫───────────────  │
│     5. _____╫───────────────  │
│  I need help with:_____     │
│  I enjoyed:_____ because _____     │
│  ──────────────────────────────────────────────  │
│  SIGNED: _____      │
│  Teacher's Comments:_____      │
│  ──────────────────────────────────────────────  │
│  ──────────────────────────────────────────────  │
│  ──────────────────────────────────────────────  │
└─────────────────────────────────────────────────┘
```

Figure 5-8. One second grade teacher designed this self-scheduling form for use with the contract system she had adapted for her students. She was often amused at the reasons children stated for having enjoyed the various activities in which they had engaged. One youngster had enjoyed chess because she had "beaten the boys." Another enjoyed math because he had "suddenly understood." A new child crossed out the section entitled "I enjoyed:" and wrote in "Nothing. This was an awful lot of work."

The final task for teachers to undertake is to guide their charges through the selection-completion-evaluation process enough times so that each student feels confidence in the task and in himself and can continue producing independently with minimal teacher supervision.

Brainstorming Exercise on Developing Student Independence

Using the direction for brainstorming described in Chapter 4, respond to each of the following questions:

What are the skills that students need to learn independently?	What are the strategies that help to develop the skills of independence?	Which strategies will you try?

Compare your answers with those that follow.

Comparing Answers to the Self-Instruction Guide

The skills that students need to function independently include those of:	Instructional strategies that develop independence skills include the frequent use of:	You are going to try the following strategies:

• identifying,
• selecting, and
• decision making concerning:
  objectives,
  resources,
  activities,
  reporting choices,
  and
  sociological,
  environmental,
  and
  learning style
    options.
• locating,
• using,
• caring,
• sharing,
• repairing and
• returning of:
  multimedia,
  self-assessment
    instruments,
  and
  teacher guides
• creating:
  priorities,
  time schedules
  and
  competence
    demonstrations
• mastering
  objectives
	• small-group techniques
	• varied instructional areas
	• options and alternatives
	• individual learning style
	• personalized time schedules
	• peer cooperation and guidance
	• cadre teams
	• motivation to obtain increased freedom
	• gradually increased responsibility
	• self-assessment instruments
	• self-selected activities
	• peer evaluations
	• multimedia resources
	• teacher guides or answer sheets
	• student talents to advantage
	• student interests as a motivation toward learning
	• increased self-image
		Only *you* know the answer to this one!

SIX

Observing Individualized
Teaching and Learning:
What to Look For

Behavioral Objectives for Chapter 6

1. You will be able to identify at least ten things that evaluators observed
    when visiting a traditional classroom that should *not* be present in an
    individualized program.
2. You will be able to identify at least ten things that evaluators should
    actually *see* when observing an effectively individualized program.

. . . .

ENCOUNTERING INDIVIDUALIZED INSTRUCTION:
A CASE STUDY OF OUTDATED CRITERIA

Professor Jensen entered the school building as quickly as he could,
hoping that the traffic delay had not caused him to miss the beginning of
the student teacher's lesson. He conscientiously stopped at the principal's
office and signed in. As he hurried along the hall toward the cooperating
teacher's room he reviewed in his mind the items he would try to evaluate
as he observed the presentation:

1. Is the lesson plan sufficiently detailed and comprehensive?
2. Does the student teacher use good questioning techniques?
3. Does she demonstrate strong knowledge of the subject matter?
4. Does she use an appropriate text or basic series?
5. Do the pupils appear to be interested in the presentation?
6. Does the student teacher maintain discipline?
7. Is there ample opportunity for the pupils to ask questions?
8. Is the room well lit and ventilated?
9. Does the student teacher use the chalkboards appropriately?

Toward the end of the first floor corridor he found room 109 and opened the door, ready to apologize for delaying the start of the lesson. Before he could orient himself he realized that the class must have just entered the room, for they were not yet seated and ready for work. (Perhaps the cooperating teacher had also been caught in a traffic jam and the principal had kept the class in the yard while waiting for her.)

He glanced about the room, hoping to recognize the young student teacher he had met only once before in the seminar at the college. In the confusion of the children's helter-skelter movement, he vaguely recognized her lithe form comfortably sitting on the floor in a corner at the back of the room. She was leaning against the wall with a small group of four or five youngsters perched up against her and they were reading what appeared to be—comic books! Professor Jensen shook his head and he rejected this initial observation as outrageously implausible. Surely she had expected him this morning! He had confirmed this observation directly with her on the telephone last week!

As he made his way toward the group seated at the rear, he stumbled over a wire extended across an assemblage of furniture labeled "Social Studies Learning Station." The wire had been connected to an overhead projector, and as he reached for something on which to balance himself the projector tipped and a series of transparencies fell to the floor. Luckily two boys adroitly caught the projector, and the cooperating teacher, who appeared from nowhere, caught Dr. Jensen!

"Good morning," she laughed. "We should have warned you about the extension cord." Amid the professor's mutterings about safety hazards and dangerous trappings, the teacher explained that wires were necessary if the youngsters were to be able to use multimedia resources while working on their behavioral objectives.

As he regained his equilibrium the professor noted that the student teacher had elevated herself and had begun to walk toward him with a broad smile on her face. He ignored her extended hand and impatiently asked for her lesson plan. The girl's face went blank. "Lesson plan?" "Yes!" he repeated. "Where's your lesson plan?"

The girl and the cooperating teacher exchanged glances of instant insight and the cooperating teacher began to explain.

"We don't use lesson plans in this school, sir." (Professor Jensen felt better at her obvious recognition of his status.) "We have an individualized program."

"How do you know what you're going to teach?" he stammered. "And how do you know what the children have learned?"

The student teacher beamed as her words flowed clearly and confidently.

"Dr. Jensen," she began, "we are required to diagnose each pupil in this class in every curriculum area and also to refer to his past achievement scores. We then write prescriptions for each child based on what he is able to learn and how he seems to be able to learn it best. Each youngster then proceeds at his own rate to learn what has been prescribed and he may learn by selecting from among several different learning resources."

Photos 6-1, 6-2, 6-3. These junior high school students are learning a foreign language through multisensory approaches. The young ladies seated on the carpeting are discussing (verbal) materials they have just read (visual). The young man is listening (auditory) to a tape through earphones to avoid disturbing classmates. Three youngsters are assembling (tactual) a map of France; in the process they are becoming familiar with French geography, names, and spelling. (Photographs courtesy of Briarcliff Middle School, Briarcliff Manor, New York.)

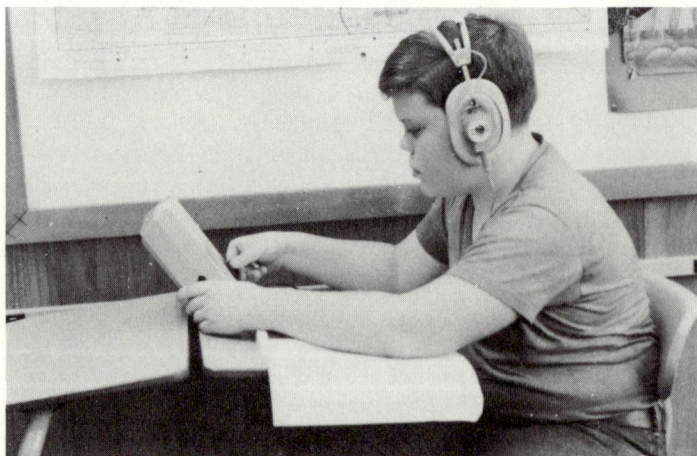

Photo 6-2

Nonsense, he thought. Philosophical theory! They are probably just taking the easy way out! Playing instead of teaching!

"How does the principal know you've taught anything at all if you can't show him lesson plans?"

The student teacher smiled patiently and asked the nearest boy for his list of objectives. The child quickly returned with a sheet of paper.

"Each child has his own set of objectives—those items that he is required to learn. He is given alternative resources (books, tapes, films, transparencies, records, etc.) through which he may find the information, but he is free to select any of the resources provided."

A gasp escaped from Dr. Jensen's mouth. "You don't mean to imply that a child doesn't have to read?" he asked incredulously.

Quietly, the classroom teacher explained that children learn through their perceptual strengths; that some youngsters learn by listening, others by seeing, and still others through tactual or kinesthetic involvement.

"Why should the child who can't read be prevented from learning science, mathematics, or social studies?" she asked. "Isn't it better that he learn through alternative materials? And, actually, most of our students not only read, they score as well or higher than those not using the individualized approach."

Dr. Jensen mentally noted that he had answers to two of the items he had originally planned on evaluating: (1) No, the lesson plan is not "sufficiently detailed and comprehensive." In fact, it's nonexistent! and (2) No, she does not "use an appropriate text or basic series." She doesn't insist that a text be used at all!

What were the other items on his list, he mused. Oh yes! Do the pupils appear to be interested in the presentation?

"When will you begin the lesson you've prepared?" he asked the student teacher.

"I'll just continue with the reading group in the corner," she responded. "We're working on developing criteria for analyzing social structure through common media."

Common media? Aaah! He shuddered. They *were* using comic books! Well, at least she recognized what was common! Her first plus for the day!

"Well, bring the class to order," he directed. "Let's see how well you teach."

"I can't teach this to the whole class," the student teacher explained patiently. "They're not all ready for so advanced a topic! I'm just working with the above-grade level students."

Dr. Jensen felt his temper rising. "Why didn't you plan something you could do with the whole class?" he all but shouted. "You knew I was coming to observe you!"

Her smile faded and her face paled as she struggled to get him to understand. "Dr. Jensen, we *never* use whole-class instruction in this room. None of the children ever learn the same thing at the same time in the same way! They can't! They learn through different perceptions, at

Photo 6-3

different rates, and through different learning styles! How could we ever teach them all the same thing at once?''

Her earnestness caused him to pause. Perhaps it was not this student's fault. After all, the college had placed her here in this school with this obviously radical teacher. The poor girl really shouldn't be blamed entirely for this fiasco. He would speak with the principal before he left the building and have her assignment changed. How could any student teacher bring order to this chaos?

He again tried to recall the items he had planned to use in evaluating her teaching ability. Well, obviously he was going to have to be negative again. The pupils can not be ''interested in her presentation'' because there is no presentation! What was left?

Did she ''maintain discipline?'' He looked about the room. Approximately 30 boys and girls occupied the premises. Each appeared absorbed in whatever it was he or she was doing. Children worked alone, with a classmate or two, or in small groups. They seemed to be either self-directed or extremely well-disciplined. After all, it certainly could not be this nonconforming cooperating teacher who would have trained all these children to work so quietly and cooperatively! Could it?

He carefully watched the cooperating teacher as she worked her way around the room. Here and there she would stop with a child or two or a small group and ask questions, give directions, or make assignments. The youngsters seemed to welcome her and to respond enthusiastically. They asked questions and received answers or suggestions right on the spot. Occasionally a pupil debated a comment with the teacher, using some of the "alternative resources" to justify the challenge. For a moment Dr. Jensen's ire was in danger of rising again. Question the teacher? How audacious! But almost before the thought presented itself his consciousness was filled with a challenging question. Wasn't this the "critical analysis" and "problem-solving" that professors urged college students to strive for? Had this quixotic teacher and her young student found a way in which to achieve this goal with elementary pupils?

The student teacher had moved on to a second group of seven or eight. She was helping the group load the filmstrip viewer and, almost simultaneously, discussing with them their objectives for this activity. She used a term that sounded like "team learning" and distributed a simple ditto sheet on which was printed a series of questions. She reviewed the procedures, questioned the pupils a bit, and then moved on to a third group. Within a moment or two she had those youngsters involved with a tape recorder and some note paper, again having focused their attention on objectives.

Then he remembered the item on "using the chalkboard appropriately." No, she did not seem to use chalkboards at all. But she did use a variety of multimedia equipment and materials that certainly appeared to facilitate learning.

He continued to think about his evaluation checklist. Did she "demonstrate strong knowledge of subject matter?" How could he tell? He thought he would ask her if she could provide any kind of *evidence* that would show that she knew the subject matter at all. As he followed her across the room, moving from child to child and group to group, he noticed that youngsters frequently seemed to return to an area where folders were on file. They would skim through an alphabetical listing, pull out a folder with what must have been their own names, and read through several pages within. They would then return the record to its (assumedly) correct place and go on with their activities.

The professor crossed over to the drawer cabinet. He casually opened the top one and noted that it included something called a "contract." Also included were "objectives," a suggested list of "alternative resources," and a series of "activity and reporting alternatives." Attached to each contract was a diagnostic test and something labeled a "self-assessment instrument." How complicated, he thought, but at least they are testing!

At the bottom of each contract he found a handwritten note to the child. The notes would read: "Dear Jimmy, since you are interested in being able to: (1) describe at least three different kinds of desert homes, and (2) list at least five ways in which your life would be different if you lived in the desert, try using the following resource alternatives and please let me know which ones: (1) you liked most and (2) taught you the most. Good luck! Kathy O'Neill (signed)."

Kathy O'Neill? That's the student teacher! Well, writing this kind of prescription does not necessarily demonstrate that she has "strong knowledge of the subject matter," but it does verify that she knows the curriculum, understands that children need to feel a personal sense of communication with their teachers, has reviewed the resources that are available and related to the curriculum, has adopted some kind of method that incorporates something called "activity and reporting alternatives" (at least it's not random chaos!), and does use testing procedures. Dr. Jensen realized that he was beginning to feel more and more positive about this young student teacher. If he could arrange for her to be housed with another teacher he might be able to salvage her!

He considered the item concerning "a well-lit and well-ventilated room."

The room was congested and appeared to be overflowing with materials, equipment, and children. (Absorbed and involved, yes, but very, very mobile!) In almost every area of the room were signs like "Interest Area," "Learning Station," "Media Corner," "Game Table," "Little Theater," and "Magic Carpet." Admittedly, each area housed individual and small groups of youngsters who were actively involved in whatever they were

Photo 6-4. Mary Ellen Ferricane, in her fourth year of teaching, develops contract activity packages based on the required curriculum. Then she explains the varied objectives, resources, and activities, and encourages student selection from among the approved alternatives. (Photograph courtesy of the Westorchard School, Chappaqua, New York.)

Photos 6-5, 6-6. Lillian Gold, teaching for 25 years, permits her youngsters wide latitude in self-scheduling learning experiences so that, at any given moment, each student may be engaged in activities that differ widely from those of others. Mrs. Gold moves from child to child and group to group constantly diagnosing and appraising progress. (Photograph courtesy of the Douglas G. Grafflin School, Chappaqua, New York.)

Photo 6-6

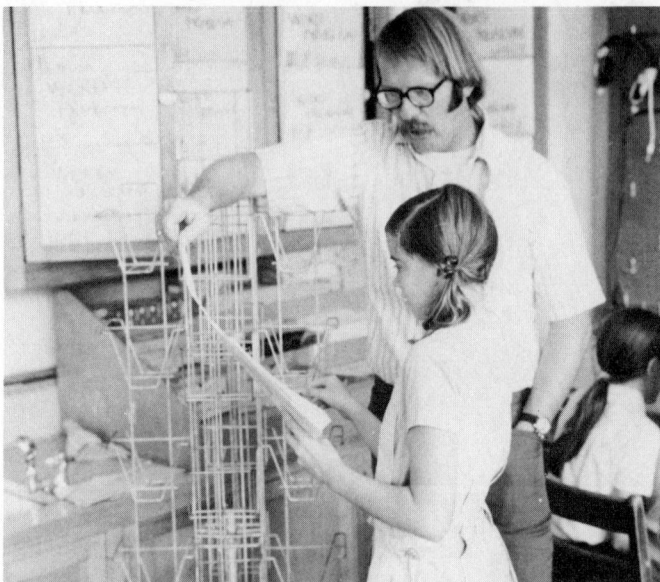

Photo 6-7. Mobility and quiet peer and student-teacher conversations are a natural part of the learning environment. Here Walter Brownsword, who has taught for 19 years, is guiding one youngster through her objectives as others work independently, in pairs, or in small groups. (Photograph courtesy of the Roaring Brook School, Chappaqua, New York.)

doing, but in this constantly moving, work and discussion-centered environment, could the pupils see well, hear well, and breathe well? He watched the children intently and recognized that they were having no trouble in this atmosphere. It was he that found the constant movement and sound disquieting.

The cooperating teacher took a moment to speak with him as he moved toward the door. "Come back soon, Dr. Jensen!" she invited. "The children love to explain to visitors what they are trying to learn and how they are learning it." It was at that moment that he realized that he had not spoken to one youngster in the room. He had been so absorbed in trying to analyze what was happening according to his preconceived list that he had not realized that the children might have given him expanded insight into the "individualization process" being used in that class.

As he stepped into the comforting solitude of the corridor, Dr. Jensen met Mr. Love, the principal.

"How are things going in there?" Love asked good-humoredly.

"It's hard to tell," Jensen responded.

A twinkle entered Mr. Love's eye. "Your first experience with an individualized program, eh?"

Professor Jensen nodded.

"Do you have any of the new Observation Instruments?" the principal asked.

Professor Jensen nodded again, only this time negatively. Mr. Love laughed good-naturedly. "Can't evaluate an individualized classroom without them!" he said. "Come into my office and I'll give you a couple. Look them over and see which appeal to you most. They all have to be used in terms of observable student and teacher behaviors. Try them all if you like, and let me know which you think are the best! I'd appreciate having your comments and suggestions."

At the college later that day, Professor Jensen tried using a few of the evaluation instruments to analyze the classroom he had visited earlier that day. To his amazement, both Kathy O'Neill *and* her cooperating teacher came out high in every positive category. Supervising an individualized program requires a different kind of itemization list, he reflected. I think I'll go back again next week and see how many of these items I can actually see!

RECOGNIZING TRADITIONAL, TRANSITIONAL AND INDIVIDUALIZED PROCEDURES: IMPLICATION FOR EVALUATORS

Like Professor Jensen, many educators have tried to evaluate what occurs in an individualized program by using criteria appropriate to traditional settings. We too, must develop new lists of identifiable items and begin to utilize sensitive behavior-observation instruments for individualized instruction.

Perhaps a comparison of the classroom procedures formerly and currently used might help us to establish a basis for identifying what a supervisor should be able to actually see when visting an individualized program.

Photos 6-8, 6-9. Students may be studying in varied learning environments in and out of classroom facilities. (Photographs courtesy of the Douglas G. Grafflin School, Chappaqua, New York.)

TRADITIONAL PROCEDURES	TRANSITIONAL PROCEDURES	INDIVIDUALIZED PROCEDURES
1. The teacher developed a class lesson plan that included each topic she expected to teach and the amount of time she anticipated spending on each phase.	The teacher develops a class plan for each topic but assigns a different number of objectives to each child, dependent upon his ability to achieve. Since plans will vary, the amount of time to complete the studies will too.	The teacher may develop a plan ("prescription") for each child or small groups of youngsters, but the students have significant control of their own programs and vary them substantially.

IMPLICATIONS FOR EVALUATORS

The supervisor knew that he could visit each class at any given hour and observe the instructor teaching a specific lesson according to plan.	The supervisor may expect that each youngster in a class is learning something about the same topic, but to varying degrees.	The supervisor may observe that each student is involved in studies that are different from those of other students. Unless he analyzes each plan he will be unable to know the scope or time allocation permitted.
Teachers were chastised if they did not "follow the schedule" or if they were "not teaching," a term used to describe anything other than the lecture, lecture-discussion, or chalk-talk method.	Teachers are sometimes admonished for not exposing every child to everything, and are cautioned not to lower standards for the less academically achieving students.	Teachers are cautioned to maintain accurate records for each pupil so that no student lacks on-going diagnosis.

2. The teacher was expected to maintain discipline at all times. Discipline was defined as each youngster's continuous attention and quiet decorum.	Since it is recognized that children's attention spans, interests, and degrees of motivation vary and have direct impact on their ability to learn, the teacher conducts some large group, some small-group, and some individualized instruction and permits the students opportunities to participate in each.	Mobility and quiet peer and student-teacher conversations are part of the learning environment. Large-group instruction is used only to introduce new topics, concepts, or generalized studies. Instruction is essentially small-group (3-8) and paired or individual. Students may work together in pairs, teams, or alone, as they prefer. Decorum is a matter of working quietly so that others may learn without interference.

IMPLICATIONS FOR EVALUATORS

When a supervisor noticed pupils who were not paying attention, the youngsters were reprimanded and the teacher cautioned to "be more aware and stronger."	Students are expected to be quiet and attentive during group instruction but are permitted discussion and peer interaction at other times.	Students may absent themselves from group instruction unless otherwise directed by the teacher. Most instruction is individualized and participatory. A lack of involvement is sufficient cause for changing the activity or environment.

TRADITIONAL PROCEDURES	TRANSITIONAL PROCEDURES	INDIVIDUALIZED PROCEDURES
3. Students were assigned the same amount of study to be completed in an identical span of time.	Students are given differing assignments to be completed within varied amounts of time.	Students help to determine their assignments and may progress at a rate consistent with their interests and abilities.

IMPLICATIONS FOR EVALUATORS

The supervisor expected each student to be working on the same assignment at the same time. Only completion was acceptable for movement to other assignments.	The supervisor may expect to see classmates working on different assignments of varied length.	The supervisor may observe students working on totally different studies that may have no relationship to each other in type, scope or time span.

4. Students completed most of their studies at their own desks.	Students may be working at a variety of different instructional areas.	Students may be studying in and out of the classroom and in and out of the school facilities.

IMPLICATIONS FOR EVALUATORS

It was easy to observe which students were "working" and which were doodling, day-dreaming, etc.	It is difficult to assess student involvement without circulating among many instructional areas and observing the students at work there.	It is impossible to assess individual progress and devotion to task without being present over a series of time intervals in a variety of places. Counseling and guidance are part of the assessment and growth process.

5. Students learned most of their knowledge from teacher lectures and books.	Students use books supplemented by multimedia resources.	Students select the resources through which they will learn and may bypass completely those that have no appeal to their perceptual strengths.

IMPLICATIONS FOR EVALUATORS

Supervisors could examine an assigned text and judge the quality of anticipated learning by testing the content of the book.	Supervisors should see a variety of available resources being used.	Supervisors should check to be certain that every stated objective can be learned through available multisensory resources.

6. Students were permitted to gain recognition only by raising their hands.	Students follow set rules for recognition during group lectures or discussions but have freedom to talk, interact, and move around at other times.	Students are treated like responsible adults. They exhibit good manners when others are talking, wait their turn, and then speak up with nicely moderated voices.

IMPLICATIONS FOR EVALUATORS

Students who did not raise their hands when wishing to speak were admonished.	Less formal procedures are used at varied times. The supervisor should become aware of the group's functioning codes.	Supervisors may recognize no apparent structure to the learning environment that appears to be consistently informal and "friendly." Guided tours by the students and teacher are essential.

These six identifiable differences among traditional, transitional, and individualized procedures relate directly to what should be observed in a class that is gradually moving toward openness and individualized learning.

Photo 6-9

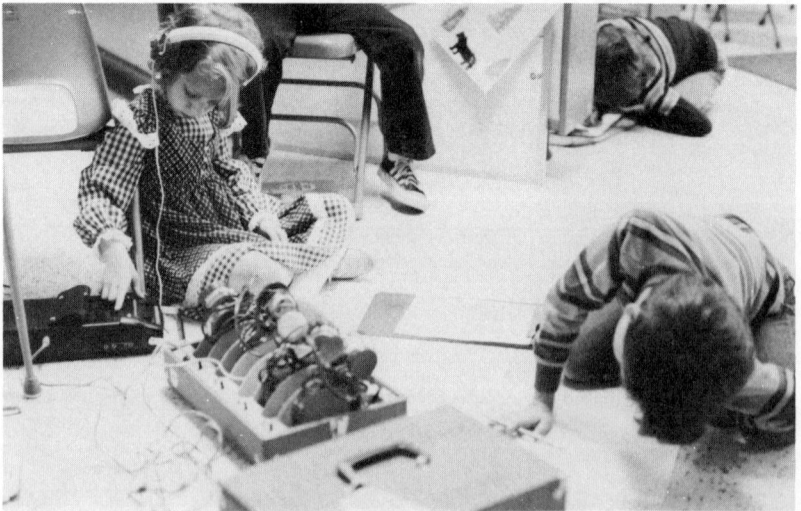

Photo 6-10. Students should select the resources through which they will learn. Multisensory alternatives should be provided to accommodate different perceptual strengths. (Photograph courtesy of the Douglas G. Grafflin School, Chappaqua, New York.)

Photo 6-11. Anthony Palladino, who has been teaching for six years, says that he treats his students like reponsible adults. They, in turn, exhibit good manners when others are talking. He believes that having varied instructional areas in the environment reduces the need for children to shout across to their peers. Rather, friends can sit together quietly and work toward completion of their objectives cooperatively. (Photograph courtesy of the Floral Park-Bellerose Elementary School, Floral Park, New York.)

Photo 6-12. Estelle Shaw has individualized instruction for four of the 14 years she has taught. She begins "slowly" each term, identifying those students who can work in small groups and then independently and those who appear to need direct supervision for a longer period of time. (Photograph courtesy of the Forest Lake Elementary School, Wantagh, New York.)

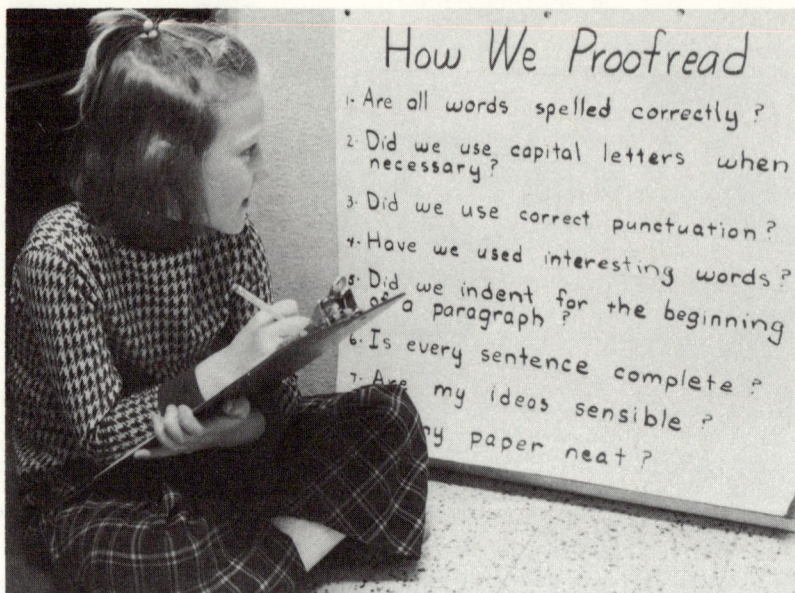

How We Proofread

1. Are all words spelled correctly?
2. Did we use capital letters when necessary?
3. Did we use correct punctuation?
4. Have we used interesting words?
5. Did we indent for the beginning of a paragraph?
6. Is every sentence complete?
7. Are my ideas sensible?
   Is my paper neat?

Photo 6-13. Individual students should be given clearly stated objectives. Varied instructional strategies should be available so that youngsters who prefer to work independently (as does this third grader) may follow directions to permit maximum personal growth. (Photograph courtesy of the Douglas G. Grafflin School, Chappaqua, New York.)

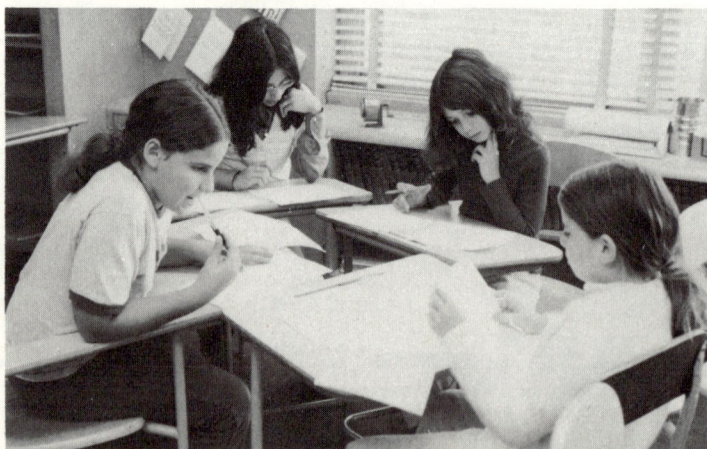

Photo 6-14. Students who wish to achieve their objectives as part of a team may use selected small-group techniques like team learning. (Photograph courtesy of Bellmore-Merrick Central High School District, Merrick, New York.)

Photo 6-15. After 15 years of teaching experience, Dorothy Haarman designs varied instructional areas to provide flexibility in the physical environment and to permit extensive opportunities for student selections and options. She claims that the "only" way to assure the progress of youngsters with learning disabilities is to individualize their instruction. (Photograph courtesy of the Floral Park-Bellerose Public Schools, Floral Park, New York.)

IDENTIFYING THE NINE NECESSARY INGREDIENTS OF ANY INDIVIDUALIZED PROGRAM

Some goals that are present in an effective traditional classroom are also appropriate for the one that is beginning to emphasize individual uniqueness, such as the development of a pleasant atmosphere or the positive rapport that should be established between the teacher and her students. There are, however, specific items that should always be observable in an individualized classroom that are rarely evident when the program is whole-group oriented. These would include evidence of:

1. Individual diagnosis prior to the development of prescription (assignments, curriculum, contracts, units, etc.).
2. Individual rather than group prescription (lesson planning, class assignments, sequential unit curricula, whole-group contracts, etc.).
3. Varied amounts of structure, determined by whether the student has

demonstrated that he can work independently, in pairs, in small groups, or that he needs to work directly under supervision.

4.   The availability of multisensory resources through which students may achieve.

5.   Publicly stated, specific objectives for each student or for small groups of similarly achieving students.

6.   Opportunity for student self-assessment.

7.   Varied instructional strategies, depending on the individual student's learning style.

8.   Varied instructional areas to provide flexibility in the physical environment.

9.   Opportunities for extensive student selection and options.

These nine necessary ingredients of an effective individualized program should be translated into *observable* teacher and student "behaviors," and then arranged so that anyone evaluating what people are doing may be able to record accurately what is *seen*. Such a compilation is called a "behavior-observation instrument." Chapter 7 identifies and

Photos 6-16, 6-17. Gregory Nash, a secondary teacher for six years, uses the multisensory strength of instructional packages to introduce language development to students who have difficulty with abstractions. He finds, however, that brighter youngsters who do not "need" packages use them for reinforcement. (Photographs courtesy of H. Frank Carey High School, Franklin Square, New York.)

Photo 6-17

describes some of these evaluation instruments and explains how they may be used by teachers, supervisors, and anyone interested in analyzing the effectiveness of an individualized program.

CIRCLE OF KNOWLEDGE EXERCISE ON OBSERVING INDIVIDUALIZED TEACHING AND LEARNING

A "circle of knowledge" is a review technique where, in coopera-tion with others, you may discover whether you remember the important elements of what you have been studying.

1. Ask from two to seven persons to join you by forming a seated circle.
2. One of the participants should serve as the group's recorder.
3. Distribute the circle of knowledge question (only one question at a time).
4. Number each member of the circle, beginning with "one" and con-tinuing around clockwise until each person has a number.
5. Beginning with number 1, each person supplies only one possible answer to the question. The recorder writes the given answer. Then number 2 supplies an answer that is also recorded, and so on. The circle continues providing answers until the time alloted has been exhausted. (A circle may continue giving answers through several rounds as long as time remains.) When time is up, the circle reviews its composite answers and each participant may then write the group's total responses to the circle of knowledge question to keep for his own use.

If a member cannot offer a new answer during a particular round he may pass or someone in the group may offer clues, either verbal or through pantomime.

Circle of Knowledge Exercise

Circle of Knowledge Question 1   Time Allotment: Four Minutes

List as many things as you can that evaluators of traditional classrooms observed that should not be present in an individualized program.

_____   _____

_____   _____

_____   _____

_____   _____

_____   _____

_____   _____

_____   _____

Circle of Knowledge Question 2   Time Allotment: Ten Minutes

List as many things as you can that evaluators should actually see when observing an effectively individualized program.

_____   _____

_____   _____

_____   _____

_____   _____

_____   _____

_____   _____

(Answers to Circle of Knowledge Question 1 may be found below, followed by answers to Circle of Knowledge Question 2.)

Comparing Answers to the Self-Instruction Guide—Chapter 6

Alternative Responses to Circle of Knowledge Question 1

                              (1)   (2)   (3)
Everyone was being taught the *same subject* at the *same time* in the *same*
                                              (4)
way. The basic teaching technique used was that of the *lecture method*.
                              (5)
Students were required to use the *same learning materials* (or resources)

(6)   (7)
and to complete the *same assignments* within the *same amount of time*.
                    (8)   (9)
Students were required to listen *in their seats* and to *raise their hands* when

they wished to ask a question or say something. Few options and oppor-
                        (10)   (11)
tunities for student *selections* or *decision-making* existed. Grades were
                    (12)
given on a *competitive basis* in comparison with how well everyone else in
                                              (13)
the group did. The classroom was a *structured environment* for all and
                            (14)   (15)
provided *little variation in instructional areas. Self-assessment*

opportunities were rarely provided for youngsters; nor were specific
                    (16)
performance or behavioral objectives identified. The teacher was the
          (17)   (18)
dominant personality in the room and rarely incorporated *student-centered*

abilities, interests and hobbies into the basic curriculum.
                        (19)
     The school *building* was the center of education and only the occasional
                                              (20)
field trip or visit took classes out of that environment. *Parents* were rarely

involved in classroom instructional activities.
          (21)
     One basic text was the main resource for learning in each curriculum
                                              (22)
area and children experienced very little *interpersonal peer relationships*

during the school day.

Alternative Responses to Circle of Knowledge Question 2

     In effectively individualized instructional programs, evaluators should
                                  (1)
be able to see that children have been *diagnosed* by inspecting their
          (2)   (3)
prescriptions, which should vary. Children may be working on *different*
                        (4)   (5)
curriculum subjects, *varied objectives,* or *self-selected activities* at
          (6)   (7)
different times and for *differing amounts of time.* Opportunities for

(8)   (9)   (10)
decision-making, *problem-solving*, and *self-selection* should exist for at

least some of the following items: (a) objectives, (b) learning resources, (c)
                                                                (11)
activities, (d) group interactions, or (e) assessment devices. *Multisensory*
                              (12)
resources should be available in a variety of *instructional areas*. Children
                    (13)   (14)
should be permitted to *self-pace* themselves and select *levels* of difficulty.
  (15)   (16)
Mobility should be acceptable at certain times as long as the *environment is*
                                      (17)
sufficiently varied so that children with different *learning styles* may func-

tion with ease.
                          (18)   (19)   (20)
    The teacher should *work with individuals*, *small groups*, and *larger*
                                                              (21)
groups when appropriate. Youngsters should be permitted to *work alone*,
        (22)   (23)
with a *friend*, or in a *small group* as long as they show evidence of
                                          (24)
direction and achievement. *Other adults and students* may interact in the
                                          (25)
instructional environment to provide contact with *different types of teach-*

ing styles.

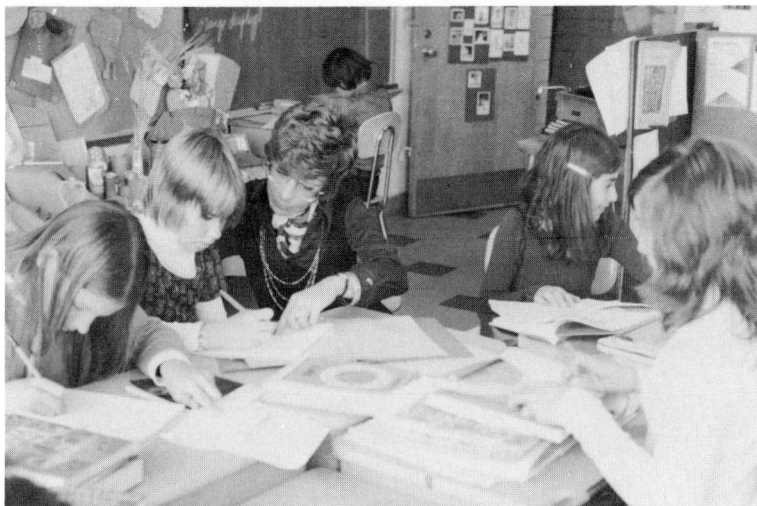

Photos 6-18, 6-19, 6-20. Mrs. Isabel Stein, who has taught for 17 years, began individualizing several years ago. She permits students to determine when they will work on the curriculum of their choice through self-selected activities. Her requirement is that they master their objectives well. Mrs. Stein indicated that she was a converted traditionalist, a teacher who ". . . did much reading and studying before slowly changing her methods." Now she finds her new program exciting for the students and for her. It helps to ". . . bring the real world into the classroom. Even skills are easier to teach this way," she concluded. (Photographs courtesy of the Saw Mill Road Elementary School, North Bellmore, New York.)

Photo 6-19

Photo 6-20

SEVEN

Supervising an Individualized Instructional Program: How to Record and Interpret Teacher and Student Behaviors

Behavioral Objectives for Chapter 7

1. You will be able to identify at least ten *teacher* behaviors that evaluators should actually see when observing an effectively individualized program.
2. You will be able to identify at least ten *student* behaviors that evaluators should actually see when observing an effectively individualized program.

. . . .

DESIGNING OBSERVATION INSTRUMENTS

Evaluators have been watching teacher and student behaviors for many years[1] in an effort to isolate those characteristics that tend to produce effective instruction. Two of the weaknesses of previous efforts were due to (1) the concentration on and the difficulty of accurately identifying common positive characteristics of teacher personality and teaching style, and (2) the human fallibility of interpreting what was seen.

Since an individualized instructional program is less dependent on teacher personality and style than on selected teaching skills and the effective management of the learning process, identification of observable teacher behaviors does not present the problems encountered by previous instrument designers. The specific skills that teachers need to possess in order to organize and manage an individualized program may be listed logically and accurately by professional educators experienced in individualization.

An itemization of teacher skills, however, is no longer sufficient to evaluate the effectiveness of either the teacher or the program. Just as students should be shown how they may demonstrate behaviorally that they have achieved their instructional objectives, teachers should be shown how they may demonstrate behaviorally that they possess the skills with which to individualize. At the point when those teacher skills that are required to individualize instruction are translated into observable teacher behaviors, objective and precise evaluation may be undertaken.

IDENTIFYING BEHAVIORAL OUTCOMES

The role of the teacher in an individualized instructional program broadens from one of transmitting knowledge to (a) diagnosing individuals, (b) prescribing curriculums, alternative resources, activities, evaluations, and small group interactions, and (c) guiding students through the learning process.[2] Since teachers may possess knowledge and skills that they either do not use or use poorly, it is the *results* of using their skills that really determine teacher effectiveness.

Evaluators need to translate Mager's[3] behavioral or performance objective processes into the identification of skills-related teacher behaviors, i.e., if a teacher functions as a diagnostician, what does she need to *do* to demonstrate that student programs reflect individual differences? The following chart synthesizes the translation of necessary teacher knowledge and skills into some selected, observable, behavioral outcomes that result from the correct use of the identified skills.

Photo 7-1. Joseph Herney diagnoses each student's progress in French and then prescribes only those objectives that the student has not mastered. (Photograph courtesy of Briarcliff High School, Briarcliff Manor, New York.)

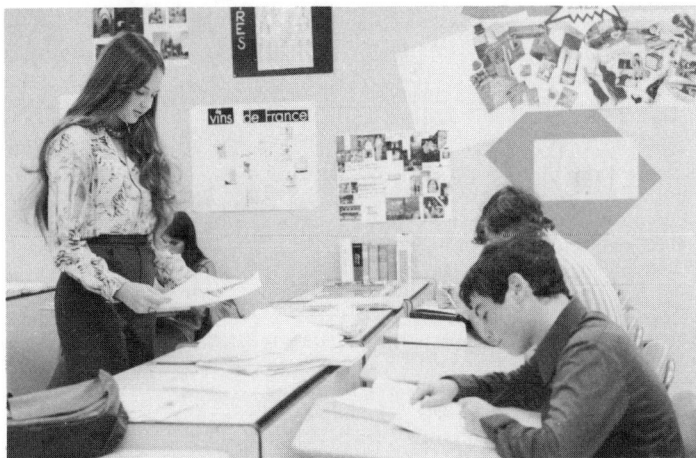

Photo 7-2. Through Joe's programed approach to foreign language, his students move ahead academically at a pace that is comfortable for each individual. (Photograph courtesy of Briarcliff High School, Briarcliff Manor, New York.)

Supervisor's Identification Chart
of the Teacher Who Individualizes Teaching and Learning

Teacher Knowledge	Use of Related Skills	Observable Behavioral Outcomes
1. The teacher recognizes that some students know more or less than their peers about a given topic.	She diagnoses each student to determine the present extent of his knowledge of those objectives that she plans to prescribe.	For each student the teacher prescribes only those objectives that the individual has not previously mastered.[4]
2. The teacher recognizes that students learn through perceptual preferences (auditory, visual, tactile, kinesthetic).	She diagnoses each student to determine the ways in which he is most likely to absorb and retain factual and conceptual information.	The teacher provides alternative multisensory and multimedia learning resources and encourages student self-selection from among approved options. She records and uses her diagnoses in future prescriptions.[5]
3. The teacher recognizes that some students learn more quickly or more slowly than their peers.	She diagnoses each student to determine his approximate rate of learning in different subject areas.	The teacher permits the student to move ahead academically at a pace that is comfortable for him.[6]
4. The teacher recognizes that each student learns information to a depth that is unique to his comprehension, retention abilities, and interests.	She analyzes each student's achievement scores, apparent motivation, and persistence.	The teacher prescribes a different number of objectives for those students who are diagnosed as being receptive to learning from those prescribed for youngsters who are diagnosed as slower or less motivated learners.[7]

5.	The teacher recognizes that students learn through different styles of study and practice.	She analyzes each student's learning style.	The teacher provides each student with environmental options of working with or without structure, peers, other adults, etc., according to the student's learning style at the time.[8]
6.	The teacher recognizes that information taught frequently, intensely, and with variety tends to be retained.	She designs a wide variety of activities, each of which reinforces the major concepts or skills in a student's prescription.	The teacher encourages student selection from among a wide variety of activities and builds each youngster's knowledge by using small-group reinforcement strategies.[9]
7.	The teacher recognizes that the element of choice provides a student with (a) a voice in the learning process, (b) opportunities in which to make decisions, and (c) experiences in self-assessment and problem-solving.	She designs activity and reporting alternatives for each prescription in greater numbers than she assigns, thus permitting extensive opportunity for selections, decision-making, self-assessment, and problem-solving.	The teacher writes optional activity and reporting alternatives into each student's prescription.[10]
8.	The teacher recognizes that required curriculums are not necessarily appropriate for all students.	She varies the curriculum requirements on the basis of individual diagnoses and often involves the student in developing his own instructional prescription. On occasion, the student may design his own course of study with teacher input or approval.	The curriculums being studied frequently vary from each other in subject matter, scope, and/or depth as prescribed for individual youngsters.[11]
9.	The teacher recognizes that different students respond to different teaching methods and that most students respond favorably to a variety of strategies.	She varies instruction according to her student's response to selected techniques.	Using many varied teaching techniques,[5] the teacher moves from individual to small group and occasionally to larger groups with ease; she encourages students to work independently, in pairs, in teams, and with adults, as they prefer. She uses independent contracts, circles of knowledge, simulations, partnerships, role playing, programed learning, games, instructional packages, etc., as needed.[12]
10.	The teacher recognizes that students need differing amounts of structure and freedom.	She provides varying amounts of structure and/or informality for all students.	She encourages some students to work within well-defined limits; others enjoy increased freedom; some determine their procedures through individual selection in appropriate locations.[13]

| 11. | The teacher recognizes that to function effectively in an individualized program a student must know how to locate, use, and share appropriate resources, personnel, facilities, etc. | She develops the requisite skills in cadres of students so that they, in turn, may teach others. | She encourages students to independently help themselves and their peers to locate, use, and share resources, personnel, and facilities effectively.[14] |

Photo 7-3. Lillian Gold permits her third graders to use multimedia anywhere in the room. (Photograph courtesy of Douglas G. Grafflin School, Chappaqua, New York.)

Photo 7-4. A corridor wall in an older building has been converted into a series of listening posts to permit independent use of media away from the formal classroom structure. (Photograph courtesy of Briarcliff Middle School, Briarcliff Manor, New York.)

USING AN INDIVIDUALIZATION INDEX

As indicated above, behavioral outcomes are essentially dependent on the teacher's translation of her knowledge and skills into observable actions or results that are readily apparent in the instructional environment. One instrument that appraises the degree to which these individualizing results are evidenced in classes or schools is known as the "individualization index."[15] Each of the characteristics listed in the index is checked by either an observer or an observation team. In section I, check the items that most closely resemble the situation that exists in the classroom. Score the points equal to the item checked, e.g., if A-3 is checked write "3" under points, if B-2 is checked write "2," etc.

In the second section, one point is allotted to each "never" response, two points to each "rarely" response, three points to each "sometimes" response, and four points to every check in the "frequently" column for each of the letters A through T.

The number of points noted for each question for each section is then added. The total score indicates the degree to which individualization techniques are being used in the class, school, or district. In section I: 10 points or below, very little implementation; between 11 and 14 points, individualization is beginning to appear in the instructional program; 15

Photo 7-5. Susan Kromol, in her sixth year of teaching, and Robert A. Leonard, district chairman of English, challenge Susan's students' critical analysis skills. Bob says, "Teachers must adjust to giving up the center of the stage. They are also afraid of noise levels and of giving youngsters freedom that they cannot handle. Teachers need to be trained to work with their students in a differently structured, but freer, environment." (Photograph courtesy of Merrick Avenue Junior High School, Bellmore-Merrick, New York.)

to 21 points, the program appears to emphasize heavy student involvement and is routinely individualized; 22 to 28 points, a well-individualized program with comprehensive reference to objectives, resources, pacing, diagnoses, curriculum, activities, and leveling.

In the second section, a score below 30 indicates that assistance is necessary if the program is to progress toward effective individualization; between 31 and 48 suggests that an individualized program is under early development. A score between 49 and 64 indicates that the program is moving toward individualization, and 65 through 80 represents highly developed programs.

Supervisors are encouraged to use this instrument as an initial means of appraising the individualization process. It should be noted, however, that this instrument indicates only the *degree* to which the individualization process has been introduced: it is *not* a measure of quality.

Remsen Individualization Index

Instructions: Check one of the choices in each of the following categories.

Section I

	✓	Points

A. *Determination of Objectives:*   A.
1. By the school; on the basis of norms established for a whole class
2. By the teacher; on the basis of individual diagnosis, hierarchical sequencing of concepts and skills is prescribed
3. By the teacher and student; on the basis of individual diagnosis
4. By the student; on the basis of his selection from among approved alternatives

B. *Determination of Resources:*   B.
1. By the school; on the basis of what is available for the whole class
2. By the teacher; on the basis of what is prescribed for the program
3. By the teacher and student; on the basis of individual diagnosis
4. By the student; on the basis of his selection from among approved alternatives

C. *Determination of Pacing:*   C.
1. By the teacher; on the basis of a set curriculum
2. By the teacher; on the basis of an individual diagnosis

	✓	*Points*

3. By the teacher and student; on the basis of individual diagnosis
4. By the student

D. *Determination of Diagnosis:*   D.
  1. By standardized testing
  2. By criterion-referenced tests in relation to cited objectives
  3. By performance prescribed by the teacher
  4. By the student from among approved alternatives

E. *Determination of Curriculum:*   E.
  1. By the school; on the basis of grade requirements
  2. By the teacher; on the basis of individual diagnosis
  3. By the teacher and student; on the basis of individual diagnosis
  4. By the student; selected from among approved alternatives

F. *Determination of Activities:*   F.
  1. By the program
  2. By the teacher
  3. By the teacher and student
  4. By the student; selected from among approved alternatives

G. *Determination of Level of Instruction:*   G.
  1. On the basis of standardized tests
  2. On the basis of criterion-referenced tests
  3. On the basis of teacher and student evaluation
  4. On the basis of student selection from among approved alternatives

Totals

Section II

Teacher Behaviors:

	Never	Rarely	Sometimes	Frequently	Points

A. Prescribes on the basis of student diagnosis   A.
B. Incorporates small-group instruction into   B.
  daily instructional methods, e.g.,
  1. circle of knowledge
  2. brainstorming
  3. team learning
  4. case study
  5. role playing

	Never	Rarely	Sometimes	Frequently	Points
6. simulation					
7. team tutoring					
8. other					
C. Asks multilevel questions C.					
D. Provides multilevel resources D.					
E. Provides for varied instructional areas, E. e.g.,					
1. learning stations (list types_____)					
2. interest centers (list types_____)					
3. media areas					
4. little theaters					
5. game tables					
6. magic carpets					
7. other					
F. Works differently with different students F.					
G. Makes assignments on the basis of indi- G. vidual student abilities					
H. Moves freely from individuals to groups H.					
I-L. Permits students to function on the basis of their individual learning styles:					
I. Environmental I.					
1. amount of sound					
2. amount of light					
3. degree of temperature					
4. physical design of area					
J. Emotional J.					
1. amount and type of motivation					
2. amount and type of persistence					
3. amount and type of responsibility					
4. amount and type of structure required					
K. Sociological K.					
1. works with large groups of peers					
2. works independently					
3. works with one other peer					
4. works with small groups of peers					
5. works with adults					
6. works with adults and/or peers					
L. Physical L.					
1. perceptual strengths and/or weaknesses					
2. amount of intake (food, liquids)					
3. time of day					
4. completes tasks in order of preference					
5. amount and degree of mobility required					

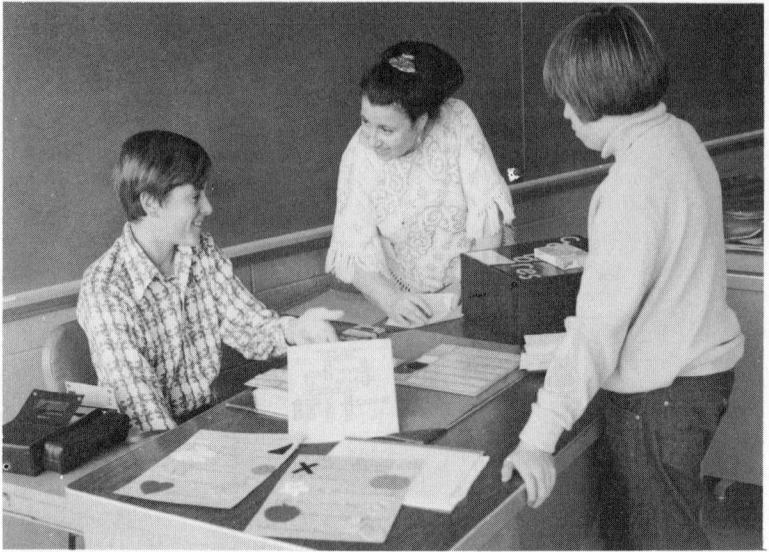

Photo 7-6. Julia Torres, who has been teaching Spanish for more than 20 years, establishes contract objectives for her students, but permits each to achieve them through self-selected resources. Some students learn to speak the language through the use of Julia's multisensory instructional packages. (Photograph courtesy of Wantagh Junior High School, Wantagh, New York.)

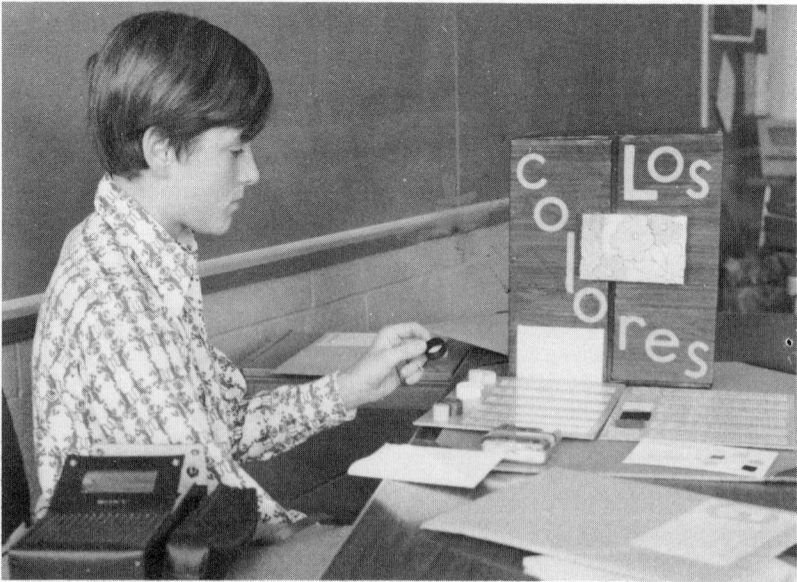

Photos 7-7, 7-8. Others listen to tapes.

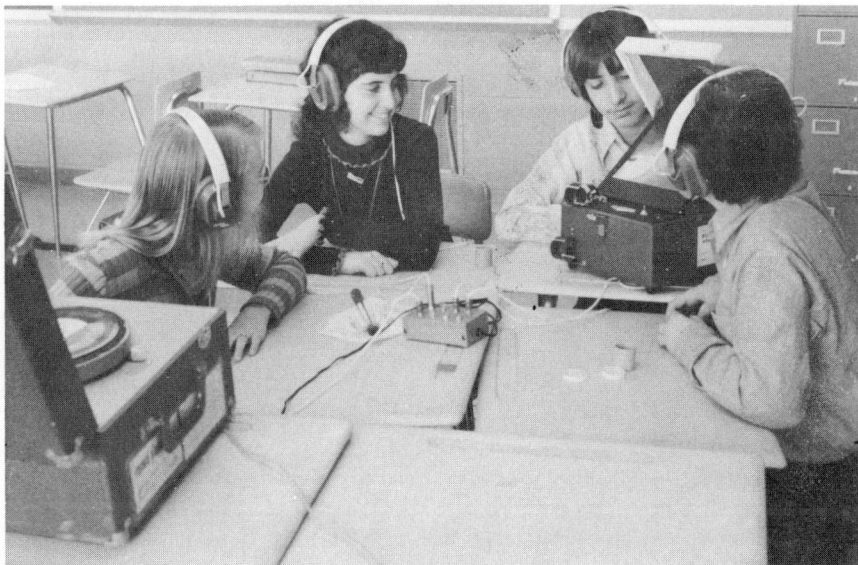

Photo 7-8

Photo 7-9. Some, using a tactile approach to language development, play games.

Photo 7-10. Other youngsters gain experience with commonly used phrases by operating a farmer's market exchange. (Photographs courtesy of Wantagh Junior High School, Wantagh, New York.)

	Never	Rarely	Sometimes	Frequently	Points
M. Trains students in use and care of resources					
N. Develops skills of independent learning					
O. Guides students toward being task-focused					

Student Behaviors:

P. Functions in small groups without teacher's presence					
Q. Functions in a variety of instructional areas without teacher's presence					
R. Demonstrates independence by:					

1. locating, using and returning resources
2. making selections from among prescribed alternatives
3. being task-focused
4. evaluating his own progress
5. seeking appropriate assistance when necessary

S. Participates in the development of his own prescription (objectives, resources, evaluation)

T. Designs his own prescription (objectives, resources, evaluation)

RECOGNIZING TEACHER AND STUDENT BEHAVIORS
IN AN INDIVIDUALIZED SETTING

Although the Remsen Individualization Index focuses essentially on behavioral outcomes, it is both desirable and realistic to have options and alternatives to instructional assessment. Evaluation diversity should be encouraged for the purpose of intelligent comparison and as a confirmation of findings.

Recent assessment instruments tend to focus on observable teacher and student behaviors. To avoid subjectivity through interpretation, the actions (behaviors) that teachers and students demonstrate in an individualized setting should be precisely identified and used in supervision, teacher-, self- and peer-assessment, and in-service courses.

The following list describes teacher behaviors that should occur in an individualized environment and then describes the student behaviors that may be seen as a result of what the teacher has done.

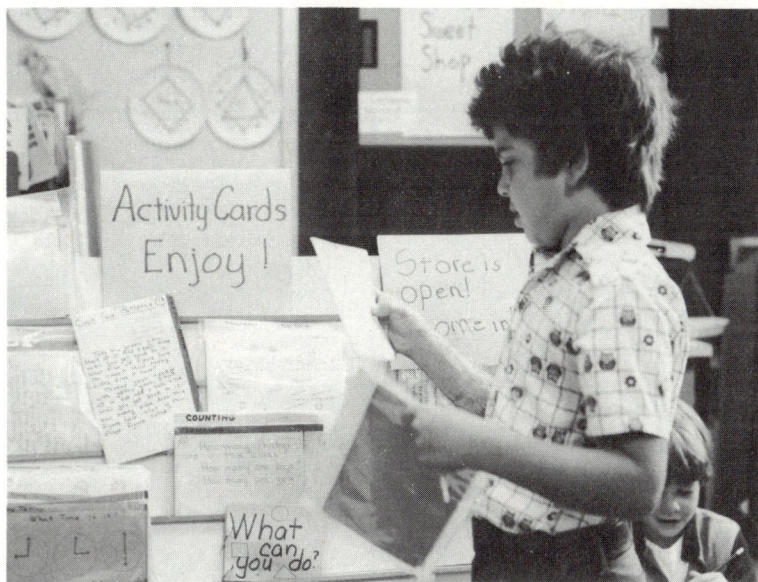

Photos 7-11, 7-12. Students should be encouraged to self-select their activities and resources and to follow through on required tasks. This third grader chooses one activity from among several options related to the same skills and then moves to the appropriate instructional area to study, evaluate his progress, and discuss his gains with his teacher. (Photographs courtesy of the Douglas G. Grafflin School, Chappaqua, New York.)

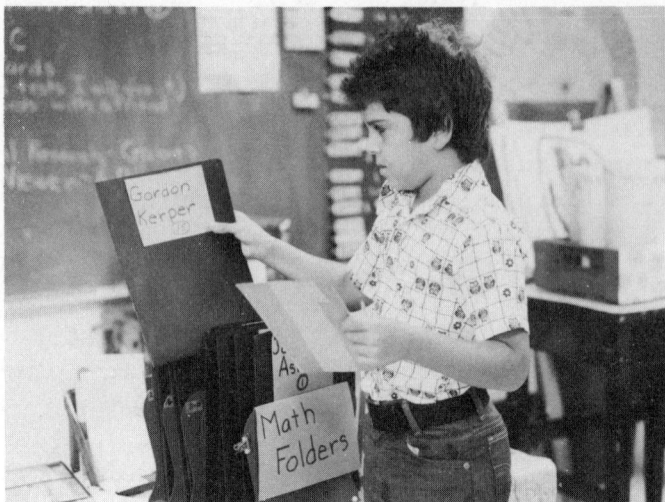

Photo 7-12

Teacher Behaviors	*Resultant Observable Student Behaviors*
1. The teacher diagnoses each student and then prescribes on the basis of the results. When the teacher diagnoses the curriculum that will be incorporated into the prescription, he or she analyzes (a) what all students should learn, (b) what most students should learn, and (c) what some students should learn. She then assesses the abilities, interests, and motivation of each student and, *using the same basic curriculum*, prescribes varied numbers and kinds of objectives. When initially focusing on the curriculum, the teacher is using a "curriculum contract process"[16] (Figure 7-1).	Each student may be working toward the completion of varied and/or entirely different prescriptions from those of other students.
2. The teacher elicits student involvement in the development of their own prescriptions.	Students select their own (a) objectives, (b) resources, (c) activities, (d) assignments, (e)

Curriculum Contract Process

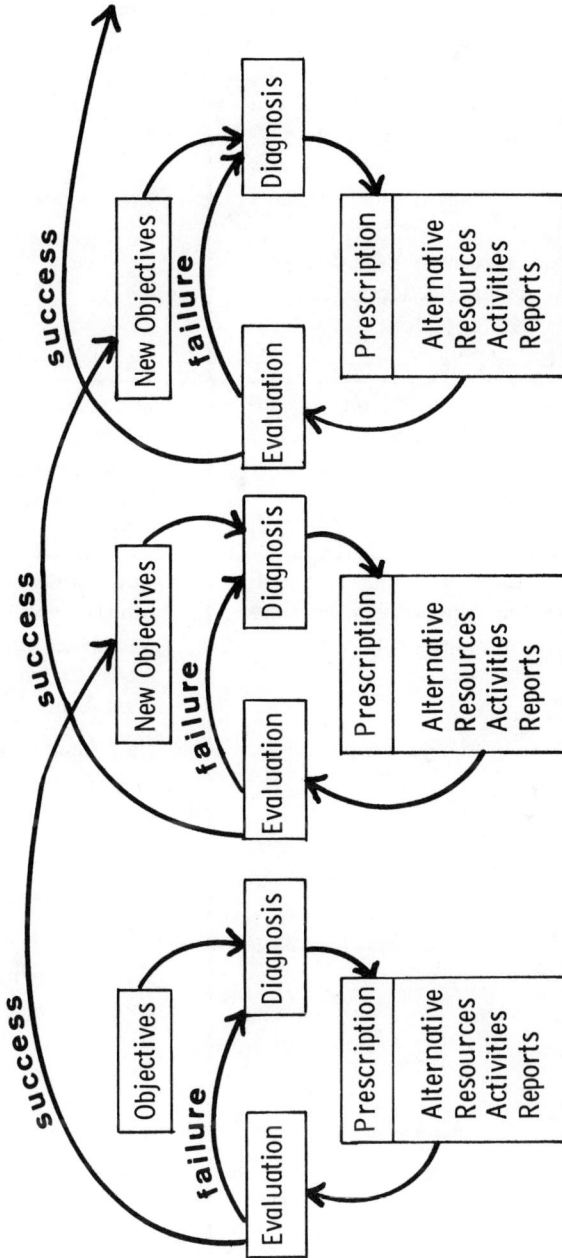

Figure 7-1

Designed by Dr. Rita S. Dunn

When the teacher designs a prescription based on the *student's identified interests and concerns*, he or she is developing a curriculum for that specific student. The teacher analyzes the possible objectives within the topic and then determines the alternative resources, activities, and reporting techniques that might be appropriate for that curriculum. When initially focusing on the diagnosis of the student, the teacher is using an "independent contract process"[17] (Figure 7-2).

small-group techniques, (f) mode of learning, and/or (g) evaluation procedures from among approved alternatives.

3. The teacher diagnoses on an ongoing basis and guides each student through the learning process.

The student is involved in individual and small-group teacher conferences (formal and/or informal) as he progresses through his prescription.

4. The teacher develops independence and responsibility (accountability) in the student.

The student uses a self-assessment instrument to continuously identify what he has already achieved and what he still must learn.

He locates, uses, repairs, shares, and replaces resources and media.

He finds assistance when necessary and assists others when he is able.

He makes choices from among approved alternatives in objectives, resources, assignments, small-group techniques, modes of learning, evaluation procedures, and when and how he will pace himself.

He learns to analyze his own progress and the achievements of his peers critically and to document his conclusions.

Independent Contract Process

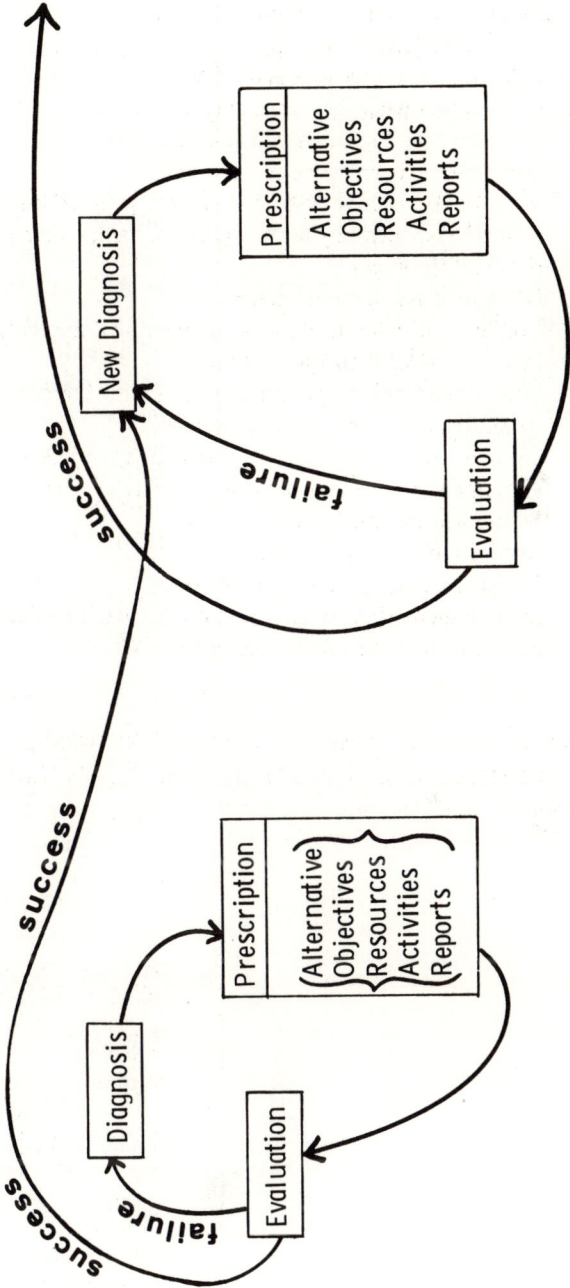

Prescription

Alternative
Objectives
Resources
Activities
Reports

New Diagnosis

Evaluation

failure

success

success

Prescription

(Alternative
Objectives
Resources
Activities
Reports)

Diagnosis

Evaluation

failure

success

Designed by Dr. Rita S. Dunn

Figure 7-2

5. The teacher provides for a variety of small-group techniques to (a) prevent alienation in the learning environment, (b) provide for student discussion, and (c) provide for reinforcement and retention of learning.	The students engage in selected small-group interactions at varied intervals, e.g., team learning, group analysis, simulations, circles of knowledge, etc.
6. The teacher establishes and equips varied instructional areas to encourage diversity, mobility, variety, and options, e.g., interest centers, little theaters, game tables, reading corners, learning stations, magic carpet areas, media corners, etc.	Students move freely about the instructional environment and work alone, in pairs, or in teams as they determine. They maintain a relaxed atmosphere, work on interdisciplinary studies at times, achieve cooperative peer interactions, use varied instructional areas and resources, participate in planning some of the activities at the various areas, establish some of their own priorities, express their thoughts and feelings in acceptable terms, show initiative and, simultaneously, maintain a discussion level that permits those who need a conversational noise level to work.
7. The teacher provides for a variety of learning experiences.	Students make selections from among many approved alternatives. They use materials and equipment available in and adjacent to the instructional setting and may also go beyond the indigenous environment for additional sources.
	Student studies may be non-school centered at times and personnel resources may be used in and out of the educational facilities.
	Students may use contract activity packages, programed learning, instructional packages,

	work-study plans and/or community contribution programs at varied times if appropriate to their learning styles, tasks, prescriptions and abilities.
	Students may experience brainstorming, independent study, case studies, group analysis, simulations, team tutoring, etc., at appropriate intervals.
8. The teacher provides for different learning rates and styles.	The students set their own pace within established or prescribed acceptable time intervals. They interact with adults and other students, as they prefer. They utilize their personal interests as one source of study focus. They involve themselves in creative activities allied with their personal talents and skills. They determine the order and extensiveness of their studies. They study in the environment they choose for time intervals with which they feel comfortable. They function within different amounts of structure and/or informality, dependent upon how they show their ability to progress independently.
9. The teacher provides for multilevel student studies that transcend "graded" materials.	Students use multilevel resources to complete their prescriptions according to their abilities and interests.
10. The teacher shares leadership with selected students as they mature and develop independent and group skills.	Students engage in paired, teamed, and small-group instruction when appropriate. They form cadres to assist others in locating, using, repairing, and replacing resources. They record their own progress. They establish some of their own priorities.

They help plan their prescriptions. They add to approved alternatives in each area. They can identify their objectives and the criteria by which they will be evaluated. They participate in planning the evaluation instrument and in assessing their own progress. They share their learning with others through alternative reporting opportunities. They can eventually design and evaluate their own prescriptions.

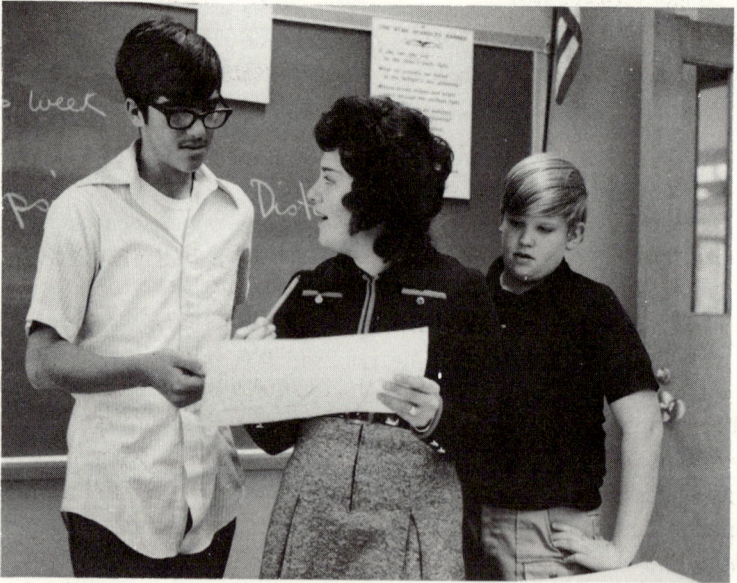

Photos 7-13, 7-14. Teachers provide for different learning styles by permitting students to select the way in which they will learn. Regina White (11 years of teaching experience), prescribes a series of objectives as part of a class contract activity package. She then permits her students to select those objectives they will complete from among her approved list. Regina moves among students and small groups assessing individual progress. (Photographs courtesy of Seaford Junior High School, Seaford, New York.)

Photo 7-14

RECORDING AND ANALYZING OBSERVABLE TEACHER AND STUDENT BEHAVIORS IN AN INDIVIDUALIZED ENVIRONMENT

Another means of determining the extent to which individualization has been introduced into a program is to watch and record quantitatively (a) what the teacher *does* and (b) what the student *does* when they are in the instructional environment. The Compain Key[18] is one newly developed scale that devotes itself explicitly to the task of identifying those behaviors.

The observer is directed to consider each of the categories in two ways: how many of the students can be observed doing what is described (all? most? some? or none?), and how much of the time do the students who do what is described actually engage in the practice (always? most of the time? sometimes? or not at all?).

When using the Compain Key, circle two items in each category —the number of students involved in the selected behavior, and the amount of time devoted to the practice.

Example: An observer using the Compain Key enters a classroom where he remains for a 45-minute interval. During that period he notices that most of the students work on tasks by themselves, but often move from the area in which they are studying to others where peers are similarly involved. Students interact with other students for what appears to be curriculum discussions and then return to where they were conducting their work. At other times, students seek assistance from the teacher and then, similarly, return to their studies either alone or with a classmate or two.

For item 1 of the Compain Key, the observer might circle *2* (most of the students) and *2* (most of the time) to provide the information that most of the students work independently most of the time.

For item 8, the observer might circle *3* (all of the students) and *2* (most of the time) to indicate that all of the students appear to be mobile most of the time.

After answering both question columns in section A, use the following scale to interpret the results:

Point Score		Point Score	
3	All of the Students	3	All of the Time
2	Most of the Students	2	Most of the Time
1	Some of the Students	1	Some of the Time
0	None of the Students	0	None of the Time

Total all of the translated points for each column in Section A and record them in the appropriate box on the graph above.

The total number of possible translated points in each category would be as follows:

All of the Students:	48	All of the Time:	48
Most of the Students:	32	Most of the Time:	32
Some of the Students:	16	Some of the Time:	16
None of the Students:	0	None of the Time:	0

Divide the total number of points recorded in each category by the maximum number of possible translated points in that category to obtain (1) the percentage of students for whom the program is being individualized, and (2) the amount of time it is being individualized for each appropriate category of students.

Example: A total number of ten is recorded on the instrument under "all students." Ten is then multiplied by three because, as the previous itemization indicated, three points should be granted for each observation of all students involved in the individualization technique. Three times ten is equivalent to the sum of 30 (3 × 10 = 30); therefore, the number 30 is divided by the total number of maximum possible responses in the category, which is 48.

$$\frac{30}{48} = 48\overline{\smash{)}30} = 62\tfrac{1}{2}\%$$

It may be assumed, therefore, that if the recorder accurately indicated what was observed, 62½% of the activities of all of the students were individualized.

Under the time portion of section A, if the total number of #3 responses were eight, eight would be multiplied by three (the amount granted for each number response), and that total of 24 would be divided by 48, the maximum number of possible responses in category 1 (all of the time):

$$\frac{24}{48} = \frac{1}{2} \text{ or } 50\%$$

It may then be assumed that all of the students in the described situation engage in 62½% of the activities on an individualized basis for 50% of the time.

Example: If the category "some of the students" is checked 12 times, and the directions indicate that each such response is granted one point, one times 12 equals 12 (1 × 12 = 12). Twelve is then placed over the total number of maximum points in that category (16) and is divided by 16.

$$\frac{12}{16} = \frac{3}{4} \text{ or } 75\%$$

It can be deduced from this procedure that 75 percent of the activities of some of the students were individualized.

The section B categories under "teacher behaviors" are scored in the same fashion; simply add the points represented by the answer *3*, all the time; *2*, most of the time; *1*, some of the time; and *0*, none of the time. Only one column, *time*, is used for part B. The maximum number of individualized responses in this section totals 66. Add the total number of responses, multiply them by the appropriate amount indicated for that response, and divide by 66 to determine the amount of time in which the teacher promotes individualized behaviors.

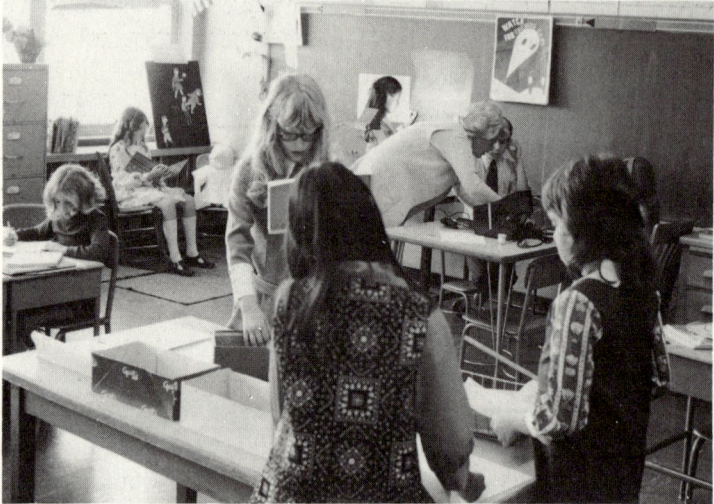

Photo 7-15. These students are selecting objectives and resources at a learning station while their classmates are each involved in varied activities at different instructional areas. The teacher (in the background) is assisting a small group at the media center. (Photograph courtesy of Seaford Manor Elementary School, Seaford, New York.)

Compain Key—By Rita Compain, C.W. Post College, 1972

Teacher_____ Time of observation_____
School_____ Date of observation_____
Form completed by_____ Subject_____Section_____

Observed Student Behaviors

Proportion Code		Time Code	
3	All of the Students	3	All of the Time
2	Most of the Students	2	Most of the Time
1	Some of the Students	1	Some of the Time
0	None of the Students	0	None of the time

		Proportion	Time	Comments
1.	Work independently	_____	____	_____
2.	Are self-directed	_____	____	_____
3.	Self-select learning resources	_____	____	_____
4.	Use multilevel curriculum resources	_____	____	_____
5.	Engage in creative work at times	_____	____	_____
6.	Work in small groups at times	_____	____	_____
7.	Are involved in self-paced learning	_____	____	_____
8.	Move freely and purposefully about the area	_____	____	_____
9.	Follow an individual prescription	_____	____	_____
10.	Use varied instructional areas	_____	____	_____
11.	Interact with peers	_____	____	_____
12.	Interact with teacher	_____	____	_____
13.	Interact with other adults at times	_____	____	_____
14.	Are aware of own goals	_____	____	_____
15.	Use a self-assessment instrument	_____	____	_____
16.	Appear to be actively involved in learning	_____	____	_____

Totals

Section B

Observed Teacher Behaviors

Time Code		
	3	All of the Time
	2	Most of the Time
	1	Some of the Time
	0	None of the Time

		Time	Comments
1.	Plans on an individual basis	____	_____
2.	Plans collaboratively at times	____	_____
3.	Organizes selected activities	____	_____
4.	Directs selected activities	____	_____
5.	Establishes varied instructional centers	____	_____
6.	Interacts with individual children and small groups	____	_____
7.	Encourages student decision-making	____	_____
8.	Diagnoses individuals	____	_____
9.	Prescribes for individuals	____	_____
10.	Guides individuals and small groups	____	_____
11.	Evaluates on an individual basis	____	_____
12.	Responds in varied ways to individuals	____	_____

13. Maintains workable noise level
14. Provides structure for those who need it
15. Provides flexibility for those who need it
16. Moves freely about the room
17. Instructs children in use and care of multimedia
18. Asks multilevel questions
19. Establishes an inter-active atmosphere
20. Employs small-group techniques
21. Works in different curriculum areas
22. Makes options available to students

Total

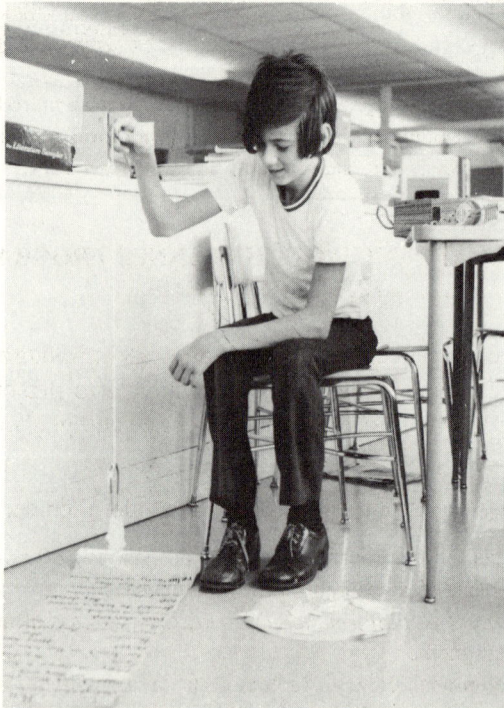

Photo 7-16. This young man is learning through an instructional package developed by Fran Kritchek, who has been teaching for 13 years. Fran says, "Packages generate enthusiasm and total involvement of the student . . . they increase concentration on the task at hand." (Photograph courtesy of Wantagh Junior High School, Wantagh, New York.)

Photo 7-17. Phil Nespeca moves freely about the room redirecting and evaluating student progress. (Photograph courtesy of Baldwin Harbor Junior High School, Baldwin, New York.)

EVALUATING THROUGH PLANNED PROGRAM BUDGET SYSTEMS

With the emergence of planning-programing-budgeting systems (PPBS), another means of evaluation is available to persons concerned with the degree to which a program is meeting the goals of those who designed it.

The five basic components of a PPBS model include:

1. the delineation of program content expressed as *program skills*,
2. the statement of measurable program *objectives*,
3. the statement of *performance criteria*, or standards of anticipated program attainment,
4. the development of achievement tests or assessment inventories that measure program *skill attainment*, and
5. the gathering of *cost data* for programs under examination.[19]

Since a necessary component of any individualized program is a statement of instructional objectives written behaviorally so that they are measurable and indicate the performance criteria (or degree of proficiency) by which the student will be judged, items 1-3 of the PPBS model are appropriate for the evaluation of such a program. Every individualized program must also include assessment instruments to determine the degree to which the listed skills have been completed (criterion-referenced tests) and, therefore, item 4 of the PPBS model also relates directly to the design of an individualized program. The only item that is not generally included in an evaluation of many of our newer programs is the cost factor indicated in item 5 and, certainly, that would be a positive addition to any form of evaluation. A PPBS model lends itself extremely well to the evaluation of an individualized program and is another source of information available to administrators and citizens interested in reliable assessment.

One note of caution should be added for those interested in adapting PPBS for the purpose of program assessment. One of the procedures used in developing program evaluation through PPBS is the identification of program skills and a comparative rating of their importance. Once this process has been completed, the projected time that will be allocated to the development of that skill is determined. It must be remembered that in an individualized program the "importance" of skills should be cooperatively determined by the *teacher and the student* and, of greater importance, *the amount of time* to be devoted to the acquisition of selected skills cannot be programed or predetermined if the concept of self-pacing, an integral part of individualization, is to be incorporated into a program.

Circle of Knowledge Exercise on Identifying Teacher Behaviors

Circle Members:
1. _____ 4. _____
2. _____ 5. _____
3. _____ 6. _____
Recorder:_____

Using the Circle of Knowledge techniques explained in Chapter 6, list at least ten teacher behaviors that a supervisor should be able to see when he visits an effectively organized individualized instructional program.
1. _____ 7. _____
2. _____ 8. _____
3. _____ 9. _____
4. _____ 10. _____
5. _____ 11. _____
6. _____ 12. _____

Circle of Knowledge Exercises on Identifying Student Behaviors

Circle Members:
1. _____ 4. _____

2. _____ 5. _____
3. _____ 6. _____

Recorder:_____

Using the Circle of Knowledge technique explained in Chapter 6, list at least ten student behaviors that a supervisor should be able to *see* when he visits an effectively organized individualized instructional program.

1. _____ 7. _____
2. _____ 8. _____
3. _____ 9. _____
4. _____ 10. _____
5. _____ 11. _____
6. _____ 12. _____

Comparing Answers to the Self-instruction Guide—Chapter 7

(Identifying Teacher Behaviors in an Effectively Individualized Program)

Teachers:

1. Diagnose each student.
2. Prescribe on the basis of the individual diagnosis.
3. Guide each student through the learning process based on an ongoing diagnosis and flexible prescription.
4. Work with individuals, small groups, and/or whole groups.
5. Use a variety of small group techniques (role playing, team learning, circle of knowledge, etc.).
6. Work at different levels with different students.
7. Guide students toward independence and self-direction.
8. Establish and equip a variety of instructional areas.
9. Provide for a variety of alternative learning experiences.
10. Train and utilize other available adults.
11. Develop a wide variety of multimedia and multisensory resources.
12. Prescribe objectives, resources and activities in conjunction with students.
13. Continue an on-going assessment of student work.
14. Use flexible room arrangements.
15. Provide access to materials within room, in adjacent area, and/or at out-of-school sites.
16. Provide for different learning rates.
17. Provide for different learning styles.
18. Design programs to provide for student interaction in a variety of positive ways.
19. Provide multiple curriculum and instructional options for students.
20. Involve students in group decision-making.
21. Provide opportunities for independent decision-making.

Photos 7-18, 7-19. Students become increasingly independent as they are required to select, locate, cooperatively use, share, repair and replace a variety of resources. (Photographs courtesy of Briarcliff Middle School, Briarcliff Manor, New York.)

Photo 7-19

Photo 7-20. Walter Brownsword sequences skills that need to be mastered and places ditto sheets describing objectives, resources and activities into mounted envelopes that indicate the level of difficulty. Students may progress through the series as quickly as they are able and may skip certain levels if they can demonstrate competence. (Photograph courtesy of Roaring Brook School, Chappaqua, New York.)

22. Instruct students in care, use and repair of media.
23. Move from student to student and group to group.
24. Identify and provide for the learning strengths and interests of individual students.
25. Provide leadership opportunities for selected students.
26. Provide opportunities for creative thinking and activities.

(Identifying Student Behavior in an Effectively Individualized Program)

Students:

1. Establish some of their own objectives.
2. Use varied alternative media and resources.
3. Use varied small-group techniques (team learning, circles of knowledge, etc.).
4. Use flexible seating arrangements.
5. Work alone (independently), in pairs, and/or in teams at times.
6. Move freely about the instructional environment.
7. Maintain a conversational noise level.

8. Create materials and resources.
9. Make choices and select from among options and alternatives.
10. Interact with adults and other students.
11. Work at different levels.
12. Self-assess their work and progress.
13. Can explain what they are doing and why.
14. Work on interdisciplinary studies at times.
15. Tutor each other at times.
16. Achieve cooperative and positive peer interactions most of the time.
17. Assume responsibility for the location, care, repair and return of materials and resources.
18. Use varied instructional areas.
19. Confer with individuals, small groups, and the teacher.
20. Select some of their own activities.
21. Use some form of programed learning, contracts, out-of-building studies and/or instructional packages.
22. Set their own pace within approximate time intervals.
23. Participate in planning some individual activities.
24. Set up and use media independently.
25. Record their own progress.
26. Establish some of their own priorities.
27. Involve themselves in creative art activities (music, art, dramatics) to capitalize on their talents and/or interests.

The responses to these two circles of knowledge were developed with the assistance of Sr. Jane Durgin of St. John's University's College of Pharmacy.

EIGHT

Analyzing Individualized Programs Through Case Studies

Behavioral Objectives for Chapter 8

1. You will be able to list ten to 20 key positive and negative behaviors of students and adults for each case study.
2. You will be able to plan steps and actions needed to improve the situation described in the case study.

. . . .

USING CASE STUDIES TO DEVELOP SKILLS
IN ANALYZING INDIVIDUALIZED PROGRAMS

Now that you have considered the alternative methods through which programs may be individualized, the seven-step process toward totally individualizing instruction, how to analyze a student's learning style and then how to redesign the environment to accommodate it, and how to observe and evaluate an individualized program, you should be ready to develop the skills that will help you to analyze your own school situation. Objective analysis of a current program is essential to change and improvement. The old industrial admonition, "If you don't know where you're going, any path will take you there," has its counterpart in education: "If you don't evaluate what you're doing, you can't improve it."

Case studies[1] can sharpen your ability to diagnose where a selected class or school program is on the individualization continuum. Once this has been determined, new objectives can be set and the next steps planned for moving toward a more effective individualized approach.

For example, should a fictitious school be described as having an administrator who coerces change toward individualization without appropriate staff involvement or training, you would be expected to note the disadvantages of such behavior and to prescribe more efficient methods for stimulating positive movement. You would then examine your own efforts toward developing faculty commitment and analyze whether or not you had adequately involved your staff. On the basis of your assessment, you might then seek to improve specific approaches and procedures.

Another case might involve a cooperative school-community effort to promote individualized techniques that capitalize on each youngster's learning style. If the case study described the protests of a small group of veteran teachers who wish to avoid the extensive testing practices that such a program would require, you would be required to analyze the behaviors of the teacher group, the administrators, the remaining faculty members, and the community representatives to determine the probable outcomes of their actions. Should a similar situation ever develop in your own school setting, you might then be better able to cope with it positively.

A third possibility might focus on community resistance to a new open school that arranges furniture in dens and alcoves and where teachers encourage various procedures that foster independent learning. Given such a situation, what are the appropriate behaviors that you should expect of the faculty, the administrators, and the board of education members? What could you do to modify negative behaviors should they occur?

Photos 8-1, 8-2. Community resistance to individualized programs can be avoided, in part, by permitting students to take instructional packages or contracts home and to have parents observe their use and value. (Photographs courtesy of the Department of Curriculum and Teaching, St. John's University, New York.)

Photo 8-2

The success of case studies for use as analysis and planning tools depends on the reality and direct relevance of the described situations to the participants. Interest is stimulated if the resulting analysis can be used to solve the selected problem or aid in improving the behavior of those involved.

Case studies perform another service; they point up errors being committed elsewhere and therefore help to prevent their duplication. They also reinforce previously learned concepts and data and sharpen our ability to compare what we know ought to be happening with what is actually occurring.

PARTICIPATING IN FOUR CASE STUDIES AT DIFFERENT LEVELS

Case studies aid in building several types of analytical and management skills in a safe, nonthreatening climate that can be stimulating and productive. These skills include the ability to compare, to rate, to suggest improvements, to contrast, to plan, to consider consequences, to list alternates, to cope with and to solve problems, and to make decisions.

In-service programs, faculty meetings, or schoolwide projects could provide opportunities for using case studies to diagnose current programs and to promote change. One or more of the four case studies that follow may be used in such a school effort to build analysis skills in diagnosing appropriate student and adult behaviors in an individualized program.

Next, you may select one of the cases as a model to construct another that might be more relevant for you and other staff members or administrators. Involve concerned peers and students in reading, role playing, analyzing and planning for improvement. You might begin with the evaluation of a single class, then a grade level or department, and finally the school.

Case Study 1: Analyzing the Innovative Primary School

The Richard K. Hart Early Childhood Center in Ivory Lane, Connecticut, was designed specifically to house an innovative primary school program. Its glass-enclosed dome and outer walls border on a tranquil, suburban woodland that is simultaneously picturesque and soothing. Its interior reflects natural daylight that brightens and cheers the huge open-space learning environment from early morning to dusk.

The school population reflects an upper-middle-class professional and business community that appreciates quality education and a program that entices children into successful learning. Taxes are high, but the school district is loyally supported by its citizens who want educational excellence. The total per-pupil annual school expenditure is somewhere in the neighborhood of $2,500, and because Richard K. Hart is a new building, its appropriations included sufficient monies for extensive multimedia resources, instructional packages, supplies, and technological equipment.

This early childhood center houses 300 pupils and boasts a staff of 12 full-time teachers, one secretary, one principal, one principal's assistant, six paraprofessionals, and two student teachers (every semester). Local parents have indicated an interest in assisting the teachers to activate the center (many mothers are former teachers), but no training program has been formulated. Therefore, the principal has not as yet utilized this volunteer service.

You are a visitor to the Hart Early Childhood Center. You enter and are immediately drawn to the breathtaking panoramas visible through each glassed wall. It is a lovely, warm, sun-drenched day, but you notice that no children are outdoors and no doors are open.

Children are clustered in various sections of the inner center areas. They are reading books, making charts, reading graphs, painting, playing with blocks and other games, or just talking to each other or to one of the available adults. Around the outside walls of the center are low bookcases, children's waist-high movable closets, boxes with materials that are still unpacked, and cartons of pupil-made booklets, reports, dolls, or creative arts.

At the middle of the center is a series of round tables that have been established as instructional areas. These "learning stations" each hold some math games, some blocks, a few brushes, two puppets, two basal readers entitled "Dick and Jane," a microscope, and some beads. No one is working at any of them. The "game tables" hold blocks, paints, a few transparencies that appear to be torn, a child's lost hat, and a huge fire engine protruding from under one of the tables. There are approximately 20 carpet squares under one of the game tables and many additional ones scattered about the center.

The 300 children appear to have been equally divided among the 12 professional teachers. Each "team" of pupils and a teacher have appropriated a part of the center for themselves. The beautiful open-spaced feeling of the building appears to be diminished by the clutter of children and resources. Wherever you walk, children are either engaged in silent reading (very young children for so many to be reading) or drawing, or are involved in independent "quiet" activity. The teachers, although they do interact with individual youngsters who seek their assistance, are engaged in examining materials from the partially opened supply cartons and are giving instructions to the student teachers who are trying to become familiar with the curriculum by reading the teachers' lesson plan books. Aides are running off dittos and writing children's names on workbooks, crayon boxes, and chairs.

The principal, Mr. James, extends an extremely cordial welcome to you. He graciously guides you through the Early Childhood Center, emphasizing the many independent activities in which the youngsters are engaged. He laughingly says that these pupils are so bright and so "mature" that they ". . . really don't need direction from anyone! They could work all day completely absorbed in their own interests!"

Teachers, too, are friendly and hospitable. They eagerly point out the learning stations, the game tables, and the multitude of media that is available. They admit that much of it is still unpacked, but add that they really must learn to use it themselves before they can permit the children to do so. They leave their plan books in a conspicuous place on their desks so that the principal may see how detailed and well planned they are. In actuality, a few teachers' plans reflect schedules two and three weeks in advance.

When questioned about the program, teachers quickly respond that this is "an open classroom modeled after the British Primary School." They explain that children self-select their resources, plan their own activities, and engage in them for as long as their interests are maintained. They add that this is "an integrated day approach."

You look around the center. The children *do* seem absorbed. There are few incidents of boisterousness or conflict. Children everywhere are working quietly, appear to be self-directed, and occasionally interact with the adults in the area. When a child does solicit counseling, the adults are responsive and warm, and in short, simple statements, they respond to the child's questions. Some children wander around and talk to each other and do not seem to mind the cluttered environment. If there is interaction with the available resources, the child who selects the materials uses them until finished, at which point another child may select them.

Individual or Group Assignment for Case Study 1

A. List all the behaviors that appear to be *inappropriate* to or absent from an effective instructional environment.

Child Behaviors	Adult Behaviors
1.	1.
2.	2.
3.	3.
4.	4.
5.	5.
6.	6.
7.	7.
8.	8.
9.	9.
10.	10.
11.	11.
12.	12.
13.	13.
14.	14.
15.	15.
16.	16.
17.	17.
18.	18.
19.	19.
20.	20.

B. List the major problems in need of correction and describe what should be done to improve the teaching-learning situation.

Problems	Procedures to Improve the Teaching-Learning Situation
1.	1.
2.	2.
3.	3.
4.	4.
5.	5.

Alternative Responses to Case Study 1: "Analyzing the Innovative Primary School"

A. List all the behaviors that appear to be inappropriate to an effective instructional environment.

Child Behaviors	Adult Behaviors
1. Students did not ask to use the outdoor facilities.	1. The principal had made no attempt to train parent volunteers.

2. Children did not use the instructional areas correctly.
3. Children did not organize their learning materials.
4. Students did not take care of, share or repair materials.

5. Students did not use the special equipment and supplies.

6. Students seemed to rely heavily on reading as the main form of learning or relaxation.

7. Students selected their own curriculum all the time.

8. Children read silently to themselves; no small group work or tutoring occurred.
9. Students worked independently all the time, never with a partner, peers or groups.
10. Students worked on their own interests without regard to their aptitudes, needs or skills.
11. Resources were not used much.

12. Children did not use media equipment.

13. Children determined their own learning activities and use of resources without direction most of the time.
14. Self-selection of activities seemed independent and focused primarily on reading or drawing.
15. The children's learning activities were not integrated with any topic or field.

2. The principal and teachers did not use parent volunteers at all.
3. The staff did not take advantage of the outdoor facilities.
4. The staff had not unpacked and sorted boxes of materials before school opened.
5. The staff had not organized the materials for learning experiences.
6. The teachers did not train pupils to work with objectives, select from among approved alternatives, follow through on options, assess themselves, etc.
7. Carpet squares were not used appropriately, or at all by teachers.
8. Teachers did not coordinate student activities.

9. Teachers did not give students prescriptions of any kind.

10. Open space was not utilized properly for appropriate instructional areas by teachers.
11. Learning activities seemed spontaneous but without direction from teachers.

12. Teachers used plan books and did not provide individual prescriptions.

13. Teachers used instructional time to unpack and examine supplies.

14. Student teachers were not participating in instruction during class time.

15. Aides were doing secretarial chores.

16. Children did not assess their own work.

16. The principal did not require teachers to correct inappropriate teaching techniques.

17. The pupils did not work in accord with their learning styles.

17. The teachers planned two and three weeks in advance without diagnosing, evaluating, or establishing an appropriate instructional environment.

18. Children did not report to anyone concerning work they had completed.

18. Teachers did not correctly describe their program; open education, the British Primary School or the "integrated day" were not accurate.

19. The principal did not recognize that some students require a great deal of structure and that most students require some.

B. List the major problems in need of correction and describe what should be done to improve the teaching/learning situation.

Problems	*Procedures to Improve the Teaching-Learning Situation*
1. Staff misunderstanding of open education, integrated day, etc.	1. In-service workshops and continuing planning with aides, principal and student teachers.
2. Lack of an effective individualized approach.	2. Program to develop diagnoses, prescriptions, organized resources, learning activities, reporting alternatives, evaluation, etc. (entire staff).
3. Poor utilization of space, indoors and out.	3. Redesign of instructional areas, correct placement of bookcases and other furniture, establishment of alcoves for small groups; development of appropriate resources at learning stations, interest centers, media corners, etc.
4. Lack of objectives, diagnosis, prescriptions and assessment activities.	4. Use of consultants and workshops to accomplish the redesign.
5. Non-use of media and resources.	5. Use of aids and secretaries, with librarian and media specialist, to establish media corners, materials at different levels, multisensory resources, etc.
6. Non-use of volunteer parents.	6. Workshops for parents and all other interested community personnel.

Case Study 2: Visiting the Beach Elementary School

You have made arrangements to visit the Beach Elementary School in Flower Bay, a small school district that has always been rather "traditional." The Beach School has a new principal, a young man named Robert Whitney who recently transferred from a low socioeconomic district in a large mid-western city. Mr. Whitney, an individualization enthusiast, provided demonstration lessons and in-service sessions for those members of his faculty who were interested. As a result, some movement toward individualization has taken place.

You enter the school and are greeted by a "task force" of sixth-grade students who have been assigned to guide you to the first discussion area. There, you are introduced to Mr. Whitney and two teachers who have volunteered to share their coffee break with you to explain the school's emerging program. You are seated, offered a cup of coffee, and given a resume of what has happened to date.

The teachers explain that only 12 of the current 30-member faculty have begun individualizing. Many of the remaining teachers have been experimenting with some of the new techniques but have elected to "go slowly" and to see how the others fare. Parents have been involved in the training process and are assisting the 12 teachers by preparing stencils and dittos, correcting papers when requested, reading textbook passages into tape recorders to assist children who have difficulty learning to read or who read poorly, working with below-level youngsters to reinforce concepts and information, and helping to supervise students as they operate equipment and media.

All of the 12 teachers have introduced several small-group techniques to their classes so that youngsters might begin to work independently without constant teacher guidance and supervision. They admit that these techniques work well with many youngsters, but that some students appear to be resistant to functioning without continuous direction. For these, the parent aides have been assigned to persuade, encourage and help such students through the learning process.

You are invited to walk through the building and to view those classrooms in which the 12 teachers have begun to individualize. You are given a list of the 12 rooms and a map of the school. Another team of students guide you to the first room. They politely explain that beyond this point the building tour is "self-explanatory." Before the students leave you ask, "How do you like individualization?" The youngsters laugh, shrug their shoulders, and say "It's all right!" They giggle and leave for their own classes.

You enter the first room. The room is arranged differently from any you have ever seen. There are only ten or 12 desks in the room, but many "instructional areas" and chairs for the 30 youngsters you count. A lounge sofa is used as a room divider toward the far right and several carpeted areas extend into corners and nooks where students are crouched over books, charts, media, and other instructional materials. Tables appear to form a nucleus of learning areas and large, well-printed signs announce: Mathematics Learning Station, Media Corner, Game Table, Little Theater, Interest Center, and Magic Carpet. The room appears to be a hub of activity as children interact freely, but quietly, moving from area to area with purpose and at their option.

You walk to the section called Interest Center and note the multitude of reading materials on varied levels. Three or four pupils are working together to achieve the objectives listed for them on their contract, but each of the students is using a different text.

You inspect the game table where some students are creating a game about the life of Benjamin Franklin and others are doing a crossword puzzle on George Washington. At the media corner two boys are beginning to project the filmstrip they have just completed on John Paul Jones.

Along the side of the bookcases are several different dittos labeled "Circle of Knowledge," "Team Learning," "Case Study," and "Simulations." You ask a few of the students what these are and they tell you that they are ways for the students to learn more about the heroes they have been studying. You pick up the ditto called "Team Learning" and note that the question on it is: "Name as many American heroines as you can in three minutes." The ditto on simulations has several paragraphs describing the way Molly Pitcher demonstrated bravery when her husband was killed at his post, and is followed by two kinds of questions. Somewhere in the material the answers can be found to the first type of question. The youngsters must think through answers to the other type of questions according to their opinions, the persuasive arguments of others, the insights they gain, etc. This is sometimes done through "roles" that the youngsters play based on descriptions of the parts they select for the simulation.

The walls are attractively covered with commercially produced charts that describe the economic bases for revolution. You wonder why they are displayed and ask a pupil whether this is an area of study for the class. The child responds that the chart is part of the *next* unit the class will be studying and that the teacher is trying to arouse the group's interest and curiosity in the topic by exposing the children to the display.

In the second room you visit, you notice that whereas small groups are busily involved in mathematics games and assignments, others are reading with the teacher, individuals are working on science experiments, and still others appear to be tutoring each other. The board has a series of assignments on it in each of the four major curriculum areas and also lists several alternatives in the creative arts. When questioned about this procedure, some of the students explain that they do have required work that must be done but that they may complete the exercises anytime at all within a two-day period. "What happens to the students who *don't* complete their work?" you ask. "They can't learn as much!" the students quickly reply.

In walking around the room you notice that although children are engaged in different activities, those who are involved in the same curriculum area are using identical materials, i.e., the same basal reader, the same

Photo 8-3. These youngsters are involved in solving a problem through small-group analysis. (Photograph courtesy of Merrick Junior High School, Bellmore-Merrick, New York.)

social studies text on the same page, the same science experiments, and the same mathematics exercises. The tapes that are available also appear to be on the same topic and at one level.

The teacher is so engrossed in individual discussions with pupils that she does not have time to speak with you, other than to nod politely. While she is talking to students, six other children appear to be vying for her attention. The youngsters around her wait, often impatiently, to receive answers to their questions.

You note that the morning has flown by quickly and that it is time for lunch. You leave the class and begin to walk toward the principal's office when you realize that groups of youngsters are walking unescorted through the halls to the cafeteria. They are talking zealously, but without much noise. One or two *do* run, but they are quickly blocked by slower moving children who will not be pushed aside. The runners slow down and alter their pace. You wonder what happened to the teachers of these pupils and whether the students are permitted to walk to their lunch area without an escort.

You then notice a teacher walking with nine pupils in the same general direction. Looking at the nine, you guess that they are probably nonconformists. One places a hand on the boy in front of him and pushes surreptitiously. Another trips a child passing alongside, while a third snatches the hat off the head of a girl directly in front. The teacher with the nine walks slowly, keeping each of the children within close range. As they begin to misbehave, she stops, rearranges the group, reprimands the instigators, and then walks on with them.

You begin to reflect on what you have seen that morning. You wonder which behavioral patterns are associated directly with the concept of ''individualization'' and which are not necessarily designed to promote individual student growth.

Individual or Group Assignment for Case Study 2

A. List every *correct* or *appropriate* (a) student behavior, (b) adult behavior, and (c) behavioral outcome evidenced in this case study.

Correct Student Behaviors	*Correct Adult Behaviors*	*Correct Behavioral Outcomes*
1.	1.	1.
2.	2.	2.
3.	3.	3.
4.	4.	4.
5.	5.	5.
6.	6.	6.
7.	7.	7.
8.	8.	8.
9.	9.	9.
10.	10.	10.
11.	11.	11.
12.	12.	12.
13.	13.	13.
14.	14.	14.
15.	15.	15.
16.	16.	16.
17.	17.	17.
18.	18.	18.

B. List every *incorrect* or *questionable* (a) student behavior, (b) adult behavior, and (c) behavioral outcome evidenced in this case study.

Incorrect Student Behaviors	*Incorrect Adult Behaviors*	*Incorrect Behavioral Outcomes*
1.	1.	1.
2.	2.	2.
3.	3.	3.
4.	4.	4.
5.	5.	5.
6.	6.	6.
7.	7.	7.
8.	8.	8.
9.	9.	9.
10.	10.	10.
11.	11.	11.
12.	12.	12.
13.	13.	13.
14.	14.	14.
15.	15.	15.

Photos 8-4, 8-5, 8-6, 8-7. In this well-organized individualized classroom, students have been trained to complete their objectives independently. The teacher, Joan Lowenthal, is free to move from one small group of students to another, thus providing many opportunities for personal and close teacher-student involvement. (Photographs courtesy of the Seaford Manor Elementary School, Seaford, New York.)

Photo 8-5

Photo 8-6

Alternative Responses to Case Study 2: "Visiting the Beach Elementary School"

A. List every *correct* or *appropriate* individualized student and adult behavior and behavioral outcome evidenced in this case study.

Appropriate Student Behaviors	Appropriate Adult Behaviors	Appropriate Behavioral Outcomes
1. Students were serving as guides for visitors.	1. The administrator provided in-service sessions and demonstration lessons for interested faculty.	1. The administrator provided leadership toward instructional improvement.
2. Students worked toward completion of their objectives . . .	2. Teachers volunteered to acquaint visitors with their program.	2. Teachers were permitted to volunteer to individualize and, therefore, were treated as individuals by the administrator.
3. . . . through their own learning style.	3. Parent volunteers assisted teachers.	3. The program was described as "emerging" and teachers were permitted to move toward individualization at their own rate.
4. Students used multilevel and varied instructional resources in room #1.	4. Teachers used small-group techniques (the first step toward individualization).	4. Room #1 was divided into instructional areas.
5. Students created resources and used them.	5. Parent aides worked directly with students who required adult assistance.	5. Parent involvement permitted more effective use of teacher time.

Photo 8-7

6. Students in room #2 were permitted to self-schedule their activities.

7. Students were permitted to walk through the halls without direct supervision and most did so politely.
8. Students were actively involved in their own learning.

9. Unescorted students who ran through the corridors were blocked properly by other children.

10. Children worked well together (perfecting multimedia or actually developing filmstrips).
11. Children learned from each other. (When a person teaches, he learns from the experience.)
12. Self-discipline was practiced.
13. Peer discipline was apparent.

6. Teachers escorted those youngsters who had not demonstrated ability to conduct themselves responsibly without supervision.
7. Teachers disciplined students when necessary.

8. Teachers permitted self-pacing and self-selection of sociological pairs and groups.
9. An attempt was made to ask high-level questions about Molly Pitcher.

10. Aides worked with those who learned more slowly.

6. Parent volunteers had been trained.

7. Walls were attractively covered, to "arouse group interest and curiosity."

8. Varied materials and multimedia resources were evident in both rooms.

9. Individualizing techniques included student latitude on time, method, and order of completing assignments.
10. An active but not frenetic classroom with self-directed learning was observable.
11. Dittoed questions went beyond the detailed factual materials ordinarily used.
12. Wall displays were used to stimulate learning.

14. Children worked on a project together but used different texts.
15. Small groups were active
and involved in varied
techniques.
16. Children interacted in
small groups through peer
sharing.

B. List every *inappropriate* (a) student behavior, (b) adult behavior, and (c) behavioral outcome evidenced in this case study.

Inappropriate Student Behaviors	Inappropriate Adult Behaviors	Inappropriate Behavioral Outcomes
1. Students should not have developed a filmstrip at the game table. (Instructional areas should be correctly used to facilitate student progress.)	1. Parents assisted only the 12 teachers involved in individualizing, rather than all.	1. In-service training is completely optional. Faculty should be exposed to techniques and then permitted to gradually adapt or discard them. Some teachers waiting to see "how others fare" may have been rationalizing their inactivity.
2. The students in room #2 had single-level resources only and even these were limited in number.	2. The principal seemed enthusiastic about individualization, but did not correct the apparent inconsistencies in the program, e.g., incorrectly established instructional areas, single-level resources in room #2, etc.	2. Most teachers had not begun to individualize instruction.
3. Basal readers should not be used in an individualized reading program.	3. Parent aides were asked to help students who did not learn in groups. (Not all children can learn in groups.)	3. Room #1 had language arts learning station resources (multilevel, single curriculum materials) inappropriately placed at an "interest center" (which should house interdisciplinary resources).
4. Children giggled and shrugged inarticulately when asked about individualization. Children needed to know more about individualization to explain the concept rather than merely to guide visitors to physical facilities.	4. Parents worked only with below-level students.	4. Some specialized areas were not well-utilized for their own unique purposes.
5. Room #2 was not individualized. Everyone involved in the same curriculum was using identical materials at the same time.	5. Children who did not complete work were not necessarily helped, nor was the work modified for them.	5. The dittoed "team learning" was a circle of knowledge; the simulation was a team learning that utilized role playing. The small-group instructional techniques were being incorrectly used.

6. Children had no involvement in the selection of topics of study.

7. Children tried to get the teacher's attention in room #2 without a set system. They were impatient and wasting time. (The teacher's role should be shared with other adults and students as resource people.)

8. The children appeared to be involved in essentially cognitive learning. No attempt was made to develop the student's affective or psychomotor characteristics. (To be whole people, we need more than cognitive learning. There is little evident expression of feeling indicated in either room.)

6. Children's materials were not posted to give recognition, to encourage creativity, and to evaluate progress.

7. Parents appeared to be disciplining and repeating instead of finding new ways of approaching the students.

8. Teacher efforts were directed toward cognitive learning only.

9. There were no teacher diagnoses of a child's inability to complete work.

10. Quality and quantity of assignments were not reassessed by teachers.

11. There was no evidence of evaluation (which is an integral part of the learning process) in either room.

12. There was no indication in room #1 that children had any exposure to science. Although there was a mathematics learning station indicated, there is no mention of anything being studied except social studies in terms of the American Revolution. (Science and math could well be integrated into this topic.)

13. No individual prescription was in operation; the same basal reader, experiments, and math problems were assigned to all.

6. Commercially produced wall charts were used. These are not as desirable as those that are student-designed.

7. Representative materials should have related directly to current (and not future) studies.

8. The teacher should have taught her students to continue work in an area where they may progress independently while waiting for her assistance. No system had been established for obtaining help when necessary.

9. Specific individualization techniques are an important part of training teachers; these were not apparent.

10. Team learning should be used to introduce new material, not for reinforcement as was the case here.

Case Study 3: Diagnosing a New Social Studies Program at the Urban Junior High School Level

You have been invited to visit an urban school system's newly established social studies program for grades 7 and 8. The information distributed included a detailed account of an individualized sequence on a contract basis that provided for many student options.

When you arrived, the chairman of the department pleasantly outlined the modus operandi of the program. Students are given:

1. Behavioral objectives for a given unit,
2. A listing of the books that contain the information they will need to learn,
3. A series of activities that they must complete,
4. A test to determine whether they may (a) proceed to the next unit, or (b) be given "remediation."

You are advised that, although the program is only in its sixth month of operation, the students are achieving beyond grade level and that many have completed 15 to 18 instructional units (almost the equivalent of both seventh- and eighth-grade social studies requirements). You are shown individual student folders containing the contracts and related tests that have been completed by the student. When asked for examples of activities that students selected, the chairman turned to the contract page entitled "activities" and showed you the following list:

Contract Activities[2]

Marquette, Francis, *Understanding India* (Englewood Cliffs, N.J.: Prentice-Hall, 1964), pp. 168-193. Do Exercises I, II, III, and IV on pp. 185, 193, 195-199.

Kleinmann, Murray and Saunders, John J, *The Fables of Southeastern Asia* (Nyack, New York: Parker Publishers, 1945). Complete "Ten Eastern Myths" on pp. 204-209 and "Heroes of Southeastern Asia" on pp. 145, 173, 196-197, and 256. Also review the birthplaces of at least four Asiatic women who actively participated in the move toward democratic socialism.

White, Ellis, *The Migrating Indian Student Population* (California: The University of California Press, 1952). Complete any eight exercises at the end of Chapters 2-11 with 100% proficiency.

Dancis, Bernice *Opening Up the Classroom in Indian Elementary Schools* (New York: The Catalyst Press, 1972). Compare your perceptions of our social studies program with Professor Dancis' recommendations for increasing student responsibility. Write a four-page essay describing the comparisons as you see them.

Increasing the Crop Yieldage in Asia (Washington, D.C.: Bureau of Agriculture, 1970). List the specific recommendations made for crop yield increases and indicate which Bureaus in the Indian governmental structure are directly responsible for implementing these suggestions. What do you think the results of United States cooperation with Indian agricultural experts will be?

You are escorted into a corridor that "houses" six different classrooms and are encouraged to visit each of the classes as you wish.

In the first room students appear to be busily engaged in reading and writing activities. The teacher is sitting with a small group of four youngsters discussing the effect of monsoons in India, and you notice that she is tape recording the session. If students need assistance they walk over to one of their peers and ask for information. The atmosphere is relaxed and informal, though industrious.

As you walk among the students, you notice that several contracts are in use at one time. For example, three boys each have a contract on "Indian Agriculture," one young lady is working on a contract entitled "The Role of Women in Indian Politics," and a few youngsters are exploring "A Mini-contract on Indian Health Codes." At your right are three very engrossed students working on something called "Contract: An Introduction to India." As you look over the shoulders of the students you realize that the topic of India must have been subdivided into several smaller phases. You wonder why this was done and make a mental note to ask the chairman.

A lively atmosphere greets you in the next room. Students are sprawled about on carpets, in chairs, on desks and against the bookcases. Two youngsters are knee-deep in clay, having constructed a huge Asiatic temple replete with Buddha and jeweled serpents. The detail work is amazing, and the students are only too happy to describe the ways in which they researched the dimensions and accoutrements of their miniature edifice.

The teacher is observing a group of seven students dramatizing a skit they wrote depicting the Indian Legislature in session. A tall, dark eighth grader is impersonating Mrs. Ghandi in argument with Mahatma Ghandi over the role of governmental regulations concerning independence. The actress vehemently declares, "One day I will lead India into a new age—an aggressive one wherein India may again take her rightful leadership place in the community of nations!" The teacher and several student observers applaud enthusiastically. The teacher then asks, "How old would Mrs. Ghandi have had to have been if she had *actually* participated in this conversation with Mahatma Ghandi?"

Several students appear to be oblivious of the varied activities in the room and are absorbed in reading from what appears to be books of encyclopedic proportions. One of the young men explained that "Bob's dad is the local librarian and he lets us take out anything we want to for our projects! He even comes in on his lunch hour on Tuesdays and Thursdays and teaches us how to find the kinds of things that interest us."

"Are other parents involved?" you ask. "Oh yes," the student responds. "Anytime we need to visit a place or interview someone for our contract, loads of parents come in to take us! We don't have to go where everyone else does; we can select our own places! Then Mrs. Newman (the teacher) lets us go with the parent escorts. They're great! They help us with our questions. When we're embarrassed they tell us how to ask the important questions so that they make sense to the people we're interviewing.

Afterwards, if we want them to, they come into class and help us to write our reports in interesting ways, or to make projects on what we've learned. Then we present them to the class. We've got lots of parents helping us!''

''Another good thing that happens,'' one student adds, ''is that our own parents begin to understand what we're doing. They want to be part of the action too! My dad took a day off from the Telephone Company to be a parent escort when Freddie and Jimmy wanted to go to the United Nations to see real Indian people. Since Dad was going, I went too. You should have seen him! He ain't afraid of anybody! He walked us right up to the Indian delegation and explained that he was a parent escort from J.H.S. #9. He introduced himself and us to the ambassador—or somebody—and then they asked us into their offices! They showed us a film about India and gave us more pamphlets than we could carry. Dad even had an idea to invite them to visit us here at school!''

''His father'll really do it!'' another boy added admiringly. ''He's got guts!''

The third room on the corridor was very quiet. Media had been established so that the room resembled a resource area where youngsters could come at will and use the tape recorders, filmstrips, films, and other software in leisure. Students were working quietly without adult supervision

Photos 8-8, 8-9. This social studies class engages in a variety of activities simultaneously. While a few of the students research needed information, others record notes taken from a filmstrip-tape presentation and two youngsters in the rear are using a game to reinforce their knowledge. The teacher is working with a fourth group (not shown) and a volunteer parent is assisting with map interpretation. (Photographs courtesy of Seaford Junior High School, Seaford, New York.)

and once, when a piece of film broke, two youngsters automatically stopped what they were doing to assist another by repairing it.

Before you could go further, the chairman caught up with you and reminded you that it was lunch time. You were surprised that the time had gone so quickly. All in all you were pleased with many parts of the program you had seen, although you believed that you could make many suggestions for improvement.

Photo 8-9

Photos 8-10, 8-11. Mary Juillerat, after seven years of teaching whole groups, has devoted the last three "to individual student needs through appropriate diagnosis and prescription." She uses learning disability tests, past records, teacher comments and interviews, case study analysis, observation, and the self-tests of students to design highly focused and appropriate tapes, multisensory materials, and large-typeface printed matter. Here two youngsters check self-assessment materials together while the student in Photo 8-11 uses a clear plastic geography puzzle as tactile reinforcement. (Photographs courtesy of the Robert E. Bell Middle School, Chappaqua, New York.)

Photo 8-11

Individual or Group Diagnosis for Case Study 3

A. List the specific student behaviors that demonstrated the program's strengths and weaknesses.

B. List the specific adult behaviors that demonstrated the program's strengths and weaknesses.

C. List the behavioral outcomes that demonstrated the program's strengths and weaknesses.

D. Itemize the recommendations that you would offer if you were a member of a consultant team invited to suggest improvements for (a) the program, (b) the first classroom, (c) the second classroom and (d) the media room.

Alternative Responses to Case Study 3:
"Diagnosing a New Social Studies Program"

A. List the specific student behaviors that demonstrated the program's strengths and weaknesses.

Student Behaviors That Demonstrated Program Strengths	*Student Behaviors That Demonstrated Program Weaknesses*
It was observed that students:	
1. Were actively using contracts to learn.	1. Did not assume sufficient responsibility for aspects of field

			work and might have been developing an overreliance on parental assistance.
2. Assisted each other.		2.	In room #1 were not using media and appeared to be learning essentially through reading and writing; students were not permitted to learn through their perceptual strengths; multimedia resources should be available.
3. Were using varied, individual, or minicontracts.		3.	In room #1 were not observed planning or evaluating and there was little evidence of interaction among peers except for assistance.
4. Learned in accordance with their own learning style.		4.	In room #1 did not appear to be learning in accordance with their learning style; rather, there seemed to be a conformity of behavior and little creativity evidenced.
5. Used their creative abilities to reinforce the information they had acquired.		5.	In room #2 varied in their understanding of the focus of the U.N. visit and reduced it to an evaluation of parental behavior.
6. Learned in varied depth despite the fact that they appeared to focus on the same curriculum topic at one time.		6.	In room #2 who were involved in role playing, incorrectly paired Mrs. Ghandi and Mahatma Ghandi in a conversation that could never have occurred in actual time; they therefore had acquired misinformation that had not been checked previously.
7. Worked independently, in pairs, and in small groups either with peers or with the teacher or other adults.			
8. Explained their program to visitors and demonstrated an understanding of the procedures.			
9. Used multimedia.			

10. Demonstrated responsibility and worked well without direct supervision.	
11. Were capable of using, sharing and repairing the software.	
12. Described positive experiences to several persons in a variety of settings that related to the instructional program.	

B. List the specific adult behaviors that demonstrated the program's strengths and weaknesses.

Adult Behaviors That Demonstrated Program Strengths	*Adult Behaviors That Demonstrated Program Weaknesses*
It was observed that:	
1. Teachers were actively involved with students in the instructional setting.	1. Teachers did not prepare effective and correctly individualized contracts.
2. Teachers worked with students in small groups, presumably on the basis of diagnosis or interest.	2. Teachers used narrow reading assignments for "contract activities." They did not provide multisensory resources.
3. In room #1 the teacher was tape-recording a lesson, presumably to provide reinforcement for slow learners, access for absentees, and advanced information for students who wished to proceed independently.	3. Teachers did not permit student selection of varied activities.
4. In room #2 the teacher showed appreciation of student efforts (applause) while simultaneously correcting errors ("How old would Mrs. Ghandi have had to have been if she had actually participated in this conversation?").	4. Teachers did not provide varied learning stations, interest centers, game tables and other instructional areas.

5. Teachers provided a wide variety of learning activities and encouraged creative expression.	5. Teachers did not provide a variety of evaluation procedures.
6. Teachers permitted (encouraged) students to use multimedia facilities.	6. Teachers did not provide or encourage small-group interaction.
7. Teachers did not dominate the classroom. Within limitations, students were permitted many options to learn from among prescribed alternatives, to use the resources available, and to select how they would learn.	7. The chairman did not correct any of the contract errors or implementation procedures. (He may not have recognized them).

Photo 8-12. Jeanne Merlino, who has been teaching for nine years, designed special materials at different levels for basic mathematics "out of a conviction that present materials were inadequate for some students' needs." She indicated that time, space, contracts and assignments tailored to individual ability had to be found for middle school students who obviously had different knowledge and ability in fractions, decimals and preliminary algebra. (Photograph courtesy of the Robert E. Bell Middle School, Chappaqua, New York.)

8. Teachers provided students with one alternative individualized approach to learning.	8. The chairman's use of the phrase "beyond grade level" evidenced a graded orientation rather than an individualized approach.
9. The chairman described pupil achievement and evidenced knowledge of the program and its procedures.	9. Teachers did not provide for student self-selection and development of contracts.
10. The literature disseminated by the administration emphasized individualization, the contract method, student options, and an invitation to visit, suggesting a clearly defined approach to individualization, specific objectives, and a willingness to demonstrate progress toward that goal.	
11. The chairman permitted visitors to observe classes that were moving toward individualization without constant supervision, therefore suggesting that he believed they would see what the literature had described.	
12. The chairman evidenced supportiveness for the instructional approach, through praise of student achievement, descriptions of the procedures and invitations to visit.	
13. The chairman initially oriented the visitors and later returned to culminate the tour and presumably to respond to questions.	

Photos 8-13, 8-14. As students become increasingly independent, they are granted more and more options to select and design objectives, to use alternate resources, to schedule their work, and to design their own prescriptions. The young ladies on the carpeting are learning through teacher-made cassette tapes; the young lady at the objectives chart is beginning to record her progress. (Photographs courtesy of Briarcliff High School, Briarcliff Manor, New York.)

Photo 8-14

C. List the behavioral outcomes that demonstrated the program's strengths and weaknesses.

Behavioral Outcomes That Demonstrate Program Strengths	*Behavioral Outcomes That Demonstrate Program Weaknesses*
1. The students were evaluated to determine the effect of the system on their achievement.	1. The contracts were written incorrectly. A contract should include behavioral objectives, alternative resources, activities, and reporting procedures. A contract should be part of a Contract Activity Package that includes, in addition to the above, a diagnostic test, a self-assessment, and a terminal teacher assessment.
2. Individual folders were maintained for each student, facilitating an organized approach to prescription and evaluation on an individual basis.	2. Students should be provided with alternative resources through which to learn (preferably multimedia, multilevel and multisensory); they certainly should not be given "... a listing of the books ..." as the only resource.
3. Teachers were using an interdisciplinary approach to their contract development as evidenced in the contract topics and activities.	3. "Activities" should be selected by the students from among alternatives; they should not be mandated without some option. "Activities" are alternative means by which students may use, in a creative way, the information they have learned through the resources. The purpose of the activities is to provide practical application of learning to assist in retention. Effective "activities" are not assignments as described in the sample contract page shown to the visitors.

4. The "independence" exhibited by the students was an outcome of their training.	4. Varied instructional areas were not provided for students, thereby necessitating use of a media room. This is not necessarily a weakness, but it does indicate a lack.
5. Teachers either had provided students with multiple contracts or had diagnosed students and then prescribed contracts on an individual basis.	5. Tests seemed to be the only evaluative technique used.
6. The classrooms appeared to be well organized and students appeared to be self-directed; these would be outcomes of training.	6. Students did not have opportunities for small group interactions, sharing, or instructional techniques.
7. Teachers involved appropriate community residents in positive ways (verbalized).	7. Teachers were not observed to be interacting with each other. In fact, the strengths of one classroom were lacking in the second and vice versa. Teacher co-planning might have eliminated some of the weaknesses of the program.
8. Teachers used the community resources for instructional purposes (verbalized).	8. Behavioral objectives were included incorrectly among the "activities" (their mandated resources).
9. Parents cooperated and contributed to the program (verbalized).	9. The sharp division of classes might have contributed to the preclusion of a better integrated program.
10. Students were able to locate, use, share and repair media; this would be an outcome of training.	10. There was no evidence of diagnosis prior to contract prescription.
	11. Volunteer parents or community citizens were not present in the media room to provide adult assistance in an emergency.

	12. No provision was evidenced for what students do after they have completed the seventh- and eighth-grade curriculum.
	13. There was no evidence of student input into the contract designs. Had students been trained to write contracts, they could have developed their own (upon satisfactory completion of required studies).

It would also seem important to have a professional in the central media room—a librarian or teacher—to help students locate what they are looking for, to make suggestions, and to order appropriate multilevel materials. If that were not possible, a parent could fulfill some of these functions.

Children, however, seem to have been well-instructed in the care and use of media and were helpful to each other.

The media room could also be used to make filmstrips and tapes, etc.

D. If you were a member of a consultant team invited to make specific suggestions for improvement of (a) the overall program, (b) the first classroom, (c) the second classroom, and/or (d) the media room, what would you suggest?

The Overall Program

1. A series of workshops should be scheduled for teachers and administrators. The following topics should be covered:
   a. writing contract activity packages that include behavioral objectives, resource alternatives, activity alternatives, reporting alternatives, and diagnostic tests, self-assessment and terminal teacher instruments.
   b. using small-group techniques to begin individualizing instruction (circle of knowledge, team learning, brainstorming, group analysis, etc.).
   c. the use of multimedia in the classroom.
   d. team-writing of contracts that could be used on a nongraded basis.
   e. the advantages of and required skills for team teaching.
   f. other ways to individualize the programs, i.e., programed learning, instructional packages, work-study experiences, etc.
2. The administration and faculty should provide for more student input into the planning of the program.
3. Establish dialog among administration, teachers and students to determine the best organizational pattern to meet the instructional and functional needs of all (no-bell, modular scheduling, open campus, sphere of interest, etc.).

4. Establish more alternatives for the social studies program (not just the use of assignment contracts).

Photos 8-15, 8-16, 8-17. Having used contracts, multisensory instructional packages, programed learning, small-group techniques, and activity and reporting alternatives, Phil Nespecca, who has taught six years, says unequivocally, "Today's students demand and deserve varied instructional approaches. They revitalize the classroom and make teaching and learning exciting!" (Photographs courtesy of Baldwin Harbor Junior High School, Baldwin, New York.)

Photo 8-16

Photo 8-17

The First Classroom

1. Introduce the teacher to alternate instructional approaches to the curriculum (aside from reading and writing).
2. Introduce the teacher to the richness of various activity and reporting alternatives.
3. Suggest that she team with her colleague in room 2 whose class is also learning about India but using different techniques.
4. Suggest that she enlist more parental cooperation to help her implement this new program.
5. Bring multimedia resources into the classroom so that students may use materials under supervision and in conjunction with other learning activities.
6. Introduce the teacher to alternative ways of evaluating students.

The Second Classroom

1. Suggest that the teacher in room 2 team with her colleague in room 1 to share their strengths.
2. Introduce the teacher to effectively designed contracts.
3. Establish parent workshops to discuss with them how they may best assist in the classroom. Discuss the parent's role of helping and guiding students so that youngsters become responsible for their own learning and behavior.
4. Help the teacher to develop instructional areas (interest centers, learning stations, media corners, little theaters, etc.).

The Media Room

1. The media room should not only be a repository of resources but, in addition, it should have facilities for moving equipment and material to individual classrooms.
2. A teacher-librarian should be present if possible. Otherwise, a parent volunteer could be enlisted so that students could be helped in all aspects of research and use of multimedia.

3. This room should also house pictures, books, magazines, vertical files and any other resource material needed by classes.
4. It should also be a place where additional media is designed, constructed and created.

Case Study 4: Adding Structure to a Community High School Program

The entrance hall of the Community School Building in Whitmore, New York, was empty and dark when Meredith Kane entered at 9:30 Monday morning. "No one's here again," she mused. "I must be dumb to believe that the kids will be here and anxious to learn on Monday morning!" She stepped inside, turned on the lights to the inner lounge area, and stepped into the office with the day's mail in her hands.

She heard steps just outside the door and Meredith's heart jumped! "It's happened at last," she thought. "Some kid cared enough to drag himself out of bed before noon!" She turned quickly toward the door in anticipation, only to find Will Brewster, the school's director.

"Don't look so disappointed," Will laughed. "Were you expecting students?" Meredith nodded. "What went wrong with this program, Will? We planned it so well! Administrative support! Community support! Direct student and teacher involvement! How could any venture so lovingly designed fall apart so quickly and thoroughly?"

"Have you read the 'Village School' story?" Brewster asked. "It takes time. . ."

"Time for what?"

"Time for kids to realize they want to learn. Starting a community school is only exciting at the beginning. It takes lots of work to get it over the dull, difficult, uninteresting moments as well as the apathy and minor problems."

"Like getting out of bed before noon so that classes might begin on time occasionally?" Meredith asked. "Or remaining through one whole course?" She sighed in exasperation. "I think we've made a dreadful mistake," she said. "These students weren't ready for the kind of freedom we gave them."

"Maybe not," Will replied. "But maybe we weren't ready for their use of freedom in a way with which we didn't agree!"

"We spent two years listening to their gripes about the irrelevant curriculum, the mandatory classes, the meaningless assignments, the dull teachers and the restrictive regulations at the high school 'prison,'" she retorted. "Throughout that entire period I distinctly had the impression that if they could study what they themselves chose, attend classes at times that they determined, demonstrate their knowledge in ways other than tests or assignments, and select their own teachers, they'd become model students. Well, they were given all of that! Now where are they? They rarely arrive before noon, are too lazy to attend the very classes they designed, and are too unmotivated to stay with the teachers *they* selected for more than four or five sessions! I predict the board and the community will react against this lack of self-discipline and abort the entire experiment. And frankly, I don't feel it's worth continuing.''

Brewster considered her ''speech'' soberly. ''I understand your reactions. Perhaps we should have prepared the students to design and select courses more carefully than they did and to see their choices through.''

''On the other hand, wouldn't that have detracted from our efforts to aid young people to mature by giving them decision-making power as they see the need?'' she asked.

''Mature young people must also assume the responsibility for carrying through on decisions they make,'' Will replied, ''Maybe it's not too late for this group. Could we build some of these elements into our structure now? Would the students buy it?''

''Buy what?'' asked a young, vibrant girl in blue jeans and a white knit body suit who had just entered the lounge. ''What are you and Meredith so upset about?''

Meredith and Will turned to greet Janey, a junior in the high school who had just entered the community school this past term.

''We've been talking about some of the problems of the school as we see them,'' Will answered, ''and were wondering whether we could gain student support for some reforms.''

''Like what?'' Janey asked.

''Like permitting free selection of courses, but then, after the selection, mandatory attendance for the length of the course—or at least until a certain point.''

Janey's face brightened. ''That would be good,'' she said, ''then courses wouldn't break up because some kids got tired of the subject before the rest of us had a chance to really get into it! What else?''

''We don't know what else,'' said Will. ''Any suggestions?''

Janey thought. ''Some of the kids are doing great work out of classes,'' she answered. ''They shouldn't have to attend meetings if they can show they know what the rest of the kids are studying. They could take a test or give a report.'' Her eyes lit up as she warmed to the idea. ''Maybe they could *teach* the part they know. After all, we all like to learn or show what we know in different ways.''

''That's a neat idea,'' Meredith said. ''We could ask—require—that each student file a list of learning objectives to be completed and the way in which the knowledge or skills acquired could be demonstrated. Students could also write in a list of resources they'd used to learn. In that way we'd know their sources of information and could suggest others if theirs seem biased or inadequate.''

Will was getting caught up in the enthusiasm. ''How will we evaluate their learning if they use resources we haven't seen ourselves?'' he questioned.

"We can evaluate their learning on the basis of completed activities they ought to design by themselves. They could actually use the information they've learned in a creative way and then, perhaps, share it with some of the other students and us. They could evaluate their own progress, and the products of their classmates, and we could do both too. You know," Meredith added, "we're really describing contracts—contracts to complete a learning task! Maybe that's what we should have used to begin with —contracts for work-study experiences, for community contribution, for independent study and for the completion of self-selected courses! Why didn't we think of it before? That's what we need for commitment by all concerned."

The director leaned back in his chair and smiled. "If we'd been able to think of everything, there'd be no problems to solve and no need for a director!"

Janey laughed, but continued to express the thought that had been gnawing at her. "How are we going to explain the contract idea to the others so that they'll be willing to try?"

Photos 8-18, 8-19. Bill Fitzpatrick, who has taught for 11 years, has refined the contract system so that most of his industrial arts students discuss their objectives with him, select resources, and progress independently toward completion of their prescriptions. (Photographs courtesy of H. Frank Carey High School, Franklin Square, New York.)

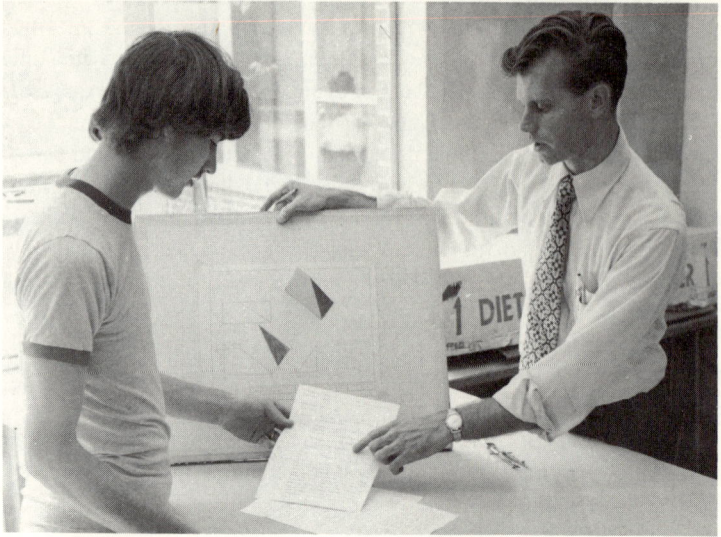

Photo 8-19

Individual or Group Assignment for Case Study 4

A. What specific behaviors are revealed in the dialog that demonstrated the program's strengths and weaknesses?

Behaviors Demonstrating Strengths	*Behaviors Demonstrating Weaknesses*
1.	1.
2.	2.
3.	3.
4.	4.
5.	5.
6.	6.
7.	7.
8.	8.
9.	9.
10.	10.
11.	11.

B. List the major problems and suggest procedures to improve the educational program at the Community High School.

Problem	*Procedure to Improve the Educational Problem*
1.	1.

2.   2.
3.   3.
4.   4.
5.   5.
6.   6.

Alternative Responses to Case Study 4: "A Community High School Program"

A. What specific behaviors are revealed in the dialog that demonstrated the program's strengths and weaknesses?

Behaviors Demonstrating Strengths	*Behaviors Demonstrating Weaknesses*
1. Administrative support.	1. Lack of sustained motivation on the part of students.
2. Community support.	2. Lack of strong expectations by the faculty.
3. Student involvement.	3. Acceptance of apathy.
4. Teacher involvement.	4. Lack of reality orientation for all concerned.
5. Concerned teacher and director.	5. Inappropriate freedom.
6. Student-selection of curriculum.	6. Lack of agreement on types of freedom.
7. Alternative means of students demonstrating their knowledge.	7. Lack of commitment on the part of students for their own schedules and selections of classes.
8. Student-selection of teachers.	8. Lack of self-discipline.
9. Student-selection of schedule.	9. Lack of structure and continuity.
10. Student decision-making opportunities.	10. Lack of training and readiness for the new approach (both teachers and students).
11. Independent study used.	11. Lack of follow-through on decisions.
12. Out-of-school studies used.	12. Lack of guidelines.
13. Bright and creative students participated.	13. Lack of assessment.
14. Willingness of staff to listen, explore, improve.	14. Lack of teaching or reporting interaction among students.
	15. Lack of specific objectives and planning of learning.

B. List the major problems and suggest procedures to improve the educational program at the Community High School.

Problem		*Procedure to Improve the Educational Problem*
1. Lack of structure.	1.	Faculty-student senate to write guidelines with power to adapt and enforce after input from all members of the school.
2. Lack of planning, commitment, involvement with others.	2.	One- to two-week planning periods to list alternative contracts with specific objectives, alternative learning resources, learning activities, reporting and teaching alternatives, self- and peer-faculty assessment.
3. Inappropriate use of time, lack of motivation, apathy.	3.	Total school involvement in establishing schedules, courses, options, and out-of-school activities with commitment sought from all through acceptance of self-selected options.

IN CONCLUSION

Education is often attacked because it is too expensive, is wasteful of human resources (the students), does not solve the problems of society, is not reality oriented, does not teach values, teaches too many values and not enough content, etc.

Individualization of the teaching-learning process provides answers for critics and a sound, evolving process that permits us to use the individual strengths of the staff as well as those of the students.

Individualized teaching and learning requires diagnosis, prescription, guidance, structure, independence, creativity, evaluation, retention and application of learning, growth, alternatives, and use of both the school and community to capitalize on the development and contribution of students and, eventually, of all members of society.

There is a caution, however. Total individualization of instruction requires more than training, knowledge, dedication and patience; it involves all of these and a total commitment to a process that must be

Photos 8-20, 8-21. Rosalie Rogers introduces seventh- and eighth-grade students to the process of individualization. Initially she works very closely with individuals and small groups but, by the time her youngsters move into the high school, they have become essentially independent. (Photographs courtesy of Briarcliff Middle School and Briarcliff High School, Briarcliff Manor, New York.)

Photo 8-21

cumulative. Unless you have been moving toward it arduously, there is no way to individualize "when school begins," "next semester," or "on Monday morning at 9:00 a.m."

For those who are beginning, proceed slowly. Introduce the first small-group technique to a class and as they begin to function effectively, introduce the second, and the third. Share your strategies with another teacher or two and exchange classes occasionally to test your ideas. Move into the planning of a learning station, a magic carpet area, and a media center and permit the students who appear to be working responsibly to study away from their desks or tables if they choose to do so. Provide alternative objectives or activities for students. Encourage them to follow through on accepted choices. Supervise them carefully so that they know that you are aware of their efforts and how well they are progressing. Redesign your instructional area.

Use programed learning materials for youngsters who respond favorably to that approach. Develop an instructional package or two and improve them as you observe students using them. Identify the few students who may be ready to set objectives based on community contribution or a work-study program and help them to begin.

Introduce some contracts to two bright youngsters and to two who have not been achieving well. Interest other staff members in starting a bank of contracts. A valuable assortment can be developed within two years through an accrual process. As additional teachers become involved, the quality of the contracts improves because revisions are made based on actual use. Use one of the five basic methods of individualizing instruction to begin the process and expand into a second method and then a third.

For those who have been developing individualized programs, take a breather and assess objectively what you have achieved. Identify, by looking at what students and teachers are actually *doing*, the aspects of your program that are effective; look for the weaknesses and try to pinpoint how to eliminate them. Look at behavioral outcomes (the *results* of behavior) and analyze how they may be improved. Talk with teachers and administrators to elicit ideas; you may choose only one part of an idea that is suggested, but that fragmented mosaic may be the one missing link between an excellent program and a superior one.

Select a second, third or fourth method of individualization and other alternative approaches for introduction into existing personalized programs. Solicit parental or student assistance with duplication of packages or materials. Photograph your program and mount the pictures in hallways, in corridors, in offices, and in the community. Recognize that

Photo 8-22. Margaret Andersen insisted that she could ". . . no longer teach 25 students at once all of the time." Her present individualized methods cause less boredom and frustration for her and for her students. "Now students are not glassy-eyed kids who aren't really with you! Instead, they are alive! Excited! And learning!" (Photograph courtesy of the Saw Mill Road Elementary School, North Bellmore, New York.)

innovators, regardless of the form of their commitment, will attract disciples and antagonists. If you build on successes and learn through errors you will ultimately serve our student population in the most effective way possible by maximizing their opportunities to achieve to their individual potential.

Individualizing instruction may be the most difficult task any of us undertake; it is certainly the most satisfying. Through personal interviews more than 700 teachers have articulated that they ". . . could never go back. . . ." Having achieved an instructional environment that provides for combined humanistic and academically directed growth, professional people can rarely retrogress to what was less than ideal. The road to nirvana is not necessarily easy, but the path is clearly set, the signs are accurate, and the trip itself is exciting and revitalizing. Once there you will understand why the successful travelers rarely glance back over their shoulders.

Appendix A

CHAPTER 1

1. Rita Dunn and Kenneth Dunn, *Practical Approaches to Individualizing Instruction: Contracts and Other Effective Teaching Strategies* (Nyack, New York: Parker Publishing Company, Inc., 1972).
2. Gerard A. Poirier, *Students As Partners in Team Learning* (Berkeley, California: Center of Team Learning 1970).
3. Dunn and Dunn, *Practical Approaches . . .* , Chapters 5, 6 and 7.
4. Jack V. Edling, *Individualized Instruction* (Corvallis, Ore.: Continuing Education Publications, Waldo Hall, 1970).
5. See Chapter 3.
6. Learning style as an aspect of *diagnosis* is usually cooperatively determined. Learning style as an aspect of *prescription* may be cooperatively written into the learner's program when necessary or appropriate ("Your grades have been lower since you've been working with Jimmy and Frank. I think you had better work alone this time and see whether you can raise your scores"), but they should, for the most part, be self-selected by the student. The teacher will observe the student functioning in the learning environment and assess the student's progress. If sufficient achievement is not evident, the teacher will then prescribe selected modes of operation in the classroom. Otherwise, students should be free to function by choice unless they prevent other students from learning.
7. Rita S. Dunn, "A Position Paper to Further Individualization of Instruction in the Schools," *Audiovisual Instruction*, 17, 9 (November 1972), 49-54.

CHAPTER 2

1. Rita Dunn and Kenneth Dunn, *Practical Approaches to Individualizing Instruction: Contracts and Other Effective Teaching Strategies* (Nyack, New York: Parker Publishing Company, Inc., 1972), Chapter 5, 6 and 7.
2. *Ibid.*, Chapter 2, pp. 68-75.
3. *Ibid.*, Chapter 3, pp. 86-95.
4. A. Zalesnik, C. R. Christensen, and F. J. Roethlisberger, *The Motivation, Productivity, and Satisfaction of Workers* (Cambridge: Harvard University, Graduate School of Business Administration, 1958), 400.

5. e.e. cummings, paraphrase of a letter written in 1955.
6. Rita Dunn and Kenneth Dunn, "Kids Must Learn How to Learn Alone," *Learning*, 1, 6 (April 1973), 17-18. Copyright 1973 by Education Today Company, Inc.

CHAPTER 3

1. George Domino, "Interactive Effects of Achievement Orientation and Teaching Style on Academic Achievement," *ACT Research Report*, no. 39 (1970) pp. 1-9. One hundred students were grouped in accordance with their perceptions of how they learned. Some of the groups were then taught in a manner consonant with their perceived "achievement orientation," while others were taught in a manner dissonant with their orientation. The testing data revealed that the students who had been exposed to a teaching style consonant with the ways they believed they learned scored higher on tests, fact knowledge, teacher attitude, and efficiency of work than those who had been taught in a manner dissonant with their orientation. A study conducted by Roger W. Haskell, "Effect of Certain Individual Learner Personality Differences on Instructional Methods," *A.V. Communication Review*, 19, 3 (Fall, 1971), 287-297, classified 145 senior high school students on the basis of their personality traits as measured by the Guilford-Zimmerman Temperament Survey and the Wonderlic Personnel Test. The students were then taught by two different methods of instruction—a linear programed instruction booklet and the more traditional lecture-discussion method. The students had also been given an academic achievement test that yielded a measure of general mental ability. By means of an analysis of covariance, adjustment was made for existing differences in general mental ability. This statistical technique revealed the existence of a positive relationship between two of the measured personality variables on the Guilford-Zimmerman test and the performance of students after exposure to the two different methods. In general, the students who were inclined to be slow and methodical and/or "easy to get along with" (traits identified as "low general activity" and "friendliness" on the Guilford test) did better under the programed learning type of instruction. Students who were more likely characterized as "aggressive" ("low friendliness" on the Guilford Survey) performed better under the more conventional lecture-discussion system. These studies support the hypothesis that when mental ability is equal, students tend to learn better if they are taught by methods that complement their individual learning style.
2. H. Munsterberg and J. Bingham, "Memory," *Psychological Review*, 1 (January 1894), 34-38.
3. Edwin Kirkpatrick, "An Experimental Study of Memory," *Psychological Review*, 1 (1894), 603-609.
4. As reported in "A Study of Visual and Auditory Memory Processes," *Psychological Review*, 3 (May 1896), 258-269, L. G. Whitehead experimented with visual and oral presentations and concluded that visual exposure produced more initial absorption but that auditory exposure pro-

duced increased retention. Similar conclusions were reached by Robert MacDougal in "Recognition and Recall," *Journal of Philosophy and Scientific Method*, 1 (April 1904), 229-233, when he obtained data verifying that a visual approach to teaching was more effective than a verbal one. This conclusion was also supported in "The Mneumonic Span for Visual and Auditory Digest," in the *Journal of Experimental Psychology*, 1 (October 1916), 393-403, and by Helen Koch in "Some Factors Affecting the Relative Efficiency of Certain Modes of Presenting Material for Memorizing," *American Journal of Psychology*, 42 (July 1930), 370-388. Koch indicated the superiority of a visual approach but concluded that ". . . the simultaneous combination of the visual and auditory presentation was . . . rather uniformly superior, and the simple auditory presentation was uniformly inferior." Conflicting studies revealed data that supported an aural rather than a visual presentation for producing acquisition and/or retention. J. O. Quantz, in "Problems in the Psychology of Reading," published in *Psychology Review Monographs*, 2 (December 1897) pp. 1-51, described comparisons made of visual and auditory learners and concluded that only small differences existed that appeared to favor the use of the aural method. Clifford Woody supported Quantz's sutdy in his report, "The Effectiveness of Oral Versus Silent Reading in the Initial Memorization of Poems," *Journal of Educational Psychology*, 13 (November 1922) pp. 477-483. In 1940, Robert Larsen and D. D. Feder in "Common and Differential Factors in Reading and Hearing Comprehension," *Journal of Educational Psychology*, 31:241-252, found that low scholastic aptitude groups were fairly even in listening and visual comprehension; the middle group demonstrated a statistically insignificant superiority in favor of the visual; and the top group had a definite superiority in learning through a visual (reading) approach. T. S. Krawiec in "A Comparison of Learning and Retention of Materials Presented Visually and Auditorially," *Journal of General Psychology*, 34 (April 1946), 193-194, indicated that the visual mode appeared to be superior for the learning of simple materials but that, for retention, neither the visual nor the auditory presentations appeared to verify better results. Henry DeWick, in a study titled "The Relative Effectiveness of Visual and Auditory Presentation of Advertising Material," reported to the *Journal of Applied Psychology*, 19 (June 1935), 245-264, stated that the auditory method seemed to be a superior teaching method, but this was refuted in 1940 by Harry Goldstein who indicated in "Reading and Listening Comprehension at Various Controlled Rates," published in *Contribution to Education* (New York: Bureau of Publications, Teachers College, Columbia University), no. 821, pp. 57-59, that listening comprehension is, in general, superior to reading comprehension; that the superiority of listening comprehension is decidedly more marked for the easy than for the difficult materials; that the relative superiority of listening comprehension is in inverse proportion to the intelligence and reading speed of the group (supporting D. D. Feder); that the relative superiority of listening over reading comprehension declines with increased rate of presentation, and that reading comprehension is more variable than listening comprehension. Goldstein's study was relatively more inclusive than many former ones, for, for the first time, he implied that the teacher must carefully analyze the physical, emotional, intellectual, and social makeup of the class (not the individual) in order to teach on a comprehension level for all. (He did not suggest methodology appropriate for such instruction.) Robert M. Friedman noted the conflicting reports in 1967 when, as part of his unpublished doctoral dissertation at New York University, "The Relationship Between the Retention Level of Orally and Visually Presented Science Material to Selected Fifth Grade Students," he concluded that neither a visual nor an auditory presentation produced significant recall differences among a small selected population (p. 76). Sam Ducker in "Listening and Reading," as reported in the *Elementary School Journal,* 65 (March 1965), 321-329, stated, "Certainly the research on the relative learning value of auditory and visual presentation reveals sharply conflicting findings. This disagreement . . . can be explained on the basis of the differences in learning materials presented, the diverse characteristics of the populations . . . and the varying means of testing employed." More recently, the focus on perceptual differences has been shifted toward other accents such as the perceptual differences between middle-class and disadvantaged children (Meryl Silver, "A Comparison Between Visual Association and Auditory Association in Disadvantaged and Middle-Class Children," *Graudate Research in Education and Related Disciplines,* 6 [Fall 1970], 229), the unreliability of learning and testing for children with low visual perceptual ability when these occur solely through their weakest perception (Howard M. Coleman, "The West Warwick Visual Perceptual Study," *Journal of the American Optometric Association,* 434 [April 1972], 452-462), and the differences between the sexes as they relate to auditory-visual integration skills and reading success (David H. Reilly, "Auditory-Visual Integration, Sex, and Reading Achievement," *Journal of Educational Psychology,* 62, 6 [1971], 482-486; Clifford J. Drew, "Research on the Psychological-Behavioral Effects of the Physical Environment," *American Educational Research Association* [Washington, D.C.], 447-465; Curtis Banion Kilbrough, "An Investigation of the Effects of Abrupt Change in Educational Environment Upon the Reported Self-Concept of Third-Grade Pupils" [Ed. D. dissertation, University of Southern Mississippi, 1969]; Paul Edward Sumter, "Learning Experiment: Effectiveness of Controlling Environmental Distractions" [Ph.D. dissertation, Iowa State University, 1969]; William Gingold, "The Effects of Physical Environment on Children's Behavior in the Classroom" [Ph.D. dissertation, University of Wisconsin, 1971]).

5. Barbara Bond and S. S. Stevens, "Cross-Modality Matching of Brightness to Lightness by 5-Year Olds," *Perception and Psychophysics,* 6 (1969), 337-339. Also, Barbara Blitz, *The Open Classroom: Making It Work* (Boston: Allyn and Bacon, Inc., 1973), criticizes that ". . . students are judged on their ability to adjust their learning styles to those of the teacher . . ." (p. 85), and then states, "All of us must learn to inhibit the conscious perception of noise and/or movement within the classroom to attend to things with any depth of concentration" (p. 196). Studies that verify the relationship between sound in the environment and achievement include David C. Glass, Sheldon Cohen, and Jerome E. Singer, "Urban Din Fogs the Brain," *Psychology Today* (May 1972), 94-98; John J. O'Malley and Alex Poplowsky, "Noise-Induced Arousal and Breadth of Attention,"

Perceptual and Motor Skills, 33 (December 1971), 887-890; and Susan J. Samtur, *Graduate Research in Education and Related Disciplines,* 4, 2 (New York: City College of the University of New York, Spring 1969), 63-81.

6. Esteban Lucas Olmeda, "Effects of Environmental Variation on Arousal and Performance of a Vigilance Task" (Ph.D. dissertation, Baylor University, 1972).

7. I. D. Griffiths and R. R. Boyce, *Ergonomics* 14 (London, England, July 1971), 457-468; John F. Wing, "A Review of the Effects of High Ambient Temperature on Mental Performance," United States Air Force Publication from the Aerospace Medical Research Laboratory, Wright-Patterson AFB (TR 1965), 65-102; also B. Givoni and Y. Rim, "Effect of the Thermal Environment and Psychological Factors Upon Subject's Responses and Performance of Mental Work," *Ergonomics* (London, England, January 1962), 99-107; I. D. Griffiths and P. R. Boyce, "Performance and Thermal Comfort," *Ergonomics,* 14, 4 (London, England, July 1971), 457-468; I. Holmber and O. Wyon of the School of Education, Malmo, Sweden, "The Dependence of Performance in School on Classroom Temperature," *Educational and Psychological Interactions,* no. 31 (1969), pp. 1-20; Frederick H. Rohles, "Thermal Sensations of Sedentary Man in Moderate Temperatures, Human Factors of Children Under Imposed Noise and Heat Stress," *Ergonomics* 13, 6 (London, England, July 1970), 598-612.

8. Blitz, *The Open Classroom . . . ,* pp. 95-109; also see Dunn and Dunn, *Practical Approaches . . . ,* 73-74; Mark Phillips, "Conceptual Systems and Educational Environment: Relationships Between Teacher Conceptual Systems and Classroom Management as Perceived by Fifth and Sixth Grade Students" (Ed.D. dissertation, University of Massachusetts, 1972); Herman Eugene LaForge, "Effect of the Open Space Design of an Elementary School Upon Personality Characteristics of Students" (Ed.D. dissertation, University of Houston, Texas, 1972).

9. Douglas McGregor, *The Human Side of Enterprise* (New York: McGraw-Hill Book Co., Inc., 1960); Elton Mayo, "The Hawthorne Experiment," *The Human Problems of an Industrial Civilization* (New York: Viking Press, 1968), pp. 53-94; Gertrude Noar, *Individualized Instruction: Every Child a Winner* (New York: John Wiley and Sons, Inc., 1972), pp. 79-81; Frederick Herzberg, "Managers or Trainers?" *Management Review* (July 1971), pp. 2-15; N. Nishikawa, "A Study of Job Satisfaction: An Empirical Test of the Herzberg Theory," *Japanese Journal of Psychology* 41 (1971), 285-294; Benjamin Schneider and Olson Lorenk, "Effort as a Correlate of Organizational Reward System and Individual Values," *Personal Psychology* 23 (1970), 313-326; Edward Lowler, "Impact of Employee Participation in the Development of Pay Incentive Plans: A Field Experiment," *Journal of Applied Psychology* 53: 467-471; Norman R. Maier and Ronald J. Burke, "Influence of Motivation in the Reorganization of Experience," *Psychological Reports* 23, 2 (1968), 351-361; Abraham H. Maslow, *Toward a Psychology of Being* (New York: Van Nostrand Reinhold Co., 1968), Chapter 2.

10. "Analysis of the Effectiveness of Tutorial Assistance in English: Performance and Persistence Among Low Achieving Students," Educational Resources Center, U. S. Department of Health, Education, and Welfare, Washington, D.C., 6, 1 (January 1971), #ED042-442, 55; Corinne C. Mumbauer, "Influence of Subject and Situational Variables on the Persistence of First Grade Children in a Test-Like Situation," Educational Resources Information Center, U. S. Department of Health, Education, and Welfare 6, 11 (Washington, D.C., November 1971), #ED052-819; also Blitz, *The Open Classroom* . . . , pp. 4, 194; David Brookes Waters, "Differential Effects of Skill and Chance on Persistence, Time and Attention Breaks as a Function of Locus of Control in Elementary School Children" (Ph.D. dissertation, Emory University, 1972); Keith Barton and James W. Barnard, "The Effects of Two Kinds of Reinforcement on the Persistence Scores of Children of Different Ability Patterns," *Journal of Psychology*, 82, 1 (September 1972), 13-19.

11. Helen Davis Dell, *Individualizing Instruction: Materials and Classroom Procedures* (Chicago: Science Research Associates, Inc., (1972), p. 13. Also see Marshall B. Rosenberg's description of the following learning styles: (a) rigid-inhibited, (b) undisciplined, and (c) creative, in "Diagnostic Teaching" (Seattle: *Special Child Publications*, 1968), pp. 38-63.

12. George A. Morgan, "Effects of a Less Prescriptive Student-Centered College Curriculum on Satisfaction and Achievement," Proceedings of the Annual Convention of the American Psychological Association, National Institute of Child Health and Human Development, 7, part 1 (Bethesda, Maryland, 1972), 505-506. This study examined the impact of change from a traditional liberal arts curriculum to one in which (1) requirements were essentially eliminated, (2) student freedom and responsibility were increased, and (3) ungraded, value-oriented discussion courses were encouraged. After a two-year period the students exposed to the new curriculum were compared with the group involved in the traditional curriculum, and it was revealed that the former expressed higher satisfaction with their study program, developed stronger intellectual values, had a feeling of better adustment than previously experienced, and scored equal or better than the latter group on academic testing measurements. On the elementary level, Blitz suggests ways that the arrangement of furniture and the teacher's presence establish a degree of structure that tends to communicate the expectations of behavior and learning to the students (*The Open Classroom* . . . , pp. 93, 194-196).

13. Herbert J. Walberg, "Social Environment as a Mediator of Classroom Learning," *Journal of Educational Psychology*, 60 (1969), 443-448; Herbert J. Walberg and Andrew Ahlgren, "Predictors of the Social Environment of Learning," *American Educational Research Journal*, 7, 2 (March 1970), 135-167; Herbert J. Walberg, "Class Size and the Social Environment of Learning," *Human Relations*, 22: 5: 465-475.

14. Gerard A. Poirier, *Students as Partners in Team Learning* (Berkeley, Calif.: Center of Team Learning, 1970), Chapter 2. Poirier's thesis is verified by Blitz, *The Open Classroom* . . . , pp. 194, 206.

15. Ralph James Ankenbrand, "An Investigation of the Relationship Between Achievement and Self-Concept of High Risk Community College Freshmen" (Ph.D. dissertation, St. Louis University, 1971).

16. James Victor Griesen, "Independent Study Versus Group Interaction in Medical Education: A Study of Non-Cognitive Factors Relating to Curricular Preferences and Academic Achievement," (Ph.D. dissertation, Ohio State University, 1971).

17. Gerald Marwell, "Types of Past Experience With Potential Work Partners: Their Effects on Partner Choice," *Human Relations*, 19-20, 437-447.

18. John W. Solocum Jr., "Group Cohesiveness: A Salient Factor Affecting Students' Academic Achievement in a Collegiate Environment," *Journal of Educational Science*, 2 (September 1968), 151-157; Paul DeHart Hurd and Mary Budd Rowe, "A Study of Small-Group Dynamics and Productivity in the BSCS Laboratory Block Program," *Journal of Research in Science Teaching*, 4 (1966), 67-73; Albert Lott and Bernice E. Lott, "Group Cohesiveness and Individual Learning," *Social Interaction in Educational Settings*, Albert H. Yee, ed. (New Jersey: Prentice-Hall, 1971), pp. 215-228; Richard Schmuck, "Some Relationships of Peer Liking to Patterns in the Classroom to Pupil Attitudes and Achievement," *School Review*, 71 (1963), 337-359; Martin Fishbein, "Prediction of Interpersonal Preferences and Group Member Satisfaction from Estimated Attitudes," *Journal of Personality and Social Psychology*, 6 (1965), 666-667; William M. Weist, Lyman W. Porter and Edwin E. Chiselli, "Relationships Between Individual Proficiency and Team Performance and Efficiency," *Journal of Applied Psychology*, 45 (December 1961), 435-440.

19. Denise B. Kandel and Gerald S. Lesser, "Parental and Peer Influences on Educational Plans of Adolescents," *American Sociological Review*, 34, 2 (1969), 213-223. Also see Albert Joseph Bidwick Jr., "A Study of the Effectiveness of Meaningful Adult Contacts on the Self-Concept, Behavior, and Achievement of Junior High School Disciplinary Problems," (Ed.D. dissertation, George Washington University, 1971); Terry D. Meddock, Joseph A. Parsons, and Kennedy T. Hill, "Effects of an Adult's Presence and Praise on Young Children's Performance," *Journal of Experimental Child Psychology*, 12, 2 (October 1971), 197-211.

20. Dell, *Individualizing Instruction* . . . , pp. 73-74. Also see H. A. Witkin, et al., *Psychological Differentiation* (New York: John Wiley and Sons, 1962), and Jerome Bruner, "Eye, Hand, Mind," *Studies in Cognitive Development*, David Elkind and John Flavell, eds. (London: Oxford University Press, 1961); Thomas Sticht, "Learning by Listening in Relation to Aptitude Reading and Rate Controlled Speech," Hum RRo *Technical Report* (Monterey, California: April 1970), no. 71-5, A.40; R. Conrad, "The Developmental Role of Vocalizing in Short-Term Memory," *Journal of Verbal Learning and Verbal Behavior*, 11, 4 (August 1972), 521-533; James David Cooper, "A Study of the Learning Modalities of Good and Poor First Grade Readers," *Dissertation Abstracts International-*

Humanities, 30, 11 (May 1970), 4676-4677; Clarence R. Calder Jr., "A Comparison of Four Methods of Teaching Psychomotor Activities to Elementary School Children from Varying Socioeconomic Levels," *AV Communication Review*, 18, 1 (Spring 1970), 25-31; Joy M. Menne and John W. Menne, "The Relative Efficiency of Bimodal Presentation as an Aid to Learning," *AV Communication Review*, 20, 2 (Summer 1972), 170-179; Alexander W. Siegel and Billie J. Vance, "Visual and Dimensional Preference: A Developmental Study," *Developmental Psychology*, 3, 2 (1970), 264-266; William G. Holiday, "The Effects of Utilizing Simultaneous Audio and Printed Media in Science," *AV Communication Review* 20 (Spring 1972), 110-111; Cynthia R. Flinder, Anne D. Pick, L. Herbert Jr., and Jacqueline J. Halis, "A Developmental Investigation of Visual and Haptic Preferences for Shape and Texture," *Monographs of the Society for Research in Child Development*, 34, 6, serial no. 130 (1969).

21. D. Braddeley, J. E. Hatter, D. Scott, and A. Snashall, "Memory and Time of Day," *Quarterly Journal of Experimental Psychology*, 22, 4 (November 1970), 605-609; Sidney Trubowitz, "The Tyranny of Time," *The Elementary School* Journal, 73, 1 (October 1972), 1-6; Blitz, *The Open Classroom* . . . , p. 61; also Jerome Kagan, Howard A. Moss, and Irving A. Siegel, "Psychological Significance of Styles of Conceptualization," *Society for Research in Child Development*, Monographs, #86, 17 (1963), 927-940. For time adaptations in industry, see "Germans Setting Own Office Hours," *The New York Times* (July 12, 1971), 1, 10; and "Flextime Seems to Lessen Tension," *The San Juan Star* (Puerto Rico, February 19, 1973), p. 36.

22. In a unanimous decision, the Massachusetts State Board of Education approved a recommendation by State Commissioner Neil V. Sullivan permitting the operation of an "open high school program in which all students need not be present all the time." The statewide program, which officials claimed to be unique in the nation in 1970, permitted students to be scheduled in programs of less than 5.5 hours of formal instruction or in programs where student learning was partially self-directed within or outside the school. Participating schools were still required to provide the regular 5.5 hour program for those students who wanted it. The decision was based on the success of three pilot programs previously conducted in Brookline, Winchester, and Falmouth as reported in *Education, U.S.A.* (Fall 1970).

23. Blitz, *The Open Classroom* . . . , pp. 74, 194.

24. Beatrice J. Farr, "Individual Differences in Learning: Predicting One's More Effective Learning Modality" (Ph.D. dissertation, Catholic University of America, 1971, University Microfilm, Ann Arbor, Michigan, July, 1971), p. 1332A. An experiment with 72 college students confirmed that individuals could accurately predict the modality in which they would demonstrate superior learning performance. The data also revealed that it is advantageous to learn and be tested in the same modality and that such an advantage is reduced when learning and testing are both conducted in an

individual's nonpreferred modality. The most desirable condition existed when learning and testing were both in the student's preferred modality; also George Domino, "Interactive Effects of Achievement Orientation and Teaching Style on Academic Achievement." *ACT Research Report*, No. 39 (1970) 1-9.

CHAPTER 4

1. Rita Dunn and Kenneth Dunn, "Kids Must Learn How to Learn Alone," *Learning, The Magazine for Creative Teaching*, 1, no. 6 (April 1973), 17-18. Copyright 1973 by Education Today Company, Inc.
2. Rita Dunn and Kenneth Dunn, *Practical Approaches to Individualizing Instruction: Contracts and Other Effective Teaching Strategies* (Nyack, N.Y.: Parker Publishing Company, 1972), pp. 68-75. Also see Barbara Blitz, *The Open Classroom: Making It Work* (Boston, Mass.: Allyn and Bacon, Inc., 1973), pp. 97-119. Also see Helen Davis Dell, *Individualizing Instruction* (Chicago: Science Research Associates, 1972), pp. 117-123. Also see Lillian Weber, *The English Infant Schools and Informal Education* (Englewood Cliffs, N.J.: Prentice-Hall, Inc., 1971), pp. 114-132.
3. Barbara Blitz, *The Open Classroom: Making It Work*, p. 103. Copyright 1973 by Allyn and Bacon, Inc. Reprinted with permission.
4 Steven Daniels, *How 2 Gerbils, 20 Goldfish, 200 Games, 2,000 Books and I Taught Them How to Read* (Philadelphia, Penna.: The Westminster Press, 1971), pp. 33-34.
5. Barbara Blitz, *The Open Classroom: Making It Work*, p. 104. Copyright 1973 by Allyn and Bacon, Inc. Reprinted with permission.
6. *Ibid.*, p. 100.
7. *Ibid.*, p. 101.
8. Three-ply cardboard can be ordered from Tri-Wall Container Corporation, 100 Crossways Park, Woodbury, New York, telephone 516-364-2800, at reasonable prices. Usually purchased in sheets of 42″ by 54″, they can, with ease, be used by children to build a variety of ideal furniture shapes. "Building with Cardboard," sketches of plans and designs for cardboard, can be obtained for about a dollar from Workshop for Learning Things, 5 Bridge Street, Watertown, Massachusetts, telephone 617-926-3491.
9. For descriptions of six varied instructional areas including learning stations, interest centers, game tables, little theaters, media corners and magic carpet areas, see Dunn and Dunn, *Practical Approaches. . . .*
10. *Ibid.*, p. 193.

CHAPTER 5

1. Rita Dunn and Kenneth Dunn, "Kids Must Learn How to Learn Alone," *Learning*, 1, 6 (April 1973), 17-18. Copyright 1973 by Education Today Company, Inc.
2. Ivan Illich, *Deschooling Society* (New York: Harper and Rowe, 1970), p. 8.

3. Norman E. Hankins, *Psychology for Contemporary Education* (Columbus, Ohio: Charles E. Merrill Publishing Company, Inc., 1973), pp. 312-333.

4. Abraham H. Maslow, *Toward a Psychology of Being* (New York: Van Nostrand Reinhold Company, 1968), pp. 63-65.

5. Rita Dunn and Kenneth Dunn, *Practical Approaches to Individualizing Instruction: Contracts and Other Effective Teaching Strategies* (Nyack, N.Y.: Parker Publishing Company, 1972), pp. 124-145. Objectives designed to meet the specific needs of individual students who require interest-centered curriculums should be developed with and for youngsters with unique learning goals or problems. Such "independent" prescriptions may vary extensively from those prescribed for students engaged in traditional curriculum studies.

6. Hankins, *Contemporary Education*, Item 8, p. 210.

7. See Chapter 2.

8. T. J. Ramirez, "Effects of Tutorial Experiences on the Problem-Solving Behavior of Sixth Graders," *California Journal of Educational Research*, 22 (1971), 80-90.

9. L. B. Kornreich, "Discovery Versus Programed Instruction in Teaching a Strategy for Solving Concept-Identification Problems," *Journal of Educational Psychology*, 60 (1969), 384-388.

10. D. T. Miles and R. E. Robinson, "Behavioral Objectives: An Even Closer Look," *Educational Technology*, 11 (1971), 39-44.

11. Laurence J. Peter, *Individual Instruction* (New York: McGraw-Hill Book Company, 1972), pp. 145-149.

12. Muriel Gerhard, *Effective Teaching Strategies with the Behavioral Outcomes Approach* (West Nyack, N.Y.: Parker Publishing Company, Inc., 1971), pp. 57-59.

13. R. Rosenthal and L. Jacobson, *Pygmalion in the Classroom: Teacher Expectation and Pupils' Intellectual Development*, (New York: Holt, Rinehart and Winston, 1968).

14. Hankins, *Contemporary Education*, p. 209.

15. Dunn and Dunn, *Practical Approaches . . .* , Chapters 3 and 4.

16. Kurt Lewin, "Forces Behind Food Habits and Methods of Change," *Bulletin of the National Research Council*, no. 108 (1943).

17. H. Stevenson and A. Siegel, "Effects of Instructions and Age on Retention of Filmed Content," *Journal of Educational Psychology*, 60 (1969), 71-74.

CHAPTER 7

1. D. Ryans, *Characteristics of Teachers* (Washington, D.C.: American Council on Education, 1960), and J. Flanagan, "The Critical Incident Technique," *Psychological Bulletin* (Long Island, 1954), pp. 327-358.

2. Rita Dunn and Kenneth Dunn, *Practical Approaches to Individualizing Instruction: Contracts and Other Effective Teaching Strategies* (Nyack, N.Y.: Parker Publishing Company, Inc., 1972), p. 63.

3. Robert F. Mager, *Preparing Instructional Objectives* (Palo Alto, Calif.: Fearon Publications, 1972).
4. Robert J. Kobler, Larry L. Barker, and David T. Miles, *Behavioral Objectives and Instruction* (Boston: Allyn and Bacon, Inc., 1970), p. 22.
5. P. G. Kapfer and G. Swenson, "Individualizing Instruction for Self-Paced Learning," *Clearing House*, 42 (1968), 405-411, and Joy M. Menne and John W. Menne, "The Relative Efficiency of Bimodal Presentation as an Aid to Learning," *AV Communication Review*, 20, 2 (Summer 1972), 170-179.
6. Barbara Blitz, *The Open Classroom: Making It Work* (Boston: Allyn and Bacon, Inc., 1973), p. 3.
7. Kobler, *et. al.*, *Behavioral Objectives* . . . , pp. 25-27.
8. George M. Hanning, "Child's Reaction to Thermal Environment Differs from Adults," *Air Conditioning, Heat and Refrigeration News*, 124 (November 15, 1971), 11; George Douglas Mayo, "Effect of Temperature Upon Technical Training," *Journal of Applied Psychology*, 39, 4 (1955), 244-246; A. S. Edwards, "The Relation of Light Intensity to Accuracy of Depth Perception," *Journal of Applied Psychology*, 37, 4 (1953), 300-301; Harry J. Jerison, "Effects of Noise on Human Performance," *Journal of Applied Psychology*, 43 (April 1959), 96-101, also Chapter 3.
9. Steven Daniels, *How 2 Gerbils, 20 Goldfish, 200 Games, 2,000 Books and I Taught Them How to Read* (Philadelphia: The Westminister Press, 1971), 33-34.
10. Blitz, *The Open Classroom* . . . , pp. 138-162.
11. Norman V. Overly, *The Unstructured Curriculum: Its Impact on Children*, (Washington, D.C.: Association for Supervision and Curriculum Development, 1970).
12. Carl R. Rogers, *Freedom to Learn* (Columbus, Ohio: Charles E. Merrill Publishing Company, 1969) pp. 134-141; Mario D. Fantini and Milton A. Young, *Designing Education for Tomorrow's Cities* (New York: Holt, Rinehart and Winston, Inc., 1970), pp. 54-58; Muriel Gerhard, *Effective Teaching Strategies with the Behavioral Outcomes Approach* (Nyack, N.Y.: Parker Publishing Company, Inc., 1971), pp. 43, 57-59; Dwight W. Allen and Eli Seifman, *The Teacher's Handbook* (Glenview, Illinois: Scott, Foresman and Company, 1971), p. 273.
13. Marshall B. Rosenberg, *Diagnostic Teaching* (Seattle: Special Child Publications, 1968), pp. 38-63.
14. Fantini and Young, *Designing Education* . . . , p. 44.
15. Ann Remsen, *Individualization Index* (New York: St. John's University, 1972).
16. Dunn and Dunn, *Practical Approaches* . . . , pp. 86-124.
17. *Ibid.*, 124-128.
18. Rita Compain, *Compain Key* (New York: C. W. Post College, 1972).
19. Roger B. Worner, "Evaluating Instructional Programs," *National Association of Secondary School Principals Bulletin*, 56, 366 (October 1972), 17-26.

CHAPTER 8

1. Guidelines for creating sample instructional case studies and for developing analysis skills are discussed fully in *Practical Approaches to Individualizing Instruction*, etc. It is sufficient to note at this point that case studies are usually short-short stories focused on a single incident, problem or situation. They are generally open-ended and stimulate analysis, different points of view, multiple potential solutions or approaches.
2. These "contract activities" (an improper label) are fictional *but* they simulate the all too usual narrow reading assignments. Learning exercises required of students as these mandated "activities" do not provide options, multisensory resources or reporting alternatives for different learning styles, levels of ability or knowledge. See Chapter 5 for appropriate activity and reporting alternatives.

Appendix B

SELECTED BIBLIOGRAPHY AND SOURCES OF
ADDITIONAL INFORMATION ON
INDIVIDUALIZED INSTRUCTION

Beggs, David W., III, and Edward G. Duffie (eds.), *Independent Study: Bold New Venture*. Bloomington: Indiana University Press, 1965.

Bettelheim, Bruno, *Love Is Not Enough*. Glencoe, Illinois: The Free Press, 1950.

Birenbaum, William M., *Something for Everybody Is Not Enough*. New York: Random House, 1971.

Bishop, Lloyd K., *Individualizing Educational Systems, The Elementary and Secondary School*. Harper and Row, 1971.

Blitz, Barbara, *The Open Classroom: Making It Work*. Boston: Allyn and Bacon, 1973.

Bolvin, J. O., C. M. Linduall, and Robert G. Scanlon, *A Manual for the IPI Institute*. Learning Research and Development Center, University of Pittsburgh, 1967.

Brown, James W., and Richard B. Lewis, *AV Instructional Technology Manual*. New York: McGraw-Hill, 1973.

Daniels, Steven, *How 2 Gerbils, 20 Goldfish, 200 Games, 2,000 Books and I Taught Them How To Read*. Philadelphia, Pennsylvania: The Westminster Press, 1971.

Dell, Helen Davis, *Individualizing Instruction*. Chicago: Science Research Associates, Inc., 1972.

Doll, Ronald C. (ed.), *Individualizing Instruction*. 1964 Yearbook, Washington, D.C., National Education Association.

Drumheller, Sidney J., *Handbook of Curriculum Design for Individualized Instruction–A Systems Approach*. Educational Technology, Englewood Cliffs, New Jersey.

Dunn, Rita, and Kenneth Dunn, *Practical Approaches to Individualizing Instruction*. West Nyack, New York: Parker Publishing Company, Inc., 1972.

Dunn, Rita Stafford, and Hamilton Blum, *Individualizing Instruction*. Jericho, New York: Board of Cooperative Educational Services, 1970.

Edling, Jack V., *Individualizing Instruction*. Corvallis, Oregon: Continuing Education Publications, 1970.

Edling, Jack V., *Individualizing Instruction for Administrators*. Corvallis, Oregon: DCE Publications.

Erger, Donald, *Understanding British Infant Schools*. Farmingdale, New York: Carley Publications, 1972.

Esbensen, T., *Working With Individualized Instruction*. Palo Alto, California: Fearon Publishers, 1968.

Gagne, Robert M. (ed.). *Learning and Individual Differences*. Columbus, Ohio: Charles E. Merrill Books, 1967.

Glasser, Joyce Fern, *The Elementary School Learning Center for Independent Study*. Nyack, New York: Parker Publishing Company, Inc., 1973.

Hankins, Norman E., *Psychology for Contemporary Education*. Columbus, Ohio: Charles E. Merrill Publishing Company, 1973.

Hoover, Kenneth, *Professional Teacher's Handbook: A Guide for Improving Instruction in Today's Secondary Schools*. New Jersey: Allyn and Bacon, Inc., 1973.

Hunter, Madeline, *Motivation Theory for Teachers* (1967), *Retention Theory for Teachers* (1967), *Reinforcement Theory for Teachers* (1967), *Teach More, Faster* (1969, *Teach for Transfer* (1971). El Segundo, California: TIP Publications.

Illich, Ivan, *Deschooling Society*. New York: Harper and Row, 1970.

Kohn, Sherwood, *The Early Learning Center*. Stamford, Connecticut: Educational Facilities Laboratories, 1970.

Livingston, Samuel A., and Clarice Stasz Stoll, *Simulation Games: An Introduction for the Social Studies Teacher*. New Jersey: The Free Press, 1973.

McLain, John D., *Year-Round Education: Economic, Educational and Sociological Factors*. Berkeley, California: McCutchan Publishing Corporation, 1973.

Open Space Schools. Washington, D.C.: American Association of School Administrators, 1971.

Osmon, Fred Linn, *Patterns for Designing Children's Centers*. New York: Educational Facilities Laboratories, 1971.

Overly, Norman V., *The Unstructured Curriculum: Its Impact on Children*. Washington, D.C.: Association for Supervision and Curriculum Development, National Education Association, 1970.

Peter, Laurence J., *Prescriptive Teaching System, Volume 1: Individual Instruction*. New York: McGraw-Hill, 1972.

Petrequin, Gaynor, *Individualizing Learning Through Modular-Flexible Programing*. New York: McGraw-Hill, 1968.

Poirier, Gerard A., *Students as Partners in Team Learning*. Berkeley, California: Center of Team Learning, University of California, 1970.

Popham, James W. (ed.). *Criterion-Referenced Measurement*. Englewood Cliffs, New Jersey: Educational Technology Publications, 1971.

Ruddell, Robert B., *Reading-Language Instruction: Innovative Practices*. Englewood Cliffs, New Jersey: Prentice-Hall, 1973.

Saxe, Robert W., *Opening the Schools*. Berkeley, California: McCutchan Publishing Corporation, 1973.

Smith, Bert Kruger, *Your Nonlearning Child*. Boston: Beacon Press, 1968.

Tanzman, Jack, and Kenneth J. Dunn, *Using Instructional Media Effectively*. West Nyack, New York: Parker Publishing Company, Inc., 1971.

Voight, Ralph Claude, *Invitation to Learning, The Learning Center Handbook*. Washington, D.C.: Acropolis Books, Ltd., 1971.

Weisberger, Robert A., (ed.), *Developmental Efforts in Individualized Instruction* (1971), *Perspectives in Individualized Instruction* (1971). Itasca, Illinois: Peacock Publishers.

Wilson, John A. R., (ed.), *Diagnosis of Learning Difficulties*. New York: McGraw-Hill, 1973.

Young, Milton A., *Teaching Children with Special Learning Needs: A Problem Solving Approach*. New York: John Day Company, 1967.

Younie, William J., *Instructional Approaches to Slow Learning*. New York: Teachers College Press, Columbia University, 1967.

Index